The Art and Times of the Guitar

THE ART
OF THE

Sometimes a thousand twangling instruments
will hum about mine ears; and sometimes voices . . .

—THE TEMPEST

AND TIMES
GUITAR

An Illustrated History of Guitars and Guitarists

FREDERIC V. GRUNFELD

The Macmillan Company   NEW YORK, NEW YORK

Collier-Macmillan Ltd.   LONDON

Library of Congress Catalog Card Number: 69-10465
Fifth Printing 1972
The Macmillan Company
866 Third Avenue, New York, N.Y. 10022
Collier-Macmillan Canada Ltd., Toronto, Ontario
Printed in the United States of America

Contents

Acknowledgments

The illustrations in this book are merely the visible fraction of an iceberg of guitar-picture research. After working in most of the major libraries of Europe, as well as the indispensable Frick and New York Public Libraries, I found that I had accumulated nearly two thousand items of iconography. In bringing this material together I had the help of librarians, curators and scholars in a score of countries, including India, Turkey, Egypt, Hungary, Romania, Portugal, Mexico and Senegal.

The sources of all the photographs used are duly identified. I should like to express my special appreciation, however, to the following people and institutions, whose assistance was particularly important in the preparation of this book:

Don J. Ricart Matas, director of the Barcelona Museum of Musical Instruments; Mrs. Henry W. Howell, Jr., librarian of the Frick Art Reference Library, and her assistant, Miss M. Steinbach; Madame E. LeBeau and Monsieur F. le Monnier of the Bibliothèque Nationale, Paris; Don Tomas Magallon Anton, Biblioteca Nacional, Madrid; Professor Jacques Barzun, Columbia University; Dr. Emanuel Winternitz, curator of Musical Collections, Metropolitan Museum of Art, and Mrs. Nada Saporiti of the museum's photographic department; Dr. Jouri Miller, Hermitage Museum, Leningrad; Don José Selva Vives, Junta de Museos de Barcelona; Doña Aurora Casanova Puig, Museo de Arte Moderna, Barcelona; Don Francisco Marques, Instituto para Alta Cultura, Lisbon; Dr. Anna-Barbara Follmann, Staatliche Antikensammlungen, Munich; Dr. Rainer Stadelmann, Aegyptologisches Institut, Heidelberg; Dr. Graf von Schoenborn-Wiesentheid, Wiesentheid, Germany; Dr. Gerhard Littmann, Baerenreiter Verlag, Kassel; Herr Franz Jahnel, Nuremberg; Mr. Vladimir Bobri, editor of *Guitar Review;* Mr. Israel Horowitz, Decca Records; Mr. Bob Cato, Columbia Records; Madame Suzanne Marquis, Time, Inc. Paris; Mrs. Walter Wood Hitesman, Jr., Bedford, N.Y.; Mrs. Ellen Maria Gorrissen, Wiesbaden; Mrs. Anita Hart Shefrin, N.Y.; Mr. Robert Graves, Deyá, and Mr. Fenwick Keyser, Towson, Md.

Special thanks is also due the staffs of the New York Public Library, the Library of Congress, the Courtauld Library, the Warburg Institute and the British Museum, whose many courtesies and kindnesses saw me through the B minor days of this manuscript. Invaluable assistance was provided in Deyá by Mrs. Dawn Brooks and Mr. Peter Kolesar. And without Miss Toby Molenaar this book would not have been possible.

Deyá, Majorca, July, 1969

Chapter 1

A Twang
for All Seasons

Psha, she's taken up with her impertinent Guitar Man.
—SIR JOHN VANBRUGH, *The Confederacy* (1705)

AFTER a century of velvet sounds, in which the blended timbres of the symphony orchestra held sway, the musical world is now in the grip of a great resurgence of pure twang. From Nashville and Liverpool, or Bombay and Yokohama, comes the incessant jangling and thrumming of plucked instruments that have suddenly become dear to our ear: the baroque harpsichord, whose effervescent ping is threatening to displace the felt-struck thud of the piano; the renaissance lute, undergoing a second golden age launched by Julian Bream; the banjo, up from slavery and now indispensable to any film score that aspires to Americana; the seven-hundred-year-old Indian sitar, which sounds like a hail of broken icicles when Ravi Shankar runs his fingers across some of its nineteen strings; its cousin the south Indian veena, which twangs for agonizing moments of indecision before finally settling down to a definite note (this is what its players call the "life" of a tone); the six-foot Japanese koto, thirteen strings, all body and no neck; the heike-biwa, the bouzouki, the samisen, the oud, the p'i-p'a, yue-chin, chirar, rebab, kayakeum, santir, ombi, vambi, nanga. . . .

But above all it is the guitar that currently finds work for idle

[1]

hands. At last guess there were fifteen or twenty million guitars in circulation in the United States alone and no foreseeable end to their proliferation. This staggering statistic must be interpreted to mean that all the major factions of society—college students, high school dropouts, peace marchers, paratroopers in green berets, and Southern gubernatorial candidates—have accepted the guitar as a universal means of communication.

The signs of this sonic revolution are everywhere. In France the tradition-minded luthiers of the Vosges have shifted over to producing guitars instead of violins and cellos. The same thing has happened in Germany. In Russia—even in Siberia, according to pictures in the Soviet press—students are playing guitars rather than balalaikas. The Book-of-the-Month Club, which began by selling books, has turned to selling the guitar records of a French gypsy named Manitas de Plata (Little Silver Hands). The Columbia Broadcasting System, in 1965, paid more money to acquire a guitar-making firm than it had paid to buy control of the New York Yankees. In Britain, where the Prince of Wales plays guitar, there are days of national mourning every now and then when one of the army of young electric guitar players is electrocuted as he goes to plug in his amplifier (house wiring in England has a tendency to be unkempt, and the voltage is a lethal 220). The Danish foreign minister, Per Haekkerup, on a visit to South America in 1966, made more friends and influenced more people than General de Gaulle, by the Machiavellian expedient of serenading his hosts on a Spanish guitar. Could *le grand Charles* have hoped to do as much on a French musette? Certainly the guitar has never had it so ubiquitous—not even in its Iberian heyday, when after a battle between Spaniards and Portuguese, the losing army took to the hills and left (it was said) 11,000 guitars upon the battlefield.

In the process of becoming universal, the guitar has lost most of its erstwhile social connotations and extramusical significance. To have played one in 1550 would have identified you as a Spanish *gracioso*, most likely a Don Juan. Around 1600 in Italy it would have stigmatized you as one of "the charlatans and saltimbanques who use it for strumming, to which they sing villanelles and other foolish

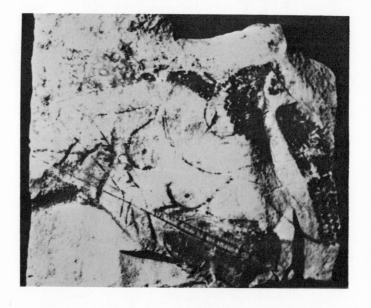

(1) Egyptian nefer player and flutist from the tomb of Pa-aten-em-heb at the necropolis of Sakkara (Memphis), eighteenth dynasty, c. 1375 B.C. Photo by Veem, courtesy of the Rijksmuseum van Oudheden, Leiden.

(2) Girl with guitar-like nefer from an eighteenth-dynasty pottery fragment found at Thebes. Photo courtesy of the Cairo Museum.

(3) Girl with nefer on the
handle of a wooden spoon,
eighteenth-dynasty, Egypt. The
instrument looks rather like a
ukulele, but with the important
difference that the neck runs
the entire length of the sound
chest. Photo by Veem, courtesy
of the Rijksmuseum van
Oudheden, Leiden.

lumpen-songs," as Michael Praetorius put it. In France, toward 1700, guitar-playing was, among other things, a royal occupation suitable for kings and courtiers. By 1800 the guitar would have marked you as a nature-loving romantic of Keatsian tendencies, for as Shelley wrote:

> The artist wrought that loved guitar
> And taught it justly to reply
> To all who question skillfully
> In language gentle as its own,
> Whispering in enamoured tone
> Sweet oracles of woods and dells,
> And summer winds in sylvan cells . . .

During the 1920's the guitar was briefly prohibited among students of Sverdloff University, Moscow, when the administration decided that "a guitar is not a class-proletarian instrument and is, indeed, an instrument favored exclusively by the bourgeois and middle classes." In the United States, on the other hand, possession of a guitar in the 1930's was almost *prima facie* evidence that you belonged to a Young Marxists' Chowder and Marching Society. Today, with the whole nation awash with the thrum and thrust of guitars, it means nothing more than that the guitarist is taking the shortest known route to what the Montgomery Ward catalogue calls "the romance of traditional folk and country-western music as well as your own mode of self-expression in song" (at prices that can range anywhere from $16 to $1,600). From a psychological standpoint, however, the guitar is still a very powerful symbol. The young man who brings a guitar to a party is serving notice, in effect, that he is a modern Leatherstocking type, sexually on the *qui vive*, a man who can "handle women." These, at any rate, are some of the associations that derive from the mystique of the footloose and fancy-free guitar—an image to which the serenader, the range-rider, Huddie Ledbetter, and Django Reinhardt have all contributed their share.

Yet the deeper, subconscious significance of twang is much older than that, and apparently lies buried in the earliest aural experiences of the human race. The original ancestor of all string instruments—

indeed the earliest instrument of which we possess a pictorial record —is the hunting bow that does double duty as a musical bow, like the one shown in a Paleolithic cave painting at Trois Frères, southern France. The sorcerer-priest in that Upper Stone Age hunting scene has a musical bow fastened to the mouth of his mask; he holds it out with his left hand and twangs it with his right. This selfsame instrument—essentially a one-string "guitar" using the mouth as a resonating cavity and the skull as a sounding board—still does yeoman service as the okongo or cora in certain parts of Africa, and produces some of the most glorious boinging and dwoinging sounds known to mankind. Another version of the mouth bow, used by American Indians, was recently revived as a concert instrument by the folk singer and guitarist Buffy Sainte-Marie.

It has not escaped the mythologists that Apollo the god of archers is also Apollo the god of music, a circumstance that might reasonably be explained by the dualism of the bow. Apollo's lyre, at any event, derives from this musical principle, and so do scores of other adaptations found the world over—fiber chords strung over turtle shells, wires mounted over clay pots, silken strings over calabash forms, gut strings stretched over wooden bowls in the shape of figs, or eggs or musk melons. But the history of what we call the guitar (as distinct from the other members of this numerous family, the chordophones) begins at the point where the form of the instrument takes on the shape of a woman's body: softly rounded at the shoulders, curving inward at the waist, and concluding with another gently rounded curve at the bottom.

Some obviously soulless organographers have described the guitar as having a figure-8 shape, whereas in actual fact its outline is simply the classic admiring gesture of man delineating the form of woman. Poets always speak of her in these terms; in languages which assign gender to such things, the guitar is invariably feminine. *La mujer y la guitarra, para usarlas hay que templarlas* says an old Spanish proverb: To use a woman or a guitar one must know how to tune them (or literally, to put them into a proper temper). Luc Dominique, the singing nun who made her debut on records as Soeur Sourire a few years ago, describes the feminine psychology of the

[6]

(4) Eros playing a pandoura (lute). Terracotta figure from Eretria, Greece, c. 330–200 B.C. Photo courtesy of the Trustees of the British Museum.

(5) Muse with pandoura (lute) from the marble relief known as the Mantinea base, dated 330–320 B.C. Though no strings are visible in this badly damaged work, the instrument shown is probably the three-stringed "trichordion" mentioned in subsequent Greek literature. Judging from the shape of the body, it is quite possible that this "lute" was skin-covered, like its modern North African relatives. Photo courtesy of the National Museum, Athens.

(6) The principal stringed
instruments of classical Greece
shown on a crater (mixing
vessel) found in Ruvo, southern
Italy. Attributed to the so-called
Sisyphos-painter, 430 B.C., the
painting depicts an angle-harp,
a U-shaped cithara, and a
lyre with a tortoise-shell body.
Photo courtesy of the Munich
Museum Antiker Kleinkunst.

(7) Psyche with lute, from a Roman sarcophagus relief of the third century A.D.
For technical reasons the sculptor has probably exaggerated the width of the
instrument's neck. Note the wickerwork chair, a design still favored in
Mediterranean countries. Photo courtesy of the Trustees of the British Museum.

guitar in one of her songs. "I would like to be like a guitar with a singing heart," she sings. "I would like to be like a guitar with a vibrant heart. *Comme une guitare que tu puisses remplir de ta chanson.* Like a guitar which you can fill with your song."

All of this may help account for the upsurge of guitarism in this age of the unfettered libido. A motivational researcher might find that the instrument's popularity is based on its singular appeal as a symbol of physical fulfillment, like the lingam and yoni of Hindu sculpture—the bowstrings of the great hunter, Apollo Argyrotoxos ("of the silver bow"), stretched out over the vibrant body of a woman.

There are also, to be sure, more mundane and practical reasons for the guitar's present high estate. These reasons have rarely been better summarized than in an advertising poster that appeared in the London tube stations in December, 1967, just as I was completing my research for this book at the British Museum. It was a poster for a Spanish guitar studio, and it spelled out the case for the guitar in a few fast lines, succinctly enough to deliver its message of persuasion before the arrival of the next train:

> *The 6 strings of the guitar have a compass of over 4 octaves: more than half that of a grand piano. They can all be played at once, giving the "little orchestra" its characteristic luxuriance of harmony. Highly responsive to the player's temperament and mood, the guitar, when skilfully played, combines a pure singing tone with deep resonance. This is not bad for an instrument 3 feet long and weighing 3½ lbs.*

Certainly one of the marvels of the guitar is the wonderful economy of the thing, compared to other ways of making music. When Andrés Segovia gives a concert in an auditorium like the Royal Festival Hall, which seats three thousand, he sits down on a low chair at the center of a stage designed for a symphony orchestra, props up his left foot on a small stool, and proceeds to pluck with his fingertips on the six strings strung across the box cradled in his arms. There is not an empty seat in the house; even the space on-stage normally taken up by the orchestra is occupied by paying guests. They are expected to quash their coughs for the next two hours so that Segovia's handmade, unamplified sonatas and sarabandes can reach to the hindmost seats in the top gallery.

Some critics seem to think that the flowering of twang is only a passing fashion, but what is actually involved here is a fundamental turnabout in our whole approach to music. And nowhere is this change better illustrated than in the curious sight of one man plucking one instrument in a hall that is patently much too large for him. The nineteenth-century sonic ideal embodied in the architecture of our concert halls was predicated on the smooth blending of massed sounds. There was a whole elaborate pattern of thinking—what might be called the "Glazunov Galaxy"—that went with this idea. An orchestra of a hundred men formed a kind of assembly line for the production of mellow, ear-filling music (the "symphony"). They worked under the supervision of a time and motion specialist (the "conductor") according to a complex, split-second plan (the "score") devised by a sonic inventor (the "composer"). If all went according to schedule, the result was a luxuriously velvet sound.

(8) Hittite juggler playing a lute (left) while another holds a trained monkey. Detail from the damaged Sphinx Gate bas-reliefs at Alaca Höyük, Turkey (New Kingdom, c. 1460–1190 B.C.). Some writers regard this hour-glass shaped lute as the earliest guitar. Photo from "Hittite Art" by Maurice Vieyra, courtesy of Alec Tiranti Ltd., London.

(9) Roman Apollo, second century A.D., holds a six-stringed cithara, or fidicula, which is played with the long plectrum in his right hand. With its shallow sound chest and cut-away shape, this unusual instrument looks as though it might be the classical prototype of the modern solid-body electric guitar. Some authorities question its authenticity. Photo courtesy of the Museo Arqueológico Nacional, Madrid.

Sometimes, in works like the *Largo* of the *New World Symphony,* the effect is so uniformly smooth that a tape recording of the thing can be played backward or forward and sound almost exactly the same.

What is conspicuously missing from such triumphs of determinism are the short lovely jabs of tone, the fractional wobbles of twang, that announce the birth of a new note on a guitar, lute, or sitar. Traditionally the sound of plucked instruments was a one-man sound, ideally scaled to small rooms and small audiences, so that the rubberoid microtones of finger striking string are not lost in the shuffle. (Guitars were never collectivized, in the interests of a bigger sound, like the violins; massed twangs, as in the balalaika orchestra, simply cancel each other.) But the microphone and the loudspeaker have changed all that. As electronic media have taken over from the concert hall, audiences have grown accustomed to the sound of the virtuoso guitar close up, as though they were sitting at the player's elbow; most recordings, in fact, are miked so close that you can hear the squeak of the fingers of the left hand as they move from fret to fret. Only then, having once acquired the taste electronically, will audiences attend the occasional "live" concerts, straining their ears and holding their breaths like so many Japanese pearl divers in hopes of hearing the telltale squeak of the moving finger.

The development of the electric guitar—whether as a bane or a boon to music remains to be seen—is also a by-product of the microphone. Throughout the nineteenth century guitar-makers had tried to give the instrument a bigger tone and greater volume. Suddenly, with electronic pick-up and amplification, every guitarist could be as loud as he liked. The electric guitar is essentially a sort of instant radio station, thanks to which the jazz guitar has been able to hold its own against instruments that would simply have overwhelmed it in the acoustic era: trumpets, drums, saxophones, and such. The Presley sound, and more especially the Beatle sound, has raised the twang of the guitar to still higher decibels: for the first time in musical history, something so intimate and individual can also be so *loud*.

Composers like Wagner and Richard Strauss used to write for vast orchestral aggregates in order to obtain an all-enveloping

[14]

(10) Player of a guitar-like
rubab, on a twelfth-century
Persian ceramic plate. The
sound chest is skin-covered;
a number of frets are indicated,
and a plectrum is being used.
Photo courtesy of the
Islamisches Museum, Berlin.

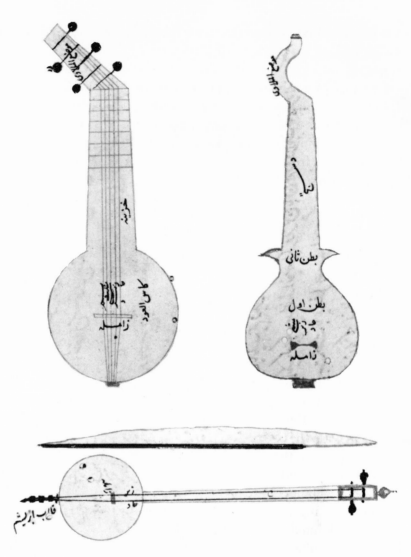

(11) Drawings of the Persian
five-string lute, bowed two-
string gizak, and guitar-like
rubab, described as having six
strings. From the Kanz al-tuhaf
("Treasury of Gifts"), an
anonymous Persian treatise of
the fourteenth century. Photos
courtesy of the Trustees of
the British Museum.

quantity of sound. Today the same thing can be achieved by four Beatles and an amplifier, with a minimum of that split-second co-ordination which is the first and most essential requirement for a performance of a Strauss tone poem. The results, in terms of musical flexibility, are incalculable; since nobody has to watch a waving stick, conductors and bandleaders have disappeared from the scene, and all sorts of improvisation are again possible. The first effects of this new sonic freedom can be heard in such wildly laissez-faire pop music as *Sgt. Pepper's Lonely Hearts Club Band,* and in experiments by serious composers like David Bedford, whose *Eighteen Bricks Left on April 21,* for two electric guitars, had its world premiere in London on November 27, 1967.

There are, of course, a dozen different varieties of guitar, some of them not even on speaking terms: Segovia's concert guitar, Joan Baez's folk guitar, Leadbelly's twelve-string blues guitar, Roy Rogers' Western screen guitar, Wes Montgomery's jazz guitar, George Harrison's solid-body plectrum guitar, and so on. They have very little in common except their history, but between them they have replaced the piano as the musical totem of the good life. The piano, in its heyday, betokened its owners' general sense of well-being; according to pianologist Arthur Loesser, a piano in the parlor expressed the idea that "God's in His heaven, dinner's at seven, all's right with the world." The guitar, however—even the $1,600 guitar—expresses the notion not of comfortable security but of youthful energy and an open mind; churches that want to demonstrate their willingness to move with the times have lately made a point of taking guitars into the fold. Although the Vatican has thus far prohibited the use of electric guitars in Catholic churches, the acoustic guitar has begun to make its appearance in such liturgical settings as the "flamenco mass" celebrated by Andalusian gypsies. In northern Spain, a folk-singing group of black-robed, guitar-toting Franciscan friars, Los 4 de Asis (The Four from Assisi), are playing the parish circuit to great acclaim. In July, 1967, a Catholic priest in Rochester, New York, conducted what was described as the first "folk song nuptial mass," with the Rev. Lawrence Gross himself strumming the accompaniments on a guitar, and joining in song with the bride and groom.

[17]

In Anglican churches the electric guitar began to appear under liturgical auspices in April, 1962, when the Rev. George Kirk of Ulley Parish Church, near Sheffield, introduced two electric guitars to replace the organ at evensong services. The players were two parishioners, fourteen and eighteen. Five years later the idea was tried at the fashionable St. James Episcopal Church, Manhattan, when a folk-rock group from St. Paul's School—the Drunken Lords —provided the music for an hour-long Sunday service. As *The New York Times* (May 1, 1967) reported: "They stepped to the microphone, tapped their feet, nodded their heads, thumped their guitars and boomed: 'Our Father, who art in Heaven, hallowed be Thy name. . . .'" After their swaying rendition of the Kyrie, the congregation was invited to join them. "Singing draws people together and gives them a chance to express, in a common way, their deepest feelings," explained the Rev. Ralph R. Warren during his sermon. "And young people are today singing out to the world and God with an exuberance and unabashed expression of what they are." Toward the close of the service, the *Times* noted, "on an aisle seat in the center of the nave, a white-haired woman smiled and tapped her cane to the beat of the Sanctus."

Not to be outdone by the churches, institutions of higher learning—American University, the Peabody Institute, and the Royal College of Music, among others—have lately begun granting academic recognition to an instrument that used to be relegated to the dormitories. Both the ultratraditionalist Mozarteum in Salzburg and the ultramodernist Darmstadt Festival offer guitar courses; Emilio Pujol, the first man to systematize the study of the guitar and its history, holds professorships both in Lisbon and at Barcelona; the Sidney, Australia, Conservatory of Music even has a "flamenco chair." But guitar-playing is usually learned at far less exalted levels, from private teachers, neighborhood studios, or self-help "methods," whose editions run into the hundreds of thousands. Millions of guitarists have learned to play by their own trial-and-error methods; that is another of the perennial marvels of the guitar, and even Segovia is intensely proud of being self-taught. The blues singer Son House once described to Julius Lester of *Sing*

quare conturbas me

(12) The "cythara" mentioned in the Latin text of the ninth-century French psalter in the Stuttgart Library is shown by the artist as a five-string instrument played with a plectrum. The player gazes pensively to one side as his *anima* (soul) looks on disconsolately from her hilltop. In the King James version, the biblical verses here illustrated suggest an entirely different musical image, since in English the word "cythara" is translated as "harp." The passage occurs in Psalm 43: "yea, upon the harp will I praise thee, O God my God. Why art thou cast down, O my soul?" Photo courtesy of Würtembergische Landesbibliothek, Stuttgart.

(13) King David plays what appears to be a skin-covered pandoura-like instrument in a detail from a psalter probably executed for the Emperor Lothar (795–855 A.D.), grandson of Charlemagne. Photo courtesy of the Trustees of the British Museum.

AGNUS STANS IN MONTE SION ET CUM EO CENTUM QUADRAGINTA MILIA HABENTES CIHARAS

HII SECUNTUR AGNUM

(14) "The lamb stands on Mt. Zion and with him 144,000 holding citharas."
Detail from the *Commentarius super Apocalypsum,* a commentary on the
Book of Revelation by Beatus of Liebana. The manuscript was executed at
León, c. 920 A.D.; some of the players are using plectra, others are plucking with
their fingertips. Photo courtesy of the Pierpont Morgan Library, New York.

(15) An historiated initial in a passional from Zwifalten, dated 1180 A.D.,
contains one of the earliest recognizable guitars in European art. St. Pelagia of
Antioch is seated on an ass and holds a rotta (another medieval descendant of the
cithara); one of her companions carries a guitar-like instrument which appears to
have three strings. Here begins the graphic association of the guitar with
erotic enterprises, for St. Pelagia "the sinner" was a dancer and courtesan, and
she is shown here before her conversion, with musical instruments as symbols of
her frivolous and fallen state. Later she was converted by a saintly bishop whose
preaching she happened to hear while passing a church with her train of admirers.
Photo by Marburg, courtesy of the Würtembergische Landesbibliothek, Stuttgart.

Out! magazine the typically unpremeditated process by which one becomes a blues guitarist:

Finally, I got the idea about how to tune it myself. I used to be a leader in the choir and they were singing the old vocal music at that time, you know, like the "do-re-mi's," so I got the idea to make the guitar go like that, and in a couple of weeks time, I was able to play a little tune. It was a little tune I'd heard Willie Wilson play called, "Hold Up, Sally, Take Your Big Legs Offa Mine." So the next time he came by I showed him I could play it. He said, "Come on and play with me tonight." It was Saturday night. I said, "I ain't good enough for that." He said, "Oh, yes, you is. You just play that. I'll back you up." So I started with him just like that. Finally, he left from around here, but I kept on playing and got better and better, you know.

Sooner or later every guitarist has to discover for himself the truism that the guitar is the easiest instrument to play badly and the hardest to play well. Even so, as Jacques Barzun has pointed out in this connection, anything worth doing is worth doing badly —a thought that may offer a certain consolation to that legion of amateurs *manqués* who will never master the technique of the thing. There must be countless millions of them. In a sense they constitute the very marrow of the history of the guitar, though we shall get to know their names only by chance, when they turn out to be very good at something else, like Mazzini, or James Joyce, or the astronaut Scott Carpenter, who was quoted as telling his wife, just before taking off on a 1962 space journey that was to land him two hundred miles off course: "If this comes to a fatal, screaming end for me I will have three main regrets: I will have lost the chance to contribute to my children's preparation for life on this planet; I will miss loving you when you are a grandmother; and I will never have learned to play the guitar well."

Never to have learned to play the guitar well! That is a regret which most guitarists are doomed to carry to the grave, a source of nagging frustration which has led to the staving-in of many a good guitar. Though most of us learn to live with it, ultimately, it seems to be responsible for the periodic outbursts of guitaristic bad temper that are reported in the press, like the dreadful case

[22]

(16) Minstrels play a guitarra latina (left) and a guitarra morisca (?) in a miniature from one of the manuscripts of the *Cantigas de Santa Maria,* collected by the thirteenth-century scholar-king, Alfonso el-Sabio of Castile and León. Photo courtesy of the Library of the Escorial.

(17) Medieval stringed instruments in Benedetto Antelami's twelfth-century sculptures for the baptistry of Parma Cathedral: King David plays a psaltery, the figure on his right a troubadour fiddle, and the figure on his left a gittern with four strings. Photo courtesy of the Ente Provinciale per il Turismo, Parma.

(18) Crowned figure with guiterne from the central portal of the
Reims Cathedral, first half of the thirteenth century.
Photo courtesy of the Service Photographique des Monuments Historiques.

(19) Angel with gittern from a canopy above one of the figures of the
apostles in the cathedral of Cologne (c. 1320). Photo courtesy of
the Rheinisches Bildarchiv, Stadtmuseum, Cologne.

of assault and battery which occurred in Wales not long ago, when a young man named Jones employed his $500 guitar to strike another gentleman on the head in what the court called "an unreasonable and unprovoked attack."

Besides being dangerous and unlawful, such uses of the guitar are a clear sign that we are living in exceptionally nervous and aggressive times. The known guitar crimes, up to now, have been mainly of the musical sort, as when, in 1381, three Englishmen (John Swetenham, William Garlthorp, and John Pycard) were sent to prison for making a disturbance with giternes. But the notion of the guitar as an instrument for venting frustrations has steadily been gaining ground. As this goes to press the pop star Jimi Hendrix has begun a new chapter in the history of the guitar by basing his whole act on the public maltreatment of the instrument. "Once I was playing away and there was a short circuit and the guitar went up in flames," he told Kevin Buckley of *Newsweek*. "It went over pretty well, so for three times after that I sprayed lighter fluid on it and then stamped out the burning pieces."

Hendrix is also in the habit of smashing his guitar, an act that grew out of another accident. "One time I was rolling around the stage and fell off into the crowd. I tried to get back, but the crowd was pressing in, so I threw the guitar back. I didn't mean to break it, but when you throw a guitar, it breaks." These tactics have demanded a whole new stylistic approach to virtuosity: "Sometimes I jump on the guitar," he explains. "Sometimes I grind the strings up against the frets. The more it grinds, the more it whines. Sometimes I rub up against the amplifier. Sometimes I sit on it. Sometimes I play the guitar with my teeth, or I'll be playing along, and I'll feel like playing with my elbow. I can't remember all the things I do."

This may not bode well for the future of the instrument, but Hendrix's ravishments may be merely the latest, most Freudian phase of man's age-old love affair with the guitar. It has been, from the very beginning, an intensely libidinous affair; indeed, as Segovia likes to tell it, the guitar was invented when Apollo

[25]

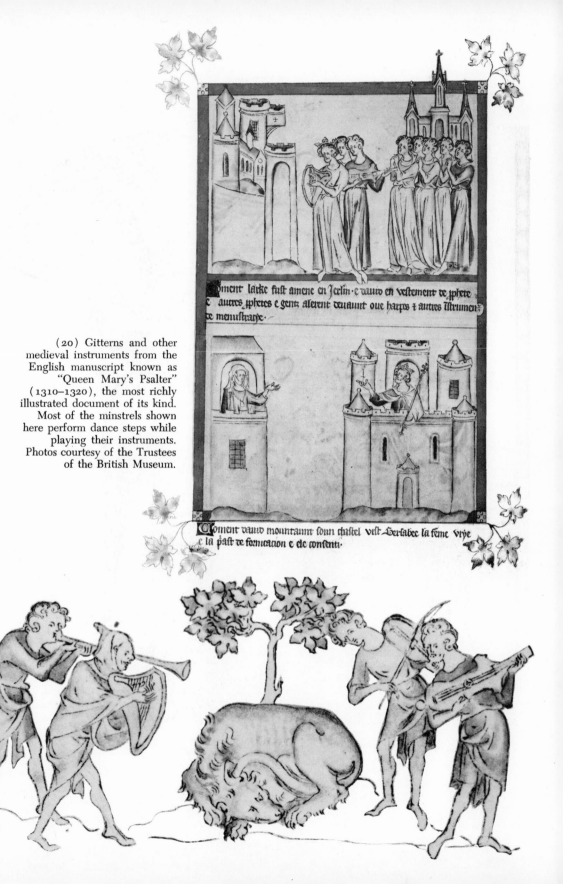

(20) Gitterns and other medieval instruments from the English manuscript known as "Queen Mary's Psalter" (1310–1320), the most richly illustrated document of its kind. Most of the minstrels shown here perform dance steps while playing their instruments. Photos courtesy of the Trustees of the British Museum.

TERPSICORE · XIII

(21) Terpsichore playing a
guitar, from the so-called
Tarocchi cards (formerly
attributed to Mantegna)—a
series of Italian Renaissance
prints, perhaps intended as a
tarot deck, engraved no later
than 1467. In Greek mythology
Terpsichore, the muse of
choral song and the dance,
traditionally carried a lyre.
Photo courtesy of the Trustees
of the British Museum.

(22) Another version of Terpsichore with guitar, from a second series of Tarocchi cards. Eight strings are shown, arranged in four courses, although only six pegs are visible. Six movable frets are clamped to the neck, and the player uses a long quill as a plectrum. The Renaissance guitar was so delicate, according to the Spanish author Diego Saavedra Faxardo, "that it won't bear the fingers, but must be touched with a fine quill to make it exert its harmony." Photo courtesy of the Trustees of the British Museum.

tried to rape Daphne—"He embraced her, Daphne was changed into a laurel, and from the wood of the sacred tree the first guitar was made."

The history of this enduring passion between the heirs of Apollo and the descendants of Daphne has been—as most of the illustrations in this book are intended to show—amazingly fruitful in terms of the visual arts. In countless prints and drawings, paintings, sculptures, the guitar serves as the mediator between music and art. When it appears in a picture, the space around it is filled with the implication of melody; it is as if the air were reverberating with the silent music that Keats heard when he saw it on a Grecian urn. Of course the other instruments can also be found in art: trumpeters playing fanfares, flutists piping serenades, violinists in string quartets, timpanists, pianists, cellists, bagpipers. But the lion's share of the attention always goes to plucked instruments; guitar, mandolin, harp, and in their day, lute and cithara. Some of the greatest painters of the Western world—Velásquez, Vermeer, Watteau, Goya, Manet, Degas, Picasso, among others—have produced masterpieces with the guitar. One wonders about the reason for this preponderance over pictures with violins or pianos; is it that the guitar is so much more pintoresque than the rest?

The answer, apparently, lies in the inherent simplicity of the guitar. A painting of a French-horn player, for example, will involve a complex set of social circumstances; the player will be a professional musician at a concert or rehearsal, or perhaps a gentleman riding to the hunt. Paintings of pianos always have to do with the bourgeois world of the nineteenth-century salon. A violin tucked under a sitter's chin distorts the face of the sitter as much as a cello disturbs his posture. Wind instruments pucker the lips or distend the cheeks. Only the guitar suffers from none of these deficiencies; holding a guitar in one's hands is almost as natural as holding a handkerchief, and leaves the face as pleasantly relaxed as any painter could wish it to be. And, equally important, a guitarist can be many things besides: a poet or a prince, an Italian actor, a Spanish peasant, a French lover, a Scottish earl, a gypsy, a street singer, a shoemaker. Angels have been known to play guitars. (Even monkeys have been taught to play it, but badly; it is the ability to play the guitar really well that distinguishes mankind from the apes.)

The guitarist, then, is Everyman, and if you riffle rapidly through the illustrations, like a flip-book cinematograph, the image of this composite hero will begin to jump before your eyes, his fingers twanging the strings of immortality. After several centuries "man with guitar" and his feminine counterpart, "*la guitariste*," emerge as a kind of hieroglyphic for music, especially the music one makes among friends. So familiar a symbol did it become that the cubists were able to use it as shorthand for "humanity" in their newly discovered geometrical world.

There is something utterly classical in the pose of man holding guitar, and the basic position has hardly changed in the four thousand years it has taken us to go from the Hittites to the hippies. Casual as it may seem, it is a decisive moment for civilization when man lays aside his arrows and devotes himself to plucking bowstrings for music. He can be very vulnerable at that point, as David discovered, in the Book of Kings, when he found himself suddenly the target of a tossed spear. But this very vulnerability is a precondition to all art, which reposes in fragile guitars rather than in swords. And thus the history of the guitar is essentially the story of some of man's best moments, even if occasionally he strikes a sour note.

(23) A lute and a guitar (shaped rather like a lira da braccio) play for allegorical dancers in "Le bon augure" (The Good Omen) by the Ferrara painter Ercole de' Roberti (d. 1496). Photo courtesy of the National Museum of Art, Bucharest.

Chapter 2

When Is
a Guitar?

There may be, for ought we know, infinite inventions of art, the possibility whereof we should hardly ever believe, if they were fore-reported to us. Had we lived in some rude and remote part of the world, and should have been told, that it is possible, only by a hollow piece of wood, and the guts of beasts stirred by the fingers of men, to make so sweet and melodious a noise, we should have thought it utterly incredible: yet now, that we see and hear it ordinarily done, we make it no wonder.

—JOSEPH HALL (1574–1656)

THE GUITAR owes its name to the ancient cithara, which was a kind of lyre, but its earliest ancestors belonged to a rival class of instruments, that of the ancient lute or pandoura. There were three basic stringed instruments in the ancient world—the harp, the lyre, and the lute, as we call them today—all of them developments of the musical bow. Pictures of these instruments appear for the first time in the art of Western Asia, notably in that great cradle of cultures between the Tigris and the Euphrates, the kingdoms of Mesopotamia, which provided the world with so many inventions still in common use, though taken very much for granted—the twenty-four-hour day, the sixty-minute hour, and the 360-degree circle, among others.

The ancient harp extended the principle of the musical bow by adding more strings and attaching a sound chest of some sort. Fritz Jahnel, the leading German authority on stringed instruments, whose *Die Gitarre und Ihr Bau* (1963) is the most exhaustive study of the technology of the guitar ever undertaken, has shown in his illustrations (Fig. 1) how an empty tortoise shell might well have served as the original sound chest. This and many

[33]

of his other drawings are reproduced here by kind permission of the author and of the publishers, Verlag Das Musikinstrument, Frankfurt. As another Jahnel drawing shows, the original form of the cithara, too, was based on a combination of turtle carapace covered with hide, and a V-frame of wood, connected at the top by a crossbar called a yoke (Fig. 3), to which the strings are fastened.

One of the classic Greek myths attributes the invention of this complex instrument to the infant Hermes, the instantly clever godling, who climbed out of his cradle to find and steal Apollo's cattle. On his way home with the stolen cows he picked up a turtle that was shuffling along in the grass. Boring out the "marrow" of the "mountain toad," he cut sticks to measure, which he inserted into holes bored in the turtle's carapace, stretched cowhide over it (as a sounding board), set the arms, connected them with a yoke, and fastened cow-gut strings to them. It was the sound of the strings and the presence of the cowhide that gave him away when Apollo came storming after his cattle. He made Hermes confess the theft and return the remaining cows. Then, as Robert Graves retells the story in *The Greek Myths:*

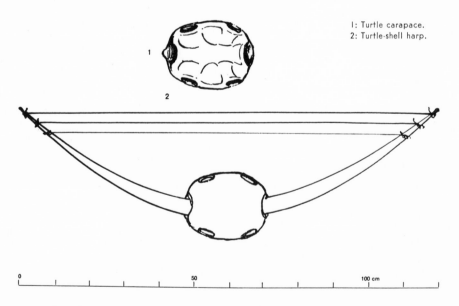

1: Turtle carapace.
2: Turtle-shell harp.

Hermes showed his newly-invented tortoise-shell lyre, and played such a ravishing tune on it with the plectrum he had also invented, at the same time singing in praise of Apollo's nobility, intelligence, and generosity, that he was forgiven at once. He led the surprised and delighted Apollo to Pylus, playing all the way, and there gave him the remainder of the cattle, which he had hidden in a cave. "A bargain!" cried Apollo. "You keep the cows, and I take the lyre." "Agreed," said Hermes, and they shook hands on it.

According to Graves's interpretation, Hermes here represents the older Creto-Helladic culture of central and southern Greece, and Apollo stands for the Indo-European Greeks, who came on the scene around 1700 B.C., and in the name of their adopted god Apollo took over and exploited the accomplishments of the earlier culture. "Some hold that the lyre invented by Hermes had seven strings; others that it had three only, to correspond with the seasons, or four, to correspond with the quarters of the year, and that Apollo brought the number up to seven."

3: Primitive cithara.
4: Primitive citharis.
5: Primitive lute.
6: Basic tanbur form.
7: Gourd resonators.

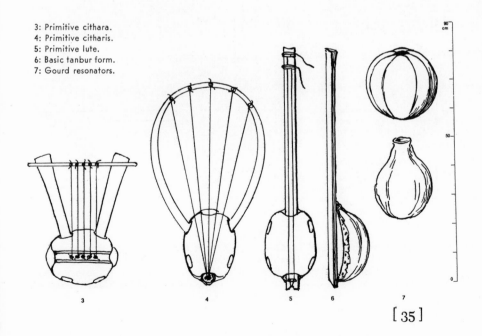

(24) Bernardino Campi (1522–c. 1590): King David playing a guitar (with a carved peg-box and lateral pegs, rather like a viol). Study for a painting on the cupola of the church of S. Sigismondo de Cremona, 1570. Photo courtesy of the Uffici, Florence.

The question of how many strings interests not only the poets but also the musicologists, who have traced the Greek instrument back to still earlier sources, such as the chetarah of the Assyrians (second millennium B.C.), the Hebrew kinnura or kinnor, and the Chaldean qitra. Perhaps these, in turn, are descended from some remote common ancestor whose name, in some hypothetical Ur-language, meant "three stringed," as does the Persian word sitar (*si-tar*, "three strings"). The sitar, incidentally, has retained its name

(25) Federico Fiori, known as Il Baroccio (c. 1526–1612): study for a painting of a blind musician playing a ghironda or hurdy-gurdy (one of the earliest guitar-shaped instruments). He looks surprisingly like a modern electric guitarist in mid-beat. Photo courtesy of the Uffici, Florence.

for centuries despite that fact that it now has six or seven main playing strings and a dozen or so sympathetic strings.

It was from the Assyrian chetarah, presumably, that the Greeks inherited the instrument Homer and the oldest Greek literary sources refer to as citharis and also as phorminx—a small, light version of the tortoise lyre. In the seventh century B.C., after the Homeric age drew to an end, two new words came into fashion: lyra and cithara. Citharis and cithara sound alike, but the musical philosopher Aristoxenus (fourth century B.C.) stated that "citharis and cithara are not the same," and that "the lyra is a citharis." The new cithara was a much heavier, technically far more complicated instrument, imported from Western Asia; in fact, Plutarch explains that the cithara was called *Asias* "because it was mostly used by the singers from Lesbos, who live over in Asia." Greek vase paintings make the distinction perfectly clear: the lyra (formerly citharis) is a light instrument with a tortoise body and delicately curved arms, while the cithara is U-shaped and has a massive wooden sound chest as a base, so that it produces a much greater volume of sound, and can also stand without a support.

What happened, obviously, is that a technically improved version, developed in a neighboring country from the same chetarah prototype, had been imported from Asia Minor by professionals wanting (as musicians always do) a "bigger sound." To avoid confusion between the new cithara and the old citharis, one of them has to relinquish its name and become the lyra. This kind of etymological leapfrogging occurs all the time in the history of musical instruments; we shall find it again when the Spanish guitarra meets the English gittern and then, as the superior instrument, quickly displaces it. The Oxford Unabridged Dictionary has a remarkably lucid note on this knotty subject that should be appended to all histories of musical instruments, which tend to be snarled in their terminology because they treat names as constants rather than variables:

Musical instruments are subject to great alteration of structure and shape, in process of time, and in different countries. Consequently, cognate names, regularly descended from the same original, come at

(26) Luca Signorelli's "Calling of the Elect" in the Cathedral of Orvieto, Italy.
The fresco, recently restored, is dated 1499–1505. Playing without plectra, the
angels all anchor their little finger to the belly of the instrument—a playing position
which was to become standard technique in later centuries.
Photo courtesy of Archivo Mas.

(27) An angel guitarist accompanies himself and members of an interracial choir in a sixteenth-century Portuguese nativity scene (*preséfio*) from the Church of the Misericordia, Abrantes. The painter is known as the "Mestre de Abrantes." Photo courtesy of the Museu Nacional de Arte Antiga, Lisbon.

length to be applied by different nations to very different types of the instrument. Sometimes, also, one or more derivative types, distinguished by diminutive or augmentative names, are used in the same country. When, as often happens, any of these national or local forms of the instrument become subsequently known and introduced in another country, they usually take their local name with them. Hence, the modern languages often use two or three modifications of the same original word applied to as many instruments which different peoples have developed out of the same type. Thus cither, cithern or cittern, citole, gittern, guitar, zither, are all found in English as names of extant or obsolete instruments developed from the cithara.

The original seven-string cithara had to undergo numerous small changes during the thousand years it reigned as the chief instrument of the public games and religious festivals of Greece and Rome; it was not as a fiddler that Nero prided himself, but as a cithara player, and as "Nero Citharoedus" he had himself sculptured in marble. The cithara seems to have begun as a three- or four-stringed instrument but soon acquired more, always against stiff opposition from the musical Establishment. The Roman philosopher Boethius reports that Timotheus of Miletus was expelled from Laconia for having presumed to add unauthorized strings to the cithara of his day. "Whereas Timotheus the Milanesian," read the decree of expulsion, "has dishonored ancient music; and whereas, by discarding the seven-stringed cithara and introducing a multiplicity of tone, he corrupts the ears of the young . . . it is decreed that the Kings and Ephors shall censure Timotheus and compel him to cut away the superfluous strings of the eleven, leaving the seven." The text of this decree, as cited by Boethius, has been exposed as a literary fraud, probably dating to the second century A.D., but it retains an essential kernel of truth, since there were many stories of this kind, all revealing the immense significance attached to such matters in classical antiquity, when numbers possessed a mystical importance on a par with their present power in the realm of science.

The cithara, favored by professional players, became in itself a status symbol and was often decked out with elaborate ornaments;

(28) Baroque angel guitarist in the Cathedral of Seville. He seems to be playing a passage on the first string, but his thumb is set to strum rasgado chords. Photo courtesy of Archivo Mas.

[42]

(29) Baroque angel in the parochial church of Llivia, province of Gerona, Spain. He holds a barred chord and strums his four-course guitar flamenco style. Photo courtesy of Archivo Mas.

(30) Trio of angel musicians—lute, guitar and lira da braccio—from an unknown painter's "Presentation of Jesus at the Temple," in the Museo Provincial of Valladolid. Photo courtesy of Archivo Mas.

a certain Evangelos, mentioned by Lucian, appeared at the Pithian games with a cithara of pure gold adorned with pearls and carved stones (it must have had a terrible tone). The lyra, meanwhile, remained in common use as the "folk guitar" of its day, affectionately known to the Greeks as chelys (tortoise) and to the Romans as testudo (turtle).

Neither the Greeks nor the Romans, however, found much use for instruments in the lute category, and they can be seen only very rarely in Hellenic art. Like the lyres, the first "lutes" may have been based on a tortoiseshell sound box, as Jahnel's drawing indicates (Fig. 5); such three-string instruments, in fact, are still being made in Tunis and Morocco, by now as much for the tourist trade as for local demand. A short neck is glued to a turtle carapace, which is covered with a piece of rabbit skin stretched tight as a drumhead but perforated along the edge by a series of small sound holes. From the looks of this shaggy construction, with bits of hair still clinging to the skin, one would hardly suspect that this is the ancestral form not only of the lute but also of the violin, the cello, and the guitar.

It is the principle of the thing that matters; the principle of the fingerboard, which seems perfectly obvious but must have represented a major technological breakthrough in its time. Both the harp and the lyre were designed basically to produce only one note per string, like a pianoforte: to play a variety of tones, one needed a lot of strings. The lute had few strings, but by pressing them against the fingerboard—i.e., by "stopping" the strings—the player had access to a whole gamut of tones. Musically, in an age of melody, the lutes opened up a new range of microtonal possibilities, just as later, in medieval Europe, they were to suggest new patterns of harmony.

The "lute" was known to the Greeks as pandoura or pandouros, but this, too, was an import from Western Asia, and the word is almost certainly derived from the Sumerian pan-tur (bow-small). This particular "small bow" is one of the great hand-me-downs of the musical world; in 4,500 years it has undergone an endless series of permutations, from pantur to pandoura, pandore, mandore, mandola, vandola, etc., so that an echo of Sumer is with us yet in the form of the mandolin (literally, I suppose, a "small bow-small"), as well as the Spanish bandurria. In a collateral branch of the family pantur turned to tanbur by the process of verbal transposition known as metathesis, and tunbur, tunbura, tamboura, etc., are current terms for long-necked lutes all the way from India to the Balkans. Meanwhile the name also attached itself to certain percussion instruments—presumably because the tanbur had a drumlike, skin-covered sound chest—with the result that a French tambour is a snare drum, while a tambourine, such as gypsies jangle, is yet another "small bow-small."

Lute players on ancient bas-reliefs are often solitary figures playing what appears to be household music—as opposed to the great religious and military processions in which harps and lyres usually participate. One remarkable set of Hittite sculptures, however, depicts a lute or pandoura player in company with a group of jugglers, including a snake charmer, two acrobats, and a man with a trained monkey. The instrument he holds in his arms (Plate 8) raises a lot of fascinating questions: since its body is shaped like an hourglass, and seven frets are clearly visible, is this, by any chance, the first "guitar"? Many writers would like to interpret it as such, to give the guitar as ancient a history as possible. One of them—Ernst Biernath—even produced a volume hopefully entitled *Die Gitarre seit dem III Jahrtausend vor Christus* (*The Guitar Since the Third Millenium* B.C.), which tries to prove, among other things, that what the Children of Israel hung up by the waters of Babylon were really guitars. But appearances can be deceiving; the sound chest of the instrument in question is almost certainly covered with skin, and the neck, instead of stopping where it meets the body, pierces it like a spear and forms a small point at the base to which the strings are attached. Its very feminine shape, however, and the fact that it is the earliest clear-cut illustration of a fretted fingerboard, entitles this Hittite lute to a place of honor among the precursors of the guitar.

A very similar type of lute, the nefer, was introduced to Egypt by Western Asian invaders in the time of the Hyksos; with the rise

(31) Angel with guitar by the seventeenth-century Spanish painter Guzman Cuesta. Five courses of strings—four double courses and a single treble "chanterelle"—are clearly visible. Photo courtesy of the Bowes Museum, Barnard Castle, County Durham.

of the New Kingdom this long, oval-bodied lute assumed a major role in musical life along the Nile. Since several actual examples have turned up in Egyptian tombs, the nefer's methods of construction are known (Figs. 8–14). Three, sometimes only two, strings were tied to the top of the neck with a loop rather than pegs; the neck itself makes several "stitches" through the skin covering the sound chest. Nefer players appear in innumerable wall paintings as part of an immensely varied and sensual musical scene that includes perfumed dancing girls and solo singers, flutists and harpists, percussion players, oboes, trumpets, bells, lyres, castanets, tambourines. Appropriately enough, the text of the song which the musician on Plate 1 (Eighteenth Dynasty) accompanies with his nefer contains an exhortation to eat, drink, and he merry: "Enjoy yourself . . . you can't take it with you," or words to that effect.

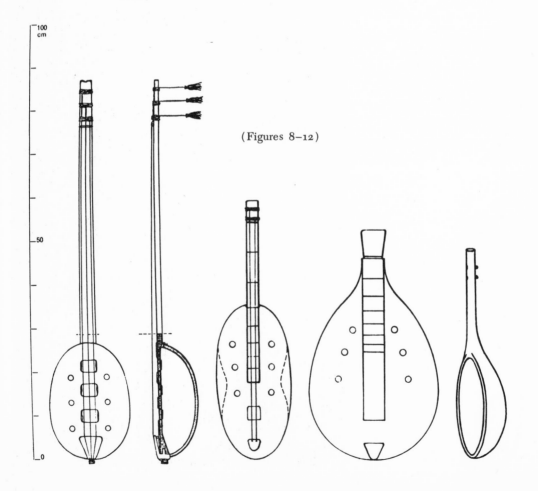

(Figures 8–12)

Long afterward, when Roman governors and Christian missionaries had swept away the pharaonic religions, the Egyptians were still among the most musical peoples of the ancient world. It was the Coptic epoch of Egypt's five thousand-year musical history that produced the first instrument that more or less answers to the definition of "guitar." Several of these small, nameless inventions, dated somewhere between the third and eighth centuries, were discovered early in the twentieth, in the ruins of the Coptic monastery of Apa (Saint) Jeremias at Sakkara and in the Coptic cemetery at Qarara. What sets these curious instruments apart from ordinary lutes is the fact that they have a clearly defined back and top, both flat, separated by at least nominally incurved sides (Figs. 15, 16; Plate 219). Another important design element not present in earlier models is the way the neck meets the body,

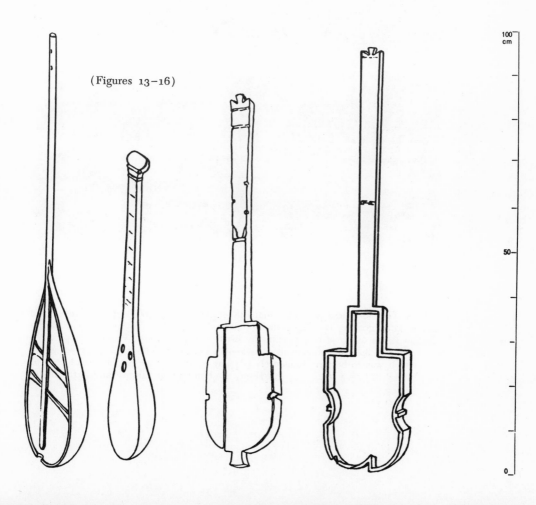

(Figures 13–16)

100
cm

50

0

(32) The Bolognese poet Giovanni Filoteo Achillini (1466–1533) singing to his guitar: an engraving by Marcantonio Raimondi, the great master engraver of the Italian Renaissance, after a portrait by his teacher, Francesco Francia. Apparently this is the earliest portrait of a known personage playing a guitar—a genre which was to become immensely popular in later centuries. Photo courtesy of the Henry E. Huntington Library and Art Gallery.

[50]

an arrangement resembling the "heel" of a Spanish guitar—though in this case neck and body are carved from a single piece of wood. These Coptic guitars are archeological oddities, however, because the next stage in the evolution of the guitar, as far as anyone can prove, did not take place until much later, in the Middle Ages. Still, when *is* a guitar? The Arabs, passing through Egypt on their way to complete the great Muslim conquest of North Africa and Spain, may well have transmitted the cardinal features of this design to the instrument makers of Western Europe.

For the time being, at any rate, the round-back lute reigned unchallenged as the queen of fingerboard instruments. Even in Rome, despite the established position of the classic cithara, the lute began to make headway as a household instrument after the second century A.D. Sculptures of lute-playing ladies—never men—are found among the sarcophagus reliefs of early Christian as well as pagan tombs (Plate 7). But with the fall of the Empire both lute and cithara vanish from sight, only to reappear centuries later in the monkish manuscripts of the Middle Ages. The cithara's descendants are legion: the medieval chrotta (rotta) and Welsh crwth have been traced back to it, the English cittern, Austrian zither, German Cithrinchen, and so on. Some have inherited vestiges of its form, others only memories of the name, which medieval Latin-descended languages turned into cithera, cetera, cetra, tschaidra, cedra, cidra, citre, citale, citola, etc.

Meanwhile another, no less prolific family was founded by the Roman fides (literally "strings") or fidicula—a term defined as "small cithara" but applied by the Romans to stringed instruments of all persuasions, including lutes and lyres. According to Ovid, the forest god Faunus was the "inventor of the curved fides," and in a figurative sense they symbolized the poet's art—in the adage *Nihil cum fidibus graculo,* for example ("Ignoramuses have nothing to do with poetry"). In due course fides-fidicula became fidula or vitula in medieval Latin, vielle in French, viula in Provençal, videle or fiedel in German, fithele or fiddle in English, viola and violino in Italian, vihuela in Spanish . . . in all, a distinguished progeny. In most instances the vielles and citolas represent two

[51]

separate and distinct species, but in Spain, for a time, vihuela was to be interchangeable with guitarra, just as fidicula and cithara had been synonymous in Rome.

At what point the Spaniards arrived at the name and style of their famous guitarra is quite impossible to say; its beginnings must have appeared, as we shall see, sometime before the thirteenth century. Whether the Moors played a decisive role in its development, as some believe, is another debatable question. It is equally possible that the first Spanish guitars were a European development, with the fidicula-cithara as its point of departure. Certain is only that the Arabic influence in Spain prepared the ground for the advent of the guitar. It was the flowering of arts and sciences under the Arab rulers that created the need for guitars and guitarists, and led directly to the first great school of guitar music, the vihuelistas.

In all the Spanish arts the Arabic influence was incalculable; whatever they touched would never again be the same. The Moorish adventure in Spain has been compared to a great torch bringing light into a world of darkness. Perhaps it was not as dramatic as that, but a disparity did exist, and is graphically illustrated in the two styles of architecture erected by the Arabs and the Christians in their respective corners of Spain: on the one hand, the heavy, windowless fortress architecture of the Romanesque style, stamped with the siege mentality of the Middle Ages and with a kind of plump, rustic feudalism; on the other, the airy, elegant lines of Moorish architecture, with its soaring columns and arches, its screens and courtyards and audience chambers, their stalactite ceilings defying the law of gravity. The Moors filled their palaces with books; 400,000 in Cordova alone, according to one report. To their Spanish dominion, Al-Andalus, the caliphs of Cordova brought a vast body of literature covering the poetry of Persia, the theology of Arabia, and the science of the Greeks. From Baghdad and other musical centers of the Muslim world they imported singers and virtuosos. The singing girls' names speak for themselves: Diya (Splendor), Basbas (Caress), Sihr (Charm), Mutayyim (Enslaving), Dhat al-Khal (Mistress of the Beauty Spot), Raiq (Bloom

(33) An allegory of music attributed to Peter Vischer the Younger (1487–1528) in the Church of St. Sebaldus, Nuremberg. The central figure is thought to be the muse of music, and the absence of the left hand to stop the strings may be due to a fault in the bronze casting. Photo by Dr. Heinz Stafski, courtesy of the Bärenreiter Verlag, Kassel.

(34) Comedian with a guitar: sculptured figure from the façade of the palace of the Counts of Montarco, Ciudad Rodrigo, Spain. The instrument is a small vihuela or *tiple* guitar with six strings, large violin pegs, a wide neck, small body and little curvature at the waist—the sort used by strolling players in the early sixteenth century. Photo courtesy of Archivo Mas.

(35) Player of the vihuela de mano (hand-plucked vihuela) from a bronze lectern by Juan Nicolas de Vergara, c. 1565, in the Cathedral of Toledo. Photo courtesy of Archivo Mas.

(36) Player of the vihuela de arco (bowed vihuela) from the other side of Vergara's lectern at Toledo. Photo courtesy of Archivo Mas.

of Youth), Mahbuba (Beloved). Both singers and players favored al-'ud, Arabic for "the wood" (*i.e.*, in its original sense, a wooden instrument, as distinct from a skin-covered one), from which we ourselves derive the word lute. Together with the 'ud came a dozen lesser members of its family, including the tunbur, the bowed rabab, a qitara that may have had a flat sound chest, and the plucked rubab, with a pear-shaped body covered half in skin, half in wood. An Arabic treatise, the *Kanz al-tuhaf* (*Treasury of Gifts*), gave directions for making rubabs: they were to be carved from apricot or plum wood that had been steeped in milk to make it more supple, and varnished with a mixture of ground glass and glue to bring out the "full tone."

With such instruments virtuosos were known to cast spells and work enchantments. The tenth-century *Ikhwan al-Safa'* contains an early forerunner of the rave review: "He played them [the strings] in a kind of way that made everyone in the assembly laugh from the merriment and pleasure, joy and gladness, which entered their souls. Then he altered them [the strings] and played them in another way, and made them all weep from the sadness of the mode [*naghma*] and grief of heart. Then he altered them again, and played them again, and made everyone go to sleep."

That infinite pains were taken over each detail of lute construction is confirmed by a conversation reported by the historian Ibn Hayan, writing about the first audition of the Persian minstrel Ziryab before the Caliph Harun al-Rashid. Ziryab (The Blackbird, so-called on account of his dark complexion) insisted on sending for his own lute rather than accept the one offered him by his own teacher, Ishak, who was also present at court.

HARUN: Why were you unwilling to use your master's lute?
ZIRYAB: If the Emir desires me to sing in my master's style, I will sing with his lute, but if I am to sing in my own style, I must play my own instrument.
HARUN: They seem alike to me.
ZIRYAB: At first view, yes; but even if the size and wood are the same, the weight is not. My lute weighs about a third less than Ishak's, and my strings are made of silk that has not been spun with hot water, which

[55]

weakens them. The bass and third strings are made of lion guts, softer and more sonorous than those from any other animal. These strings are stronger than any others and withstand better the striking of the plectrum.

When Ishak's understandable jealousy drove Ziryab from Baghdad, he made his way to Spain, there to become the shining ornament of the court of Cordova, a man of wealth and influence, founder of a great school of music whose influence lasted for centuries. Some say that its echoes can still be heard when the cantaores unlimber their voices in Andalucía. It was here, in Al-Andalus, that Ziryab invented the fifth string of the lute, and a plectrum made of an eagle's talon. And it was here that the taste for the twanging of plucked instruments brought a perpetual quiver of music to the narrow streets of the cities—a sound that has not yet deserted the old towns of Spain. What that musical life was like is vividly recorded in a manuscript written by an Oriental Arab, Ahmed bin Muhammad Al-Yemeni, who visited Al-Andalus during its golden age of lute playing:

I was in Malaga, a Spanish city, in the year 406 of the Hegira [1015 A.D.] and was housed for a long time by illness. Two friends, mindful of my delirium, cared for me tenderly. It was at night especially that I felt wakeful. All around my house there was an incessant jangle of singing, and of lutes, tomburs, and lyres, which disturbed me intensely and added to the restlessness and suffering caused by my illness. These toccatas and songs nailed themselves to my mind without hope of respite, so that I was filled with aversion for them, and would have liked to find a house away from all the noise. But this was difficult in Malaga, for the people are absolutely dominated by their passion for music. One night I awoke after dozing a little, and noticed that the tumult of odious voices and turbulent tunes had calmed down, leaving only a breath of sound, tranquil and lovely. I felt that my soul understood this music and could find repose in it, with none of the repugnance I had felt for the other. It was purely instrumental, without the human voice. Then it began increasing slowly in volume. I was drawn to it and disposed to listen even when it had reached the fullest possible strength. I found myself forgetting my misery in the emotional enjoyment, which almost caused me to image that the walls and floor were floating around me. I said to myself: "For instru-

(37) Orpheus plays a six-course vihuela in the frontispiece of Luys Milan's
El Maestro, published in Valencia, 1535. This is the first of the great collections of
music for vihuela. Photo courtesy of the Biblioteca Nacional, Madrid.

mental music, nothing could be more perfect. What kind of voice will the musician have? How will it end?" Scarcely was the question asked before there came the sound of a woman's voice, clear and beautiful. I could not contain myself and got up, leaving my two companions sleeping. I opened the door of my room and followed the sound until I reached the part of the house whence I could overlook the neighbors. I saw a large garden with about twenty people in the center, seated in a row with sweets, fruits, and drinks before them. The girl who was singing sat apart from the others, and held her listeners spellbound. She sang and sang, and I, hidden above, could watch without being seen. As she sang a verse, I learned it, till I knew quite a number. Finally I withdrew to my room, thanking God, as though I had come out of a great trouble and were no longer ill or suffering. The next morning I got up, and went to see a friend, the Ulema of Cordova, who was living in Malaga, and told him what had happened. I recited the verses and described the house. He smilingly answered: "That is the house of the minister so and so, and the slave girl comes from Baghdad, one of the best singers of Al-Mansur bin Abi Amir. She came into the possession of this minister after Al-Mansur's death. Those poems were written by the Spanish poet, Muhammad bin Carloman."

This is an extraordinary picture of the pleasures of music and poetry at a time when the cold countries to the north were just learning to read and write. "Where else in the world was there such a phenomenon in the eleventh century?" asks the Spanish musicologist Julian Ribera, from whose *La Música de las Cantigas* this account is taken (in the translation by Eleanor Hague and Marion Leffingwell). Where indeed but in Moorish Spain? Besides Malaga the likeliest place for such a concert would have been Seville, a beehive of musicians and instrument makers. "I do not know why it should be so," said a musician from Seville to his rival from Cordova, in the presence of the Caliph, "but it is a fact that if a scholar dies in Seville his books are taken to Cordova to be sold; but if a musician dies in Cordova his instruments are sold in Seville."

(38) Boy on a dolphin plays the vihuela in Luys de Narvaez's *Delphin de Musica* (Dolphin of Music) published in Valladolid, 1538. The title and illustration refer to the legend of the Greek poet Arion of Methymna, who was saved from drowning and borne to land by a dolphin who had been charmed by his music. Photo courtesy of the Biblioteca Nacional, Madrid.

(39) Title page of the first book of music specifically intended for the guitar. *Le Premier livre de chansons, gaillardes, pavannes*, etc., was one of a series of four such books printed by Robert Granjon and Michel Fezandat in Paris during the early 1550s, with tablature by Guillaume Morlaye. The guitar is a four-course French instrument with three double courses and a single "chanterelle." Photo by Gebrüder Zumbühl, courtesy of the Viadana Bibliothek, St. Gallen.

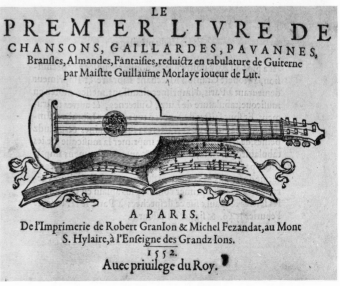

LE
PREMIER LIVRE DE
CHANSONS, GAILLARDES, PAVANNES,
Branfles, Almandes, Fantaifies, reduictz en tabulature de Guiterne
par Maiftre Guillaume Morlaye ioueur de Lut.

A PARIS.
De l'Imprimerie de Robert GranIon & Michel Fezandat, au Mont
S. Hylaire, à l'Enfeigne des Grandz Ions.
1552.
Auec priuilege du Roy.

(40) "Quintern" (*i.e.*, guitar) player from the series of ten "Women Musicians" attributed to the Swiss artist Tobias Stimmer (1539–1584). The woodcuts are thought to have been made in Strasbourg in the 1570s. "It is obvious that the quintern was modeled on the fiddle," says the accompanying poem. "One can tell by the looks of it that it served as an introduction to the lute, for accompanying songs, for reciting old tales and a good many other things. We should preserve this tradition of our elders." Photo courtesy of the New York Public Library.

Chapter 3

Guitarra and Vihuela

Among the creatures of the earth, God placed music with
the greatest reason and perfection in man, and among
stringed instruments in the vihuela.
—ENRIQUEZ DE VALDERRÁBANO

A N OBSCURE Swiss poet named Amarcius, writing in eleventh-
century Latin, has left us a brief account of what minstrelsy
was like in Northern Europe during the Middle Ages:
"When the citharist appears, after arranging for his fee, and proceeds
to remove his instrument from its cover of oxhide, the people assem-
ble from far and near, fix their eyes upon him and listen with soft
murmurs as he strikes the strings with fingers stretched far apart;
strings which he himself has fashioned from sheep gut, and which
he plays now tenderly, now with harsh booming sounds."

The word cithara in Amarcius' poem might have referred to any
of the plucked instruments of his time. Perhaps he was talking
about the kind of "cythara" illustrated in the ninth-century Stuttgart Psalter (Plate 12), a five-string, paddle-shaped model that
is fairly typical of the various medieval precursors of the guitar
(Figs. 17–24). Still closer to the mark is the pear-shaped gittern
—alias guiterre, gyterne, gytryn, etc.—which makes its appearance
in the poems and manuscripts of the next two centuries. The *Roman de la Rose* (c. 1280) mentions harps, fiddles, rebecs, guitarres,

[61]

and lutes in a single breath. An early English translation of the *Roman* advises:

> And if thy voice be faire and cler . . .
> Thou shalt maken no great daunger
> Whanne to singe they goodly preye;
> It is thy worship for t'obeye:
> Also to you it longith ay
> To harpe and gitterne, daunce and play. . . .

Gitterns are played by both men and angels in the pages of Queen Mary's Psalter, a British Museum manuscript, dated 1310-1320, said to be the most richly illustrated of all medieval psalters (Plate 20). The British Museum also owns the only actual gittern still in existence (Plate 220), an ornate instrument carved from a single block of wood with a back like a ship's keel and sides tapering from a slim tailpiece to a massive neck, as elaborate as the rest. There is an oval hole in the neck so that the player can grasp the instrument much as a painter holds a pallette. This is not a typical example of the species, however, perhaps because it

(Figures 17–24)

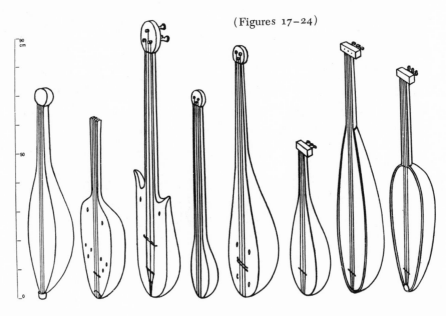

(41) Dutch guitarist by an
unknown seventeenth-century
engraver plays a four-course,
eight-string instrument.
Collection of the author.

(42) A page of stringed instruments from the great *Syntagma Musicum* of Michael Praetorius, published at Wittenberg and Wolfenbüttel, 1615–1620. The illustrations are from a supplement entitled *Theatrum Instrumentorum sea Sciagraphia*. It identifies the guitar as "quinterna"; most of the others belong to the lute family. Photo courtesy of the New York Public Library.

(43) A page of stringed instruments from Athanasius Kircher's *Musurgia Universalis*, published in Rome, 1650. He refers to the guitar as "cythara hispanica," and shows a five-course model. Photo courtesy of the New York Public Library.

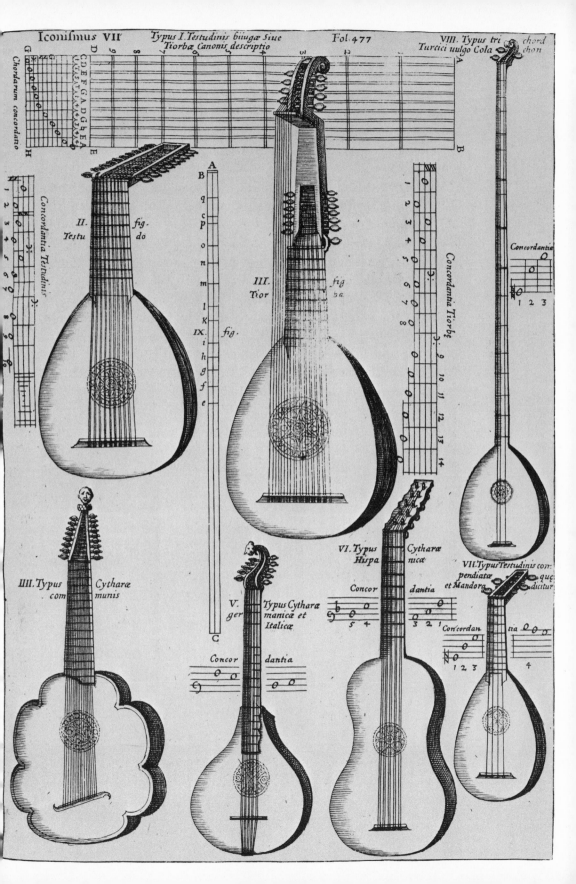

was a wood sculptor's showpiece rather than a playing instrument. And the original form has been badly tampered with. At some point in its history, someone tried to convert it into a "violin" by adding such anachronisms as a violin fingerboard, bridge, and soundboard.

Much simpler and more playable gitterns can be seen in the hands of cathedral sculptures throughout northern Europe (Plates 18–19). Strummed with a plectrum, they sometimes look remarkably like modern solid-body electrics. But the gittern cannot really qualify as a bona fide guitar: while it curves inward quite elegantly at the waist, the shoulders flare out on both sides of the neck as though the stubs of wings were attached to them. The significance of these curious bulges has been explained by Emanuel Winternitz, curator of musical collections at the Metropolitan Museum of Art, in a long and ingeniously reasoned essay on *The Survival of the Kithara and the Evolution of the English Cittern*. Apparently the "wings" are vestigal remains of the two arms of the classical cithara,

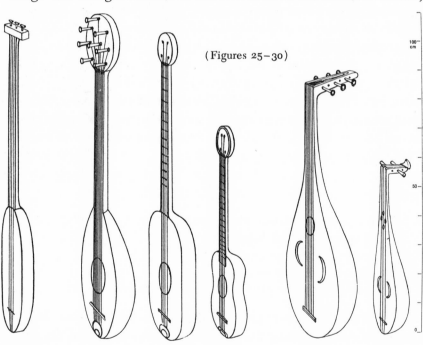

(Figures 25–30)

and the gittern itself represents a major link in a chain of evolution stretching from Apollo's lyre to the English drawing-room cittern.

It was the cittern, and not the guitar, that inherited the form and function of the medieval gittern. The very word *cittern,* in fact, was a sixteenth-century formation that came into use in England just at the time when the obsolete gittern was being supplanted by the bigger and better-sounding Spanish guitar. In the ensuing conflict between "gittern" and "guitarra" one of the names had to go; in effect, it was the same process of etymological displacement that had taken place in Greece when the Asian cithara outflanked the Homeric citharis. The cittern that emerged from this collision —wire-strung and played with a plectrum—never really recovered from the blow. Flat, tear-drop versions of it continued to be made down to the eighteenth century, when it enjoyed a brief vogue as the "English guitar" before fading out completely.

The gittern, then, was uncle rather than father to the guitar. Both of them, however, showed the same deplorable penchant for traveling in fast company. Despite the patronage of saints and angels, a certain air of licentiousness and loose living clings to the gittern and its boon companions. John Wycliffe, the English church reformer, sternly denounced the sinners who used "veyn songis and knackynge and harpynge, gyternynge and daunsynge, and othere veyn triflis to geten the stynkyng love of damyselis." Chaucer, who took a much more tolerant view of such triflis, welcomed the gittern as an aid to love, and has his heroes serenading by moonlight: "He syngeth in his voys gentil and smal . . . ful wel acordaunt to his gyternynge." In the "Pardoner's Tale" it plays a lusty accompaniment to all sorts of wanton sports and pleasures:

> In Flaunders whilom was a compaignye
> Of yonge folk that haunted en folye,
> As riot, hasard, stywes, and tavernes,
> Where as with harpes, lutes, and gyternes,
> They daunce and pleyen at dees bothe day and night. . . .

The minstrels and jongleurs who recited the *chansons de geste* (songs of deeds) during the age of the troubadours used the gittern

(44) Title page of an early edition—probably the third—of Juan Carles y Amat's *Guitarra Española y Vandola*. This edition, published at Gerona in 1639, with a foreword by Fray Leonardo de San Martin, fails to mention the author by name; as a result, the treatise is sometimes mistakenly attributed to San Martin. It influenced guitar tutors for well over a century. Photo courtesy of the Biblioteca Nacional, Madrid.

(45) Finger positions for the coded chords in Carles y Amat's *Guitarra Española*. Photo courtesy of the Biblioteca Nacional, Madrid.

not so much to accompany the poem as to provide musical interludes between couplets. They were not merely entertainers in the modern sense: their real function was to educate the illiterate courts of the Middle Ages. Kings and princes who wanted to instruct their vassals in the ways of chivalry "commanded the minstrels and jongleurs to appear with their lutes and viols and other instruments so that they might play and sing the ballads composed about the famous deeds of knights."

To keep body and soul together in those precarious times, a wandering *jongleur* was in any case well advised to cultivate more than one string to his lyre. "I can play the lute," a minstrel could boast, "the violin, the pipe, the bagpipe, the syrinx, the harp, the gigue, the gittern, the symphony, the psaltery, the organistrum, the regals, the tabor, and the rote. I can sing a song well and make tales to please young ladies and can play the gallant for them if necessary. I can throw knives into the air and catch them without cutting my fingers. I can do dodges with string, most extraordinary and amusing. I can balance chairs and make tables dance. I can throw a somersault and walk on my head."

The finest pictures of medieval minstrels and their instruments are to be found in the collection of *Cantigas de Santa María* made for the thirteenth-century scholar-king, Alfonso el Sabio ("the Learned") of Castile and León. The Cantigas are songs in praise of the Virgin and her miracles—over four hundred of them, recorded in four magnificent manuscripts, which have been preserved in Spanish and Italian libraries. They are illustrated with hundreds of miniatures covering virtually every phase of life in the Middle Ages, from architecture and costume to warfare and shipbuilding. Included, too, is a detailed picture of instrumental music at the court of a great Spanish monarch: musicians perform on flutes and bagpipes, trumpets are played in pairs, bell music is tapped out on small carillons, minstrels and *juglares* perform on the guitarra morisca and the guitarra latina (Plate 16).

For the next two hundred years or so we hear a good deal about this distinction between the "Moorish" and the "Latin" guitar—not only in Spain but also in France, where in 1349 Duke Jehan of Normandy is known to have employed specialists in the guiterre morische and the guiterre latine. The former, obviously a Moorish import, was shaped like an almond, with a vaulted back, long neck, and eight strings. The latter—at last, a recognizable forebear of Segovia's guitar—had a slightly incurved body with a flat back and no more than four strings.

What made it the "Latin" guitar? According to one hypothethis, it was latina not because it came from Rome but because it was the indigenous instrument of Mediterranean Europe. The musicologist Karl Geiringer has explained the distinction by quoting a definition from the thirteenth-century *Sachsenspiegel:* "The name Latini was bestowed on the indigenous population, the original settlers and colonists in regions over-run by the Barbarians." Musically, the main distinction seems to have been that while the guitarra latina was strummed *rasgado,* by "ripping" the thumb across the strings, the guitarra morisca was played note-for-note, *punteado,* in the melodic style still employed by North African Arabs on the instrument they call the kitra. The poet Juan Ruiz —author, epicurean, and Archpriest of Hita, in Spain—describes both kinds in rhyme as part of the long procession of instruments in his *Libro de buen amor* (Book of Good Love):

> Allí sale gritando la guitarra morisca
> De las voces aguda e de los puntos arisca
> El corpudo laúd que tiene punto a la trisca
> La guitarra latina con esos se aprisca.

> Here comes the Moorish guitar with its clatter
> Its strident notes and high-pitched chatter;
> The corpulent lute that beats time for the dance
> Joins the Latin guitar, and all three advance.

The Moorish guitar gradually disappeared from Spain, for its work, in any case, was better performed by the lute. But as late as the sixteenth century it could still be said of a Spanish musician that he played *a la morisca y a la castellana*—in the Moorish and in the Castillian style.

The prevailing confusion on this point is further compounded,

DONA POLICARPIA
Meſtra de Vióla.

LIC,AM
INSTRUMENTAL
DA VIOLA PORTUGUEZA,
ou de Ninfas, de cinco ordens,

(46) Title page of an unacknowledged but almost literal translation of Carles y Amat, entitled *Liçam Instrumental da Viola Portugueza,* and published in Lisbon, 1752. The title vignette, also adapted from Dr. Carles's book, here seems intended to portray the "author" of the treatise, "Dona Policarpia, Mestra de Vióla." Photo courtesy of the Biblioteca Nacional, Madrid.

(47) Another plagiarized version of the work of Carles y Amat, "augmented" and published by Andrès de Sotos in Madrid, 1764. Photo courtesy of the Biblioteca Nacional, Madrid.

ARTE PARA APRENDER CON facilid, y ſin Maeſtro, à templar, y tañer raſgado la Guitarra de cinco ordenes, ò cuerdas; y tambien la de quatro, ò ſeis ordenes, llamadas Guitarra Eſpañola, Bandurria, y Vandola, y tambien el Tiple. Demueſtraſe con grande claridad la formacion de los 12. puntos naturales, y 12. b. mollados con Laminas; y principalmente ſe pone una tabla, que por ella ſe puede cifrar qualquiera tono, tocarle, y cantarlo por doce modos diſtintos, ſacado de las mejores Obras, y Maeſtros: diſpueſto, recopilado, y aumentado por Andrès de Sotos. Año de 1764.

Con Licencia: En Madrid, en la Imprenta de Cruzada. Se hallará en caſa de dicho Andrès de Sotos, mas abajo de la Portería de San Martin.

of course, by the fact that the larger versions of these early guitars were also known as vihuelas (for reasons already explained in the last chapter). At first vihuela was a generic term for all stringed instruments with a neck and fingerboard, as opposed to those of the harp or lyre family. Spanish writers then distinguish between the vihuela de arco, played with a bow (*arco*) like a violin, and the vihuela de peñola, played with a quill plectrum (*peñola*) and belonging to the guitar family. When it was played with the fingers instead of a plectrum it was known as the vihuela de mano. The thirteenth-century *Libro de Apolonio*, written by an anonymous cleric, relates how the Princess Luciana played the vihuela at court:

> *Aguisósse la duenya, fiziriénola logar,*
> *tenpró bien la vihuella en un son natural,*
> *dexó caer el manto, paróse en un brial,*
> *començó una laude, omne non vio atal. . . .*

"The lady sat down, taking her place, and tuned the vihuela to a natural tone. She let fall her cape, revealing a rich silken skirt, and began a song more dazzling than any ever heard. She created such beautiful sounds and beautiful ballads that those who understood were left open-mouthed. She made the vihuela say cheering notes that seemed like spoken words. Both the nobles and the commoners agreed that the lady and the vihuela went so well together, it was a pleasure for all who saw her."

Several modern writers, including Walter Starkie and J. B. Trend, have classified vihuela music as lute music, and refer to the vihuelists as "lutenists of the Spanish renaissance." But the lute and the vihuela always coexisted at Spanish courts, and each had an independent music of its own. If the word *vihuela* has to be translated at all, it will have to be rendered as *guitar*—as indeed it was during the sixteenth century. An inventory of musical instruments belonging to Henry VIII of England (the whilom husband of a Spanish queen) mentions "four gitterons with iiii. cases *they are called Spanish Vialles.*" In Portuguese to this day the Spanish guitar is called violão, and in backwoods Brazil peasants still play a "viola" that is almost an exact duplicate of the archaic vihuela. Neither of

Adviertaſe, que al formar los puntos en la guitarra, ſe han de piſar las cuerdas con las puntas de los dedos, poniendo la mano arqueada, y no ſe ha de piſar en los traſtes.

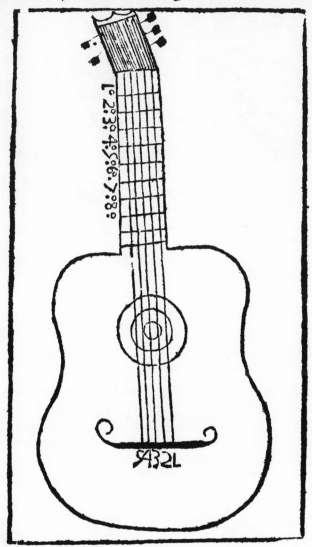

(48) A page of explanations from Lucas Ruiz de Ribayaz's *Luz y Norte Musical* (Musical Guiding Light) for guitar and harp, published in Madrid, 1677. Photo courtesy of the Biblioteca Nacional, Madrid.

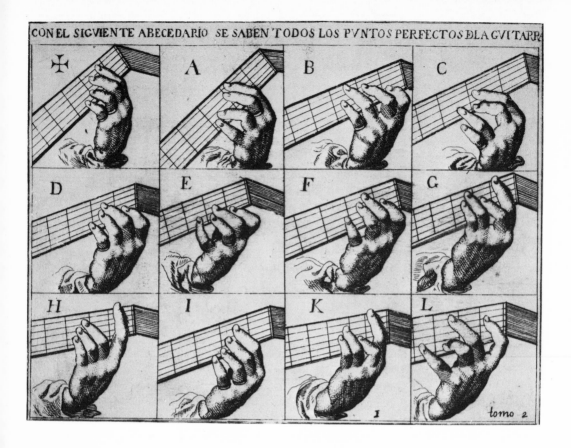

(49) Finger positions for stopping the standard chords, from *Instrucción de Musica sobre la Guitarra Española* by Gaspar Sanz. Engraved at Zaragoza in 1675, the plates are signed by Joannes Blauet. Sanz's numerical system is an adaptation of Carles y Amat's. In his instructions, he cautions readers to apply equal pressure on all fingers stopping a chord. A ring in the illustration indicates that the finger wearing it does not touch the strings.
Photos courtesy of the Biblioteca Nacional, Madrid.

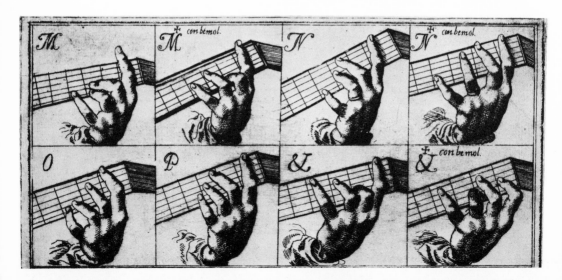

these, needless to say, is to be confused with its distant Italian cousin, the bowed viola of the string quartet.

There were vihuelas of all sorts and sizes: the Franciscan friar Juan Bermudo, in his great treatise *Declaración de instrumentos* (1555), mentions versions with as few as four and as many as seven strings. The latter is preferable, he says, and if the frets are positioned correctly on the neck so that all semitones can be played comfortably, the instrument is *perfectisímo*. By that time the Moors themselves had been expelled from Spain—Granada had capitulated in 1492—but this matter of the frets on the fingerboard was decidedly an Arabic contribution. As Henry George Farmer explains in his *Historical Facts for the Arabian Influence*, "The European citharist and harpist had only their ears to guide them when tuning their instruments, whereas the Arabian lutenist, pandorist and guitarist had their notes determined by frets on the necks of their instruments, which were adjusted by *measurement* [his italics]."

The standard vihuela had six courses of strings. It was "double strung" like the lute, mandolin, or the modern twelve-string guitar —which is to say its strings were arranged in pairs ("geminated"), tuned in unison or an octave apart. Only the top string was a single "chanter." In the absence of tuning forks and a fixed "do," vihuela tunings were very arbitrary. In theory, however, its tuning, like the lute's, was G–c–f–a–d–'g'; in other words, at intervals of a fourth, with a major third occurring between the third and fourth strings. Music for vihuela can easily be played on the modern guitar by transposing the instrument up a minor third with a capotasto and by lowering the third string a semitone.

Technically, the distinction between the vihuela and the common or garden-variety guitarra was chiefly one of range. Bermudo states unequivocally that "the guitar is nothing but a vihuela shorn of its sixth and first strings." Its tuning, therefore, was like that of the four inner courses of the vihuela: c–f–a–d'. A fifth course was afterward added to it, and its pitch raised a tone to A–d–g–b–e', which has remained the tuning of the five upper strings ever since.

The vihuela's two or three extra strings gave it a very considerable

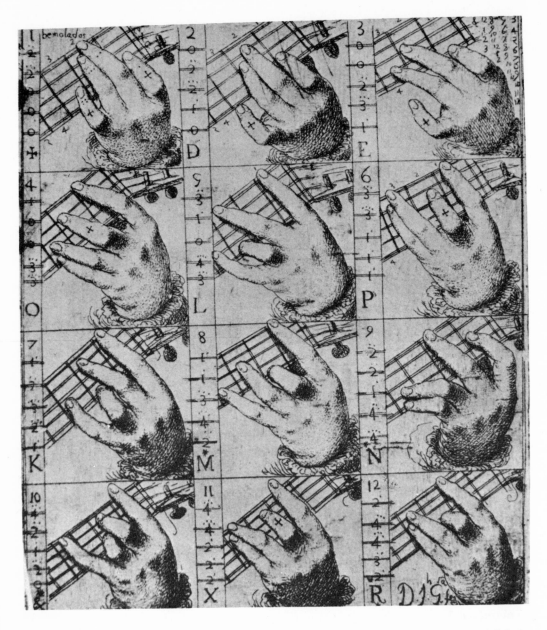

(50) Finger positions for standard chords, from José García Hidalgo's
Principios para estudias el nobilisimo y real arte de la pintura (Principles for
Studying the Most Noble and Royal Art of Painting), published in Madrid, 1693.
Hidalgo, a painter and engraver whose main subject was art, included guitar-playing
among a series of plates dealing with activities for hands and fingers.
Adapting Sanz's system, he indicated nonplaying fingers with a small cross.
Photos courtesy of the Instituto de España, Madrid.

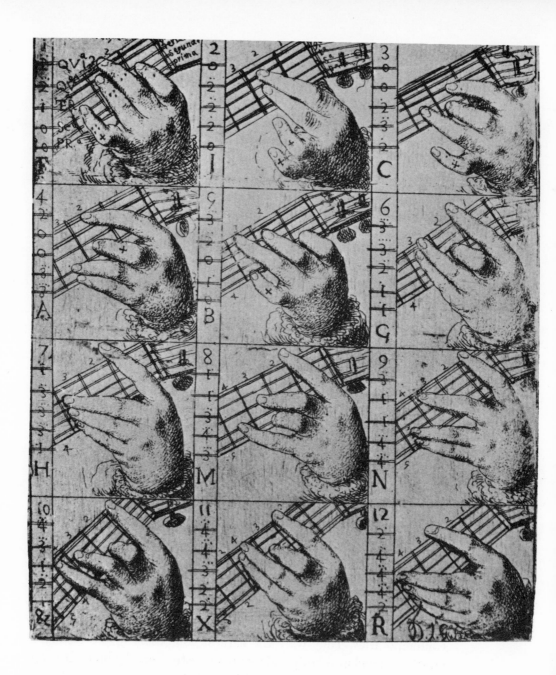

social and musical edge over the guitarra; one was an aristocrat's instrument suitable for serenading duchesses, the other a plebeian affair suitable for peasants and townsfolk. It was customary to keep a guitar hanging in a barbershop so that a customer waiting to be shaved could strum away the time until his turn came. Pieter Bruegel painted a slightly sarcastic example of it in *The Fight Between Carnival and Lent* (Plate 62), and the aristocratic poet Luis de Góngora devoted an ironic ditty to it:

En mi aposento . . .	In my lodgings . . .
Una guitarilla tomo,	I take a little guitar
Que como barbero templo	Which I tune like a barber
Y como bárbaro toco.	And play like a barbarian.

The vihuela, at the other end of the social scale, bore the same relationship to this kind of music-making as does Segovia's playing to Southern hillbilly picking. The age of the vihuela was an age of great polyphonic music, and of superb virtuosos who could improvise the most elaborate counterpoint. "In my youth," wrote Don Luys Zapata in his book *Miscelanea,* "there was in Valladolid a player of the vihuela called Narváez who had such extraordinary skill that over a four-voiced organ composition in a book he would instantly improvise another four—a marvel for those with no knowledge of music, and for those who understood, an even greater miracle."

Luis de Narváez was one of the five or six major figures responsible for the flowering of the vihuela in sixteenth-century Spain; they were the composers who gave the guitar its first and in many ways finest body of repertoire. Today there is hardly a classic guitar recital, or an LP anthology, which does not commence with a group of pieces by Narváez, Milán, Mudarra, Fuenllana, or one of their contemporaries. They were the earliest composers in the history of music to develop a truly independent instrumental idiom that was not merely a translation from the vocal style.

We know from hearsay that these composers were preceded by a whole school of vihuelistas whose music is lost because it was never published. We know some of their names, and the fact that

[78]

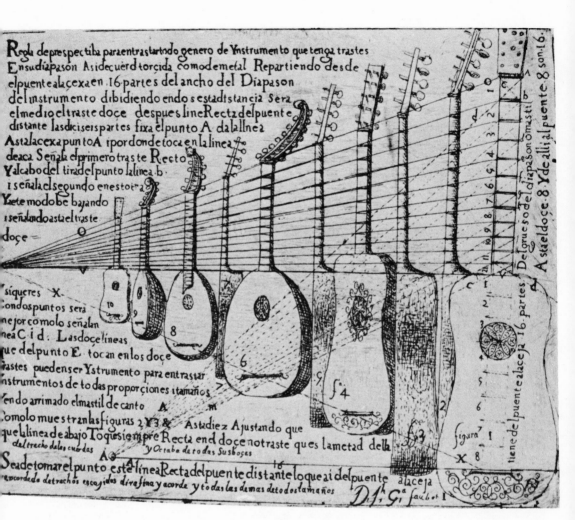

(51) The art of tying frets to the necks of stringed instruments is explained in García Hidalgo's *Principios* as a practical application of his principles of perspective. His method calls for twelve frets, spanning exactly half the distance between the bridge and the nut. Photo courtesy of the Instituto de España.

Franca Trippa.   Fritellino.

(52) Jacques Callot (1592–1635): the clowns Franca Trippa and Fritellino from the series of *commedia dell'arte* engravings entitled *Balli di sfessania* (sfessania are lascivious Neapolitan carnival dances). Photo courtesy of the Trustees of the British Museum.

(53) Melchior Gherardini (d. 1675): a young man dancing and playing a guitar, seen in two versions. Photo courtesy of the Metropolitan Museum of Art (Whittelsey Fund, 1951).

one Guzmán played so beautifully that his fingers "made the strings speak," and that a certain Macotera was "ingenious on the vihuela, and such a marvelous composer and so learned, that he plays on four strings of the vihuela such variations, harmonies and accompaniments that those who hear him are filled with admiration."

But the first great vihuelist to break into print was Luis Milán, whose *Libro de Música de vihuela de mano Intitulado El Maestro* (*Book of Music for Hand-plucked Vihuela, entitled The Teacher*) appeared at Valencia in 1535. *El Maestro* was not just a collection of music; it was designed as an instruction manual with graded pieces for those who wanted to master the instrument, starting with simple directions for tuning it. (You were to start with the highest string and work downward.) Most of the contents, however, are at the virtuoso level—fantasias, love songs, sonnets, and romances that reflect the leisurely elegance of life at a Spanish court. Milán (c. 1500–c. 1561) was a courtier and musician-poet at the court of Queen Germaine de Foix at Valencia, and one of his incidental accomplishments was a Spanish adaptation of Castiglione's school for gentlemen, *Il Cortegiano* (*The Perfect Courtier*). We know that he was something of a dandy and that modesty was not his long suit, for *El Maestro* is decorated with a vignette of Orpheus playing, not a classical lyre, but a six-string vihuela, and the motto that runs along the borders proclaims confidently:

> *El gran Orpheo, primero inventor*
> *Por quien la vihuela paresce en el mundo*
> *Si el fue el primero, no fue sin segundo. . . .*

> Great Orpheus, first inventor
> Who brought the vihuela into the world;
> If he was the first, he was not the only one. . . .

Soon after Milán brought the first vihuela book into the world, Narváez followed suit with his *Seys libros del Delfín de Música*, published at Valladolid in 1538. Its title, *The Dolphin of Music*, is an allusion to the Greek legend of Arion, a lyre virtuoso who was saved from drowning by a music-loving dolphin. The book's woodcut illustrations (Plate 38) show "Arion on the Dolphin's backe,

[81]

still fumbling on a gittern," as the playwright Thomas Heywood once described the scene. Narváez was a native of Granada (his dates are not known) who became *maestro de vihuela* to Philip II and wrote magnificent counterpoint. He was the first composer to publish *diferencias*—the Spanish word for variations—in a purely instrumental style. Some of his most famous variations, often heard on concert programs, are based on the tune *Guárdame las vacas,* a folk song that made the rounds of Western Europe and ultimately came to Britain as *The Sheepheard Carillo his Song:*

> I pre-thee keepe my kine for me
> Carillo, wilt thou. Tell.
> First let me have a kiss of thee,
> And I will keep them well.

In 1546 the third great master of the vihuela school, Alonso Mudarra of Seville, produced his *Tres libros de Música en cifras para vihuela. Música en cifras* refers to the fact that the music, as in all of these collections, was written not in ordinary staff notation but in "cipher"—a system of tablature using numbers, similar to the symbols of Renaissance lute tablature, or the diagrams found in modern guitar and ukelele editions. Instead of showing the actual notes to be sounded by the strings, tablature symbols indicate the positions of the fingers necessary to produce them. The six lines of the tablature correspond to the six strings of the vihuela; the ten frets are numbered, and a 5 placed on the top line, for example, indicates that the player's finger is to be placed on the fifth fret of the sixth string. Time values—quarter notes, half notes, and so on—are placed above the *cifras* of the tablature. Though some composers altered certain details of the system to suit themselves (Luis Milán, for example, counted his strings from the top line down) number tablature was actually one of the most practical and accurate methods of musical notation ever devised. It has clarified for us a number of points that were left vague or undefined in the conventional notation of the day, such as the question of whether leading notes were to be sharped or not (a detail of particular interest to musicologists tracing the evolution of medieval modes

Dame en Habit De chambre

Ce Vend à Paris proche les grands Augustins aux deux globes avec Privil du Roy

I. D. De Saint Iean del.
1675

(54) "Dame en habit de chambre," a Parisian print dated 1675, marks the guitar's rise to ubiquity among fashionable French ladies. This is an early treatment, by I. D. de Saint Jean, of a subject which was to become immensely popular in French art. Photo courtesy of the Bibliothèque Nationale, Paris.

Dame de qualité joüant de la Guitarre

se vend a Paris chez A. Trouvain rue S.t Jacques au grand Monarque atenant les Mathurins avec privilege du Roy 1694.

(55) "Dame de qualitè jouant de la guitare" was published in 1694 by A. Trouvain, a printmaker in the rue St. Jacques. Photo courtesy of the Bibliothèque Nationale, Paris.

into major-minor scales). In its day it was a great boon for beginners, who needed neither theory nor sight-reading before starting to play from tablatures.

Mudarra's collection—parts of it have been recorded by Segovia and others, and all of it is available in a modern transcription by Emilio Pujol—contains a superb cross-section of what the well-versed vihuelist was expected to play: fantasias, galliardes, pavanes, villancicos (love songs), romances (ballads), psalms, and motets, either written by Mudarra himself or adapted from such Flemish masters as Josquin des Prés and Adriaan Willaert. There are settings of texts by Ovid and Virgil, and sonnets by Petrarch and Sannazaro. This is an art of high seriousness even in its dances; rhythmically very flexible and harmonically some of the most exciting music ever written for plucked instruments.

Mudarra and more than forty other vihuela masters taught the nobility of Spain how to play with elegance and clarity (*tañer con limpieza, distinción*). For another three decades the repertoire grew by leaps and bounds: Enriquez de Valderrábano brought out his *Silva de Sirenas* at Valladolid in 1547, Diego Pisador his *Libro de Música* at Salamanca in 1552, Miguel de Fuenllana the *Orphenica Lyra* at Seville in 1554, Luis Venegas de Henestrosa a *Libro Nuevo* at Alcala de Henares in 1557, Friar Tomás de Santa María his *Arte de Tañer Fantasías* at Valladolid in 1563, and Esteban Daza his *El Parnaso*, again at Valladolid, in 1567.

"Dear reader," writes Valderrábano, speaking as one vihuelista to another, "as a lover of God and the vihuela, when my childhood talents were discovered I set myself to improve them, though at first it was more to satisfy my own longings and fancies than to make a name for myself as a musician. Even so I undertook to learn what I could of this art by virtue of divine grace, industrious application, and my own native endowments. After many years of study I created this work, to which I gave the name *Silva de Sirenas* [*The Siren Anthology*] on account of the diversity of things that are in it. I wanted my music in *cifras* to teach people how to play, and thereby increase the number of aficionados capable of performing great things, or those of lesser difficulty, each according to his technique and ability. And I wanted my work to be of equal benefit to all who are engaged in this honest occupation."

Valderrábano proudly points out that there are many novelties in his immense collection, one of the richest of all vihuela books. Included are thirty-three fantasias, counterpoint in four and five voices, romances, duets for two vihuelas with different tunings, and magnificently simple love songs like the *villancico, De dónde venís, amore:*

De dónde venís, amore?	Whence comest thou, my love?
Bien sé yo de dónde.	Full well do I know whence.
Cavallero de mesura	My caballero, my lord,
do venís la noche oscura?	on this dark night abroad,
De dónde venís amore?	Whence comest thou?
Bien sé yo de dónde.	Full well do I know whence.

"Man is music, and is composed of music," says Valderrábano in the introduction to his sirens. Perhaps there was never an epoch more receptive to this proposition, a time when men and music were as intimately related as they were in the age of the vihuela. It has been suggested that one reason for the guitar's continuing fascination is that it is the most unmechanical of instruments, and the most human. Guitar and lute are the only instruments in which the fingertips of both hands are in immediate contact with the sounding strings and produce the tone—as opposed to the violin, for example, where a bow does half the work, or a piano, whose hammers intervene between player and strings. It is this sense of the organic that Valderrábano and his colleagues, lyric poets almost to a man, expressed in both words and music. Man *is* music, in that context. Not until Frederic Chopin created his unique genre of piano fantasy was there to be another music so utterly attuned to its instrument, so remarkably spontaneous in its design that no shadow seems to fall between the conception and the execution.

Yet their golden age, like Chopin's, was short-lived. By the beginning of the seventeenth century, when the guitarra had replaced the vihuela and new musical winds were stirring, Milán, Narváez, and the rest had already been forgotten. They became faded names on the title pages of rare books—exceedingly rare but

Dame de Qualité
Joüant de la Guitarre

(56) Competing for the same market, the engraver Berey also issued a
"Dame de qualitè jouant de la guitare." Berey's print shop was located
just down the street from Trouvain's in the rue St. Jacques.
Photo courtesy of the Bibliothèque Nationale, Paris.

Amants donnant̄vne Serenade

Ces deux belles au balcon
Escoutent la serenade

Que ces Amants Sans facon
Leur donnent en guise d'aubade

Sceemb 1693

(57) "Amants donnant une Serenade," an anonymous French engraving of 1693, shows two "unceremonious" lovers performing an aubade (literally, a serenade at dawn) so early in the day that the ladies are still in nightcap and peignoir. Photo courtesy of the Bibliothèque Nationale, Paris.

Çaffe di Roma *se vend rüe St Jacques au â Monarque* Le Caffé de Rome

Chi sara stato in Roma, cognoscera
Giorgio nella sua Bottega, sto Turco,
fa il Gatto morto, ma per lui la
Musica è il suono delli Quatrini

Ceux qui auront esté a Rome conoitront
le St George dans sa Boutique ; ce Turc
est plus fin que l'on ne pense, la Musique
qu'il aime le plus est le son de l'Argent

(58) "Le Caffé de Rome" (sic) by Nicholas Bocquet of the rue St. Jacques, shows a Roman coffee house run by a Turkish proprietor named Giorgio: "the music he loves best is the tinkle of money." Photo courtesy of the Bibliothèque Nationale, Paris.

unimpressive little volumes, full of mysterious signs and numbers which no one remembered how to read, kept in the dustier recesses of Spanish libraries. The whole school was not rediscovered until the 1870's, when a Spanish nobleman of Irish descent, the Conde de Morphy, undertook the laborious task of deciphering the *cifras* and translating them into modern notation. Living in Paris in self-imposed exile after one of the periodic crises in the Spanish dynasty, he spent seven years producing his path-breaking anthology of *Les Luthistes [sic] espagnols du XVIe siècle* before returning to Madrid as advisor to the young Alfonso XII. It must have been like discovering the buried art of some forgotten kingdom to come suddenly on whole volumes filled with treasures like Milán's fantasias, Narváez's diferencias, and Mudarra's setting of the lament for King David:

Triste estaua el rey David	It was a sorrowful King David,
Triste y con gran passión	Sorrowful and forlorn,
Quando le vinieron nueuas	To whom they brought the tidings
De la muerte de Absalón.	Of the death of Absalom.
Palabras tristes dezía	And sorrowful words did he utter
Salidas del coraçón . . .	That from his heart were torn . . .

Chapter 4

La Guitarre Royalle

Ma guiterre, je te chante	My guitar, I sing of thee;
Par qui seule je deçoy	'Tis with thee that I decoy
Et j'enchante	And ensnare enchantingly
Les amours que je reçoy.	The ladies I enjoy.

—RONSARD

IT WAS THE four-course guitar, rather than the six-course vihuela, that first made its way across Europe in the sixteenth century, as the vade-mecum of pickers and pluckers. "In my earliest years," wrote the author of an anonymous French treatise in 1556, "we used to play the lute more than the guitar, but for twelve or fifteen years now everyone has been guitaring, and the lute is nearly forgotten in favor of Heaven knows what kind of music on the guitar, which is much easier than that for the lute."

The honor of having published the first complete book of music for four-course guitar belongs to the Frenchman, Master Guillaume Morlaye *joueur de lut*, and to two Parisian music printers, Robert Granjon and Michel Fezandat. Between 1551 and 1553 they issued a set of four *Livres de chansons, galliardes, pavannes, bransles*, etc., containing a wide choice of what were then called *danseries*, as well as adaptations of lute pieces in guitar tablature. Morlaye also helped himself to Melchoir de Barberis' *Fantasie per sonar sopra la chitarra da sette corde*, the first Italian guitar imprint, which had just appeared in Venice, 1549, as part of the lute collection *Opera Contina*. Morlaye's tablatures were intended primarily for

(59) Title page of *I Quatri Libri della Chitarra Spagnola* by the musician who called himself L'Academico Caliginoso, detto il Furioso (The Obscure Academician, called Mr. Furious). Date and place of publication are not given, but according to Gaspar Sanz's *Instrucción* the author was an Italian named Foscarino. Photo courtesy of the Biblioteca Nacional, Madrid.

(60) A typical page of seventeenth-century Italian guitar tablature from il Furioso's *Quatri Libri*. The work in question is a courante (corrente) entitled *La Gratiosa*. The letters represent coded chords, and the notes above the five "strings" indicate time values. Photo courtesy of the Biblioteca Nacional, Madrid.

amateurs, and their common denominator is a certain sturdy functionalism in keeping with the simplicity of the instrument shown on the title page of the *Livres* (Plate 39): a four-course, seven-string guitar with only eight frets. "The guitar, more than the lute, is in touch with some vital and ageless currents beneath the polished and courtly surface of sixteenth-century music," writes the American musicologist Daniel Heartz, who rediscovered the only existing copies of these remarkable *Livres* in St. Gallen, Switzerland, and published the first article on them in 1960—more than four hundred years after they came off the press at the Granjon-Fezandat workshop in the University quarter of Paris.

Their collection probably inspired a similar set of *Livres* issued by a competitor of Fezandat's, the music publishing firm of Adrian Le Roy and Robert Ballard. In addition to music for guitar, Le Roy and Ballard brought out a guitar tutor, now lost, which offered *Briefue et facile instruction* in such matters as tuning, reading tablature, and positioning the hand *sur la guiterne*. These books were expensive, and the sort of customer who bought them is shown in various engravings of the time: buxom, visibly well-to-do ladies like those in Tobias Stimmer's *Women Musicians* (Plate 40), dated about 1570. There are other indications that the guitar was moving up the social ladder. Ronsard, the "prince of poets," speaks of it as a passkey in the matters of love:

Il est des dames pensives	It is the ideal instrument
L'instrument approprié:	For ladies of great learning.
Il est des dames lascives	Lascivious ladies also play,
Pour les amours dédié.	To advertise their yearning.

Across the Channel, in Tudor England, the old-fashioned gittern could be heard thrumming its last, often side by side with its wire-strung offspring, the cittern. "Sumtyme I foote it with dauncing; noow with my Gittern, and els with my Cittern," writes Robert Laneham, a great ladies' man and favorite of the Earl of Leicester. Young gentlewomen, he adds, are much impressed by his performances. "Then carroll I up a song withall, that by and by they cum

La
Guitarre Royalle
Dediée Au Roy
De La Grande Bretagne
Composée
Par Francisque Corbett
Grauée par H. Bonneüil
et
Se Vend A Paris Chez ledit Bonneüil Rüe au
Lard proche la Boucherie de Beauuais au dessus
de la halle aux Cuirs

Auec Priuilege du Roy

(61) Title page of Francesco Corbetta's *Guitarre Royalle*, dedicated to Charles II of England, but published in Paris, 1671. Three years later Corbetta produced a second collection with the same title, this time dedicated to Louis XIV. Photo courtesy of the Biblioteca Nacional, Madrid.

flocking about me lyke beez too hunny: and ever they cry, 'anoother, good Laneham, anoother!' "

The thin-voiced, narrow-chested gittern had trouble competing
with the lute except in the dance department. At night, under a
lady's window, it was easily outclassed by the latter's resonant
twangings. The disparity is graphically illustrated in the earliest
English comedy, Nicholas Udall's *Ralph Roister Doister* (c. 1550),
where the hero's amatory exploits are catalogued by instrument
and sound effect:

> With every woman is he in some
>   love's pang:
> Then up to our lute at midnight,
>   twangledom twang!
> Then twang with our sonnets, and
>   twang with our dumps:
> And *Heigho!* from our heart, as heavy
>   as lead lumps.
> Then to our recorder, with
>   toodleloodle poope
> As the howlet out of an ivy bush
>   should hoope.
> Anon to our gitterne, thrumpledum
>   thrumpledum, thrum;
> Thrumpledum, thrumpledum, thrumpledum
>   thrumpledum, thrum.

The onomatopoeia confirms that the lute excelled as a twanger of
courtly counterpoint, while the gittern made short shrift of countri-
fied accompaniments. But the advent of the Spanish guitar re-
dressed the balance of tone power and abolished with the old division
of labor. "Give me my gittara: and room for our Chiefe," announces
a leading rogue in Ben Jonson's play *The Gypsies Metamorphosed*
(1621), sounding a new note of confidence—and inaugurating a
new terminology—in the fretful world of plucked instruments. From
then on we hear no more of gitterns but only of guitarres, gittars,
guittars, and so on; by the 1680's the word had become so thoroughly
naturalized in Britain that a young dandy could be described meta-

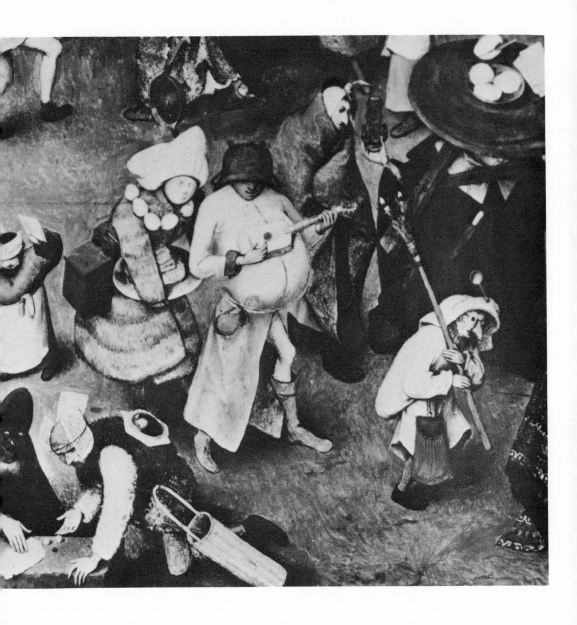

(62) Pieter Brueghel, in "The Fight Between Carnival and Lent" (1648),
was one of the first Flemish painters to include a plebeian guitar among his stage
properties. The instrument wielded by his puffed-up Carnival singer is obviously
a peasant instrument, and has only a meagre six frets. Photo courtesy of the
National Gallery, Vienna, and *Horizon* magazine, New York.

phorically as "the general guitar o' the town, inlay'd with every thing women fancy."

But it was the addition of the fifth string that marked the next big step in the instrument's rise to universal eminence. In Spain the "invention" of the fifth string was credited to the swashbuckling poet Vicente Espinel (1551–1624), who figures in many histories as the father of the modern Spanish guitar. We know, of course, that Espinel no more originated the idea than Elvis Presley invented the electric guitar; Juan Bermudo, even before Espinel was born, had already written about guitars with five strings, or more accurately said, five courses of strings. But Espinel gave the fifth course the benefit of his very considerable influence and great personal charm as a musician, poet, and propagandist. "I could tell you things about the famous Espinel that pass human understanding," testified his friend Cervantes in his pastoral *La Galatea*, published in 1585. And again, in the *Viage del Parnaso* of 1614: "*Es el grande Espinel que en la guitarra tiene la prima y en el raro estilo*"—in other words, "It is the great Espinel who has primacy [and the first string] on the guitar, and great style in matters of art."

Espinel is remembered today chiefly as the author of a picaresque autobiographical novel, *Vida del escudero Marcos de Obregón*, which casts a rather jaundiced eye on the Spanish folkways of his day. At one point a young barber with a good voice and a guitar comes to pay regular visits to the narrator:

Seated at the threshold he sang some tonadillas, to which I contributed a poor bass, but well harmonized, and there are no two voices which do not sound well when they sing correctly. Thus, thanks to our concert and the voice of the boy, which was excellent, we brought the neighborhood together to hear our harmony. The lad always played the guitar, not so much to show that he knew how, as to scratch himself with the movement of his wrists, which were covered with a sort of mangy rash. . . .

The sardonic Espinel was his own most romantic and improbable character. Born in Ronda and educated at Salamanca, he was expelled from the university, tried soldiering, was imprisoned by Algerian pirates, took holy orders and became a chaplain, was deprived of his office for malfeasance, then appointed choirmaster at Pla-

(63) "Young Woman Playing a Guitar": Fresco painting from a villa near Venice by an unknown painter of the seventeenth-century Venetian school. Photo by Anderson, courtesy of the Real Accademia, Venice.

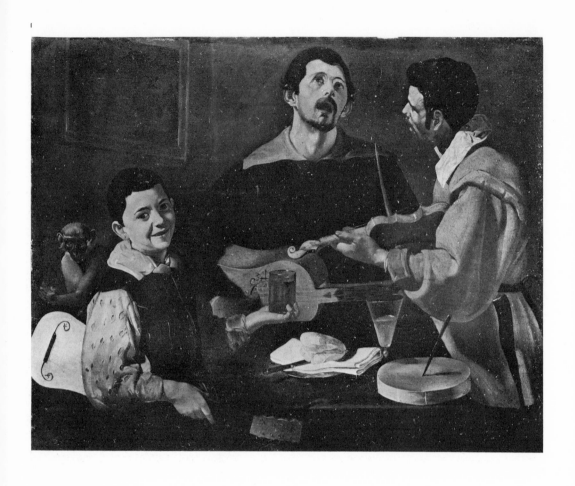

(64) "Three Musicians" by Diego Velazquez play two guitars and a pochette fiddle.
This is one of Velazquez' early tavern pictures, painted in Seville about 1620.
Photo by Walter Steinkopf, courtesy of the Gemäldegalerie, Berlin.

(65) "Three Musicians" by Theodoor Rombouts (1597–1637): they sing to the accompaniment of a guitar strummed rasgado while a lute lies unused on the table, perhaps because it would be too much trouble to tune its eighteen strings. Photo courtesy of the Munich Pinakothek, Bayerische Staatsgemäldesammlungen.

sencia, did translations of Horace, and wrote many poems of his own, most of them too licentious to be published in Spain. Among other things he revived the verse form called *décimas*—and also *espinelas*, in his honor—consisting of a stanza of ten lines of eight syllables.

"May Heaven forgive that Espinel!" exclaims a character in Lope de Vega's play *La Dorotea* of 1632. "He has brought us those new verses, décimas or espinelas, and the five strings of the guitar, so that now everyone forgets the old noble instruments as well as the old dances, what with these wild gesticulations and lascivious movements of the chaconne, which are so offensive to the virtue, the chastity and the seemly silence of the ladies!" Even here, then, on its traditional stamping grounds, the guitar cannot escape the charge of contributing to the delinquency of those who are so inclined.

At the end of the century, when the five-course guitar had become standard throughout Spain, the stage was set for Dr. Joan (or Juan) Carles y Amat's modest but memorable guide, *Guitarra Española y Vándola*, the first book ever published on the common man's *Spanish Guitar and Vándola* (the latter, in this context, was simply another name for a four-string treble guitar like the one shown in Plate 105). The sixty-page treatise first appeared in 1596, but the earliest known edition—represented by a single copy unearthed by an American dealer—is dated 1627, and there were many subsequent reprintings, plagiarisms, and adaptations until 1764. Joan Carles, *Doctor en Medicina* and author of several medical texts, was an aficionado rather than a professional musician, and he explains that his main reason for writing this one "was the choleric short temper of Spain, for I see that nothing is as tedious as the process of teaching the art of playing the guitar. Those who desire to be instructed in this art should not be surprised if after three days their teachers tire of showing them, for this choleric temperament lies heavy upon all of us Spaniards, and everything we undertake, however short it may be, seems very long to us." To speed things up, and to spare the student "such misery as we derive from our short temper," Dr. Carles has devised a simple method "for tuning and playing *rasgado* the guitar of five strings, called 'Spanish' because it is more popular

(66) In Rombouts' "Musicians," the guitarist plays a chitarra battente (curved-back guitar) with his thumb, Burl Ives style, and a lute again lies unattended at his feet. Photo by Alinari, courtesy of the Kansas City University Museum.

(67) "A Musical Gathering,"
by David Ryckaert (1612–
1661); the combination of lute,
guitar, cello, harp, singers and
dogs is visually fascinating but
seems musically improbable.
Photo by Marburg, courtesy of
Count von Schönborn-
Wiesentheid.

(68) Detail from another
Ryckaert painting of
"Hausmusik," also dated c. 1650.
The bearded old man shown
singing in the previous picture
is here strumming a guitar
resting on the table—a rare
position, possible only with a
small guitar. Photo courtesy of
the Liechtenstein Galerie,
Vaduz.

in this country than in others." Another preface is cast in the form
of a sonnet in which the subject addresses the reader. "You'll see
that I am gallant, a guardian and a guide":

> *Verás que soy galana, guarda, guía,*
> *graciosa, gala, gracia, gallarda,*
> *gustosa, general, grata, guitarra.*

The instrument Joan Carles wrote about had nine strings arranged
in five courses: A–a, d–d', g–g, b–b and a single chanterelle e'. Working within the range of the first four frets, he devised a method of
numbered chords with which he could perform things "that may
seem impossible" at first glance. "The good and practical painter
brings together all the colors that are necessary so that he may
paint according to his fancy a man, or a lion, or a bull [a very
Spanish choice of subjects, this]. In the same fashion we have
assembled all the chords which are like the materials and colors of
the painter, and with which . . . one can play vacas, passeos, gall-
ardas, villanos, italianas, pavanillas and similar things [the song
and dance forms of the day]."

It was this eminently danceable instrument, known at home as the
"Castilian" guitar and abroad as the chitarra spagnuola, that fascinated the painters as well as the musicians of Europe. Though
there were earlier examples, the great age of guitar paintings begins,
properly speaking, with Spanish pictures like the *Three Musicians*
of Velásquez and Zurbarán's *Temptations of St. Jerome.* Soon the
Italian, French, Dutch, and Flemish schools were equally busy with
guitarists; it was a seemingly inexhaustable subject that produced,
before the century was out, a great many first-rate pictures by such
artists as David Ryckaert, Rutilio Manetti, Le Valentin, Gonzales
Coques, and Sir Peter Lely, as well as at least one masterpiece—
the Vermeer *Guitarist* now in the Kenwood Museum, London
(Plates 64–82). This great outpouring of art is a sign of the guitar's
coming of age; of its acceptance—documented by the paintings
themselves—by all levels of society and throughout Western Europe.
In Spain itself the five-course guitar replaced the vihuela in a single
generation. "Until our time," wrote the Inquisitor Sebastián de Co-

varrubias in his Castilian dictionary of 1611, "the vihuela has been much valued and has had excellent musicians, but after guitars were invented those giving themselves to the study of the vihuela have been very few. This has been a great loss, because all kinds of music were played on it, whereas now the guitar is no more than a cowbell, so easy to play that there is no stable boy who is not a musician on the guitar."

Among lute players there was little love lost for a rival who threatened to debase the currency of all fretted instrument music. A French savant, Pierre Trichet, stated the case for the lute party when he defined the guitar in his treatise on musical instruments (a work written in the 1630's, which remained in manuscript until it was published in the *Annales Musicologiques for* 1955-1956):

The guiterre or guiterne is a musical instrument widely used by the French and Italians, but still more among the Spanish, who were the first to make it fashionable, and who know how to play it more madly than any other nation, using it particularly for singing and for playing their sarabands, galliardes, espagnolettes, passemezes, passecaglias, pavanes, allemandes, and romanesques with a thousand gestures and body movements which are so grotesque and ridiculous that their playing is bizarre and confused. Nevertheless even in France one finds courtesans and ladies who turn themselves into Spanish monkeys trying to imitate them, demonstrating that they prefer foreign importations to their own native products. In this they resemble those who, though they could dine well at their own table, would rather go out to eat bacon, onions and black bread. For who is not aware that the lute is what is proper and suitable for the French, and the most delightful of all musical instruments? Still there are some of our nation who leave everything behind in order to take up and study the guitar. Isn't this because it is much easier to perfect oneself in this than in lute-playing, which requires long and arduous study before one can acquire the necessary skill and disposition? Or is it because it has a certain something which is feminine and pleasing to women, flattering their hearts and making them inclined to voluptuousness?

He neglected to add that the lute was a nuisance to keep in tune; in the course of time it had become overloaded with strings—up to two dozen in extreme cases—which had the annoying tendency to

(69) "Gypsy Guitarist" by Louis or Jean de Boullogne (the latter known as
le Valentin) also supports his guitar on the table. Photo by Alinari,
courtesy of the Uffici, Florence.

(70) Francisco Zurbarán's "Temptations of St. Jerome" affords a back view of the early Spanish guitar, revealing the movable frets that were tied around the neck as specified by García Hidalgo. The picture is one of a series that Zurbarán painted for the monastery of Guadalupe, 1638–1639, illustrating the life of the Roman scholar-saint. Here again the guitar is seen in frivolous company, for beautiful women were among the saint's most distracting temptations. Photo courtesy of the Monasterio de Guadalupe, Cáceres, Spain.

go limp at the slightest provocation. As one French wag put it, "One can see the lutenists tuning up, but one never hears them play." And the German baroque critic Johann Mattheson was moved to observe that if a lutenist reaches the age of eighty, "you can be sure that he has spent sixty of his years tuning and fixing broken strings."

The case for the guitar, on the other hand, is vigorously summed up in Luis de Briçeño's *Método mui facilíssimo para aprender a tañer la Guitarra a lo Español,* published in Paris in 1626. Briçeño (who had the misfortune of seeing his name misspelled on the title page) does not stop to wonder why guitars are attractive to women; he takes that for granted and addresses himself directly to them:

There are many, my lady, who make fun of the guitar and its sound, but if they would consider carefully they would find that the guitar is the most suitable instrument for our time one could imagine, for nowadays one looks for savings of purse and trouble. The guitar is a veritable theatre of savings. And furthermore it is convenient and appropriate to singing, playing, ballet-dancing, jumping, running, folk-dancing and shoe-dancing. I can serenade with it, singing and expressing with its help a thousand amorous passions. . . . It has none of the inconveniences to which the lute is subject; neither smoke nor heat nor cold nor dampness can incommode it. It is always fresh as a rose. If it gets out of tune easily, it is just as easy to tune it again. . . . In my and many other people's opinion, the guitar has a great advantage over the lute, which requires many attentions to be properly maintained: it has to be a good instrument, well played, well strung, and listened to carefully, in silence.

But the guitar, my lady, whether well played or badly played, well strung or badly strung, is pleasant to hear and listen to; being so easy to learn, it attracts the busiest of talented people and makes them put aside loftier occupations so that they may hold a guitar in their hands. They desert the lute, mandora, harp, violin, sinfonia, lyre, theorbo, cittern, and clavichord, all for the guitar. Many things could be said in favor of these instruments, but here one consideration is paramount: two thousand people now entertain themselves and express their thoughts and troubles through the guitar. And as further proof of the value of my guitar ask yourself whether kings, princes and gentlemen lay aside the guitar for the lute as they now leave the lute for the guitar?

(71) "The Guitarist," by Jean Daret (1613–1668), plays with his right hand
well forward of the sound hole—a position that Mexican guitarists often use.
Photo by Giraudon, courtesy of the Musée Granet, Aix-en-Provence.

(72) "Lady Playing a Guitar," by Caspar Netscher (or after him), signed
and dated 1680. The lady has a nice bend to her left wrist, but a purely imaginary
right-hand position. Photo courtesy of the Boston Museum of Fine Arts.

Briçeño's tract must have made many converts; a more eloquent argument for the guitar has never been written. And, as he points out, as France moved into the age of the *grand monarque* the guitar did find its way into the boudoirs of power and become the instrument of kings.

Louis XIV himself and Charles II of England led the list of exalted personages who could be heard twanging the guitar at all hours of the day or night. It was said of Louis that "he was never taught anything but how to dance and play the guitar," but in both of these subjects he was an extraordinarily apt pupil. He was only fifteen when he first appeared as Le Roi Soleil in the thirteen-hour long *Ballet of the Night*, dressed in the famous costume bedecked with sun symbols and beams of light shining from his head and body. Thereafter he ruled in life, as on stage, as "The Sun King," while continuing to take daily dancing lessons—for twenty-two years—from his ballet master, Pierre Beauchamps. The guitar was less of an obsession with him, but as a young man he used to perform almost daily together with his courtiers Butaut and La Chesnaye; when the council of state met in the palace chambers, the king might be found whiling away the time in his *cabinet de bain*, playing the guitar with Butaut or discussing plans for a ballet. Pierre Bonnet writes in his *Histoire de la Musique* of 1715 (the year of Louis' death): "I believe it is proof of the greatness of His Majesty that they say he equalled, after eighteen months, the guitar master whom Cardinal Mazarin had brought from Italy to teach him to play this instrument, much in vogue at the time."

Louis' Italian guitar master was Francesco Corbetta, alias Francisque Corbett, the foremost guitarist of the age. It is reported that the Duke de Guise discovered him in Florence and recruited him for the royal household. Born in Pavia about 1615, Corbetta published his first book of tablatures at Bologna in 1639 and another in Milan, 1643. The known facts about his life are scanty: He seems to have been attached to the court of Mantua for a time, and also to that of Leopold William, Archduke of Austria, to whom he dedicated another book of guitar tablatures that appeared in Brussels in 1648. Eight years later he was in Paris, and it was afterward his

(73) "The Five Senses" by Jean de Boullogne, called le Valentin (c. 1594–1632). Engraved by Hubert and Le Vasseur. Photo courtesy of the Bibliothèque Nationale, Paris.

(74) "The Duo" by Gonzales Coques (1614–1684). The Flemish painter
was virtually an exact contemporary of Francesco Corbetta; this picture could
almost serve as an illustration of Grammont's tales of courtly guitar playing and
intrigue. Photo courtesy of the Musée de Peinture, Brussels.

[114]

proud boast that "His Majesty [Louis XIV] permitted me to supply an interlude of several guitars . . . for a ballet composed by the very famous composer Jean Baptiste Lully, *maistre de la musiq.*" Louis was then eighteen years of age, and he himself danced the lead (what else?) in the ballet, which was entitled *La Galanterie du temps* and had been commissioned by Mazarin.

During the early 1660's Corbetta went to London to join the newly established court of Charles II, where he became the center of a fashionable guitar clique headed by the king himself. "The court was an entire scene of gallantry and amusements," report the *Memoirs of Count Grammont,*

with all the politeness and magnificence which the inclinations of a prince naturally addicted to tenderness and pleasure, could suggest: the beauties were desirous of charming, and the men endeavoured to please: all studied to set themselves off to the best advantage: some distinguished themselves by dancing; others by show and magnificence; some by their wit, many by their amours, but few by their constancy.

There was a certain Italian at court [Corbetta], famous for the guitar: he had a genius for music, and he was the only man who could make anything of the guitar: his style of play was so full of grace and tenderness, that he would have given harmony to the most discordant instruments. The truth is, nothing was so difficult as to play like this foreigner. The king's relish for his compositions had brought the instrument so much into vogue, that every person played upon it, well or ill; and you were as sure to see a guitar on a lady's toilet as rouge or patches.

Nothing could happen at Charles' court without becoming embroiled in sex and subterfuge; according to the *Grammont Memoirs,* Corbetta's music was soon in the thick of it:\

The Duke of York played upon it tolerably well, and the Earl of Arran like Francisco himself. This Francisco had composed a saraband, which either charmed or infatuated every person; for the whole *guitarery* at court were trying at it; and God knows what an universal strumming there was. The Duke of York, pretending not to be perfect in it, desired Lord Arran to play it to him. Lady Chesterfield [Arran's sister, and the real object of the Duke's maneuvering] had the best guitar in England. The Earl of Arran, who was desirous of playing his best, conducted his Royal Highness to his sister's apartments: she was lodged at court, at her

[115]

(75) "Two Ladies of the Lake Family" by Sir Peter Lely (1618–1680), a fashionable Dutch-born portraitist of the English aristocracy. Photo courtesy of the Tate Gallery, London.

(76) "The Guitar Player" by Jan Vermeer (1632–1675): one of the painter's late masterpieces, and easily the most important of all seventeenth-century guitar pictures. Photo courtesy of the Iveagh Bequest, Kenwood, and the Greater London Council.

father's, the Duke of Ormond's; and this wonderful guitar was lodged there too. Whether this visit had been preconcerted or not, I do not pretend to say; but it is certain that they found both the lady and the guitar at home; they likewise found there Lord Chesterfield, so much surprised at this unexpected visit, that it was a considerable time before he thought of rising from his seat to receive them with due respect.

Jealousy, like a malignant vapour, now seized upon his brain: a thousand suspicions, blacker than ink, took possession of his imagination, and were continually increasing; for, whilst the brother played upon the guitar to the duke, the sister ogled and accompanied him with her eyes, as if the coast had been clear, and no enemy to observe them. This saraband was at least repeated twenty times: the duke declared it was played to perfection: Lady Chesterfield found no fault with the composition; but her husband, who clearly perceived that he was the person played upon, thought it a most detestable piece.

Francisco Corbetta afterward published a collection of his pieces, *La Guitarre Royalle*, dedicated to Charles II. It consists of a great many court dances—gavottes, jigs, minuets, etc.—along with the "allemande cherished by His Highness the Duke of York, the sarabande composed on the death of Madame d'Orleans, a little gavotte beloved by Monsieur the Duke of Monmouth . . . and also preludes to allemandes, two of which will be seen to be full of tenderness, one on the death of the Duke of Gloucester (Duc de Clocester), the other on the imprisonment of the Duke of Buckingham (Bouquingam)." This last is not a very long piece, for Buckingham spent less than a month in the Tower of London (charged with treasonable intrigue and having cast the king's horoscope) before being restored to royal favor.

We catch another glimpse of Corbetta in the diary of Samuel Pepys, an unreconstructed lute player who had little use for the guitar—"methinks it is but a bauble." On August 5, 1667, Pepys wrote: "After done with the Duke of York, and coming out through his dressing room, I there spied Signor Francisco tuning his gittar, and Monsieur de Puy with him, who did make him play to me, which he did most admirably—so well as I was mightily troubled that all the pains should have been taken upon so bad an instrument."

(77) "The Guitarist" by David Teniers the Younger (1610–1690) suggests a hidden parallel between music and soap bubbles as basically ephemeral pursuits. Photo by A. C. Cooper Ltd., courtesy of the Royal Collections, Buckingham Palace.

Corbetta returned to Paris about 1671, where he obtained royal permission to publish first the "English" collection and then a second, "French," *Guitarre Royalle* of 1674, containing pieces obviously written under the influence of the French court, bearing such titles as *Saraband la Dauphine* and *Sarabande le Depart du Roy*. There is some evidence, cited in Richard Keith's articles on Corbetta, that he went back to London to teach the future Queen Anne; perhaps also the future Queen Mary. His death, in the year 1681, inspired a musical tribute or "tombeau" by the royal chamber guitarist, Robert de Visée, and an epitaph in verse by another of his pupils:

Ci git l'Amphion de nos jours,	Here lies the Amphion of our years,
Francisque cet homme si rare	Francisque that rare man from afar
Qui fit parler à la guitare	Who taught the voice of the guitar
Le vrai langage des amours. . . .	To whisper love into our ears. . . .

(78) A second "Guitarist" by David Teniers the Younger in an engraving by Vandenberg and De Launay le Jeune. Collection of the author.

[120]

Mefiez vous Philis de cet aimable Maître;
Il vous fera bientôt aimer à l'vnisson:
Vos regards et ses yeux peuvent faire conoître,
Qu'en amoureux Duo finira la lecon

L'Amour est un Prothée habile a nous seduire,
Il prend, pour vaincre un coeur la forme qui luy plaist:
Et quand ce foible coeur ne peut plus s'en dedire,
Le traître se demasque et fais voir ce qu'il est.

A Paris chez Dupuis rue de la Vannerie et chez Duchang Graveur du Roy rue S. Jacques

(79) "The Dangerous Lesson" by Jean Raoux, engraved by N. Dupuis, Jr.
The printer's inscription warns Phyllis to beware of her amiable teacher and
the amorous duo which will finish the lesson. Photo courtesy of the
Bibliothèque Nationale, Paris.

(80) "Les Charlatans Italiens" by Karel Dujardin (1622–1678): a Dutch
painter's view of traveling mountebanks and their tent, with a harlequin
guitarist as the main drawing card. Photo, Archives Photographiques,
courtesy of the Louvre, Paris.

Chapter 5

The Age of Figaro

Figaro (to Count Almaviva): Play it with the back of the hand like this; thrum, thrum, thrum, thrum. If you sang without a guitar in Seville, faith, you'd be found out at once, and hunted down.

—BEAUMARCHAIS, *The Barber of Seville*

THE GUITAR made the transition from Baroque to Rococo without skipping a beat; it entered the eighteenth century cradled in the arms of Jean Antoine Watteau's beautiful people. Far from being merely incidental or decorative, its presence actually serves a very vital function in Watteau's art: there is so much open air in his pictures, compared to the crowded compositions of his predecessors, and this emptiness, which gives his figures room to play in, Watteau fills with the vibrations of a silent, palpable music. Sometimes it is a lute that performs in his palace gardens, but usually he prefers to take a guitar for his strolls through the countryside; it doesn't get in the way of casual seductions, and it stays in tune (Watteau's lutenists, significantly, are always busy tuning).

One never sees brasses or any loud instruments in any of these pictures; only plucked strings and the occasional flute. "Music," writes the critic Edmund Hildebrandt, "winds like a rondeau from group to group, joining each pair of lovers to the next; in a man's hands it is his chief means of self-advertisement, and it unites even the lone figure with the world around him. . . . This musicality is neither an ornament nor an afterthought, but rather one of the essential creative elements of Watteau's psyche as an artist. It permeates his whole language of forms, in the way he composes his subjects, in his line and coloring, even at such times as no music is being made." The guitar becomes a sort of hieroglyph for happiness; when a group is gathered around a girl in a swing there will be a guitar lying in the grass as a symbol of that sensual promise and fulfillment which is the underlying theme of all these paintings.

Watteau, with his magnificent sense of fantasy, was never concerned with *trompe l'oeil* exactitude, but he was a meticulous observer, and his guitars were lovingly drawn from nature. Scarcely more than a dozen of his sketches of guitarists have been preserved; he must have made dozens more during his all-too-brief life (1685–1721) as preliminary studies for his paintings. Often he chose to depict guitarists in curiously affected attitudes, as though they were just reaching up to pluck harmonics at the neck—a gesture probably intended to make his visual music all the more piquant and intriguing to a guitar-conditioned audience (Plates 85-92).

What sort of music was it that Watteau's lovers would actually have played at their *fêtes galantes?* Most probably the minuets of Robert de Visée and François Campion, or the passacalles of Gaspar Sanz, these being the three leading guitar composers of the time. Visée (c. 1650–c. 1725) was, as we know, a student of Corbetta, chamber musician to the Dauphin and a protégé of Louis XIV's master of finances, Colbert. Composer of three influential books of dance pieces, he was often to be heard at soirées given by the king's indispensable Madame de Maintenon; he is also supposed to have furnished the incidental music when Charles Perrault, author of the classic French fairy tales, gave recitations for his friends. Campion, a noted virtuoso and official "*maitre de theorbe* [archlute] *et de guitare*" of the royal musical academy during the first decades of the new century, published a series of "new discoveries for the guitar" which were fairly studded with *tremblements, martellements, chuttes,* and *tirades*—the guitaristic equivalents of the trills, shakes, and mordents that were becoming so popular on the harpsichord.

Gaspar Sanz (1640–1710) was guitarist to the viceroy of Aragon,

(81) Another of Karel Dujardin's "Charlatans" affords a closer view of the Italian guitarist, whose playing posture has the makings of a modern pop style. Photo courtesy of the Staatliche Kunstsammlungen, Kassel.

(82) "Young Woman Playing a Guitar," by the French painter Augustin Quesnel, 1681. Photo courtesy of the Museum of Fine Arts, Budapest.

Juan José of Austria, natural son of Philip IV; on the title page of his famous *Instrucción de música sobre la guitarra española* he proudly describes himself as a Bachelor of Theology of the University of Salamanca. Despite his clerical training, his music is vividly charged with rhythms borrowed from the marketplace and the popular theater: the dance of *las hachas* (torches, not hatchets), the *canario* (supposedly from the Canary Islands), or the *passacalle* (originally danced in the streets by people passing through the *calles*). He also undertook to reproduce on the guitar "all the sounds of the palace," including *The Cavalry of Naples, The Trumpets of the Queen of Sweden, Bugle Calls of the Musketeers of the King of France,* and so on. His method of instruction, carefully illustrated, teaches its readers how to play *rasgado* and *punteado* in the "Spanish, Italian, French and English styles," no less. Like Luis Milán 150 years earlier, Sanz was a thinking man's guitarist, and something of a philosopher besides. "Some have spoken of the perfection of this instrument," he writes in the introduction, "some saying that it is perfect and others that it is not":

I take the middle way and assert that it is neither perfect nor imperfect, but what you make of it. Its faults or its perfection lie in whoever plays it, and not in the guitar itself, for I have seen some people accomplish things on one string for which others would need the range of an organ. Everyone must make of it what he can, good or bad. A guitar is a woman to whom the saying, "Look at me but do not touch me," does not apply; her rosette soundhole is the very opposite of a real rose bud, for she will not wither, no matter how much you touch her with your hands. On the contrary, when she is touched and played by a master hand, she will produce ever-new blossoms whose fragrant sonorities will please the ear.

Sanz's music—now being gradually revived in modern editions— rings down a delayed curtain on the era of great guitarists and vihuelists at the courts of Spain. From here on, composers who play the guitar are the exception rather than the rule; aristocratic amateurs and serious professionals take to the harpsichord, violin, or cello. And although it never lost its popularity in Spain, where *cualquiera sabe un poco de latín y un punto en la guitarra* (everybody knows a little Latin and a chord on the guitar), the day of the

(83) Drawing attributed to Claude Gillot (1673–1722): a scene from the comedy, *Jupiter curieux impertinent*, presented at the fair of St. Germain, on February 3, 1711. The third act of the pantomime is in progress: Columbina, with guitar, is seated in a group that includes Pulcinella and Mezzetino. Scaramouche stands at left, and in the center, Pierrot. Photo by Giraudon, courtesy of the Louvre, Paris.

(84) "The Amours of Pantalon and Harlequin": a German view of the *commedia dell' arte* by Johann Jacob Schübler (d. 1741), engraved by Johann Balthasar Probst (1673–1750). Photo courtesy of the Bibliothèque Nationale, Paris.

(85) "Scène d'amour" by Antoine Watteau (1684–1721). The very high hand position—preferred by many of Watteau's guitarists—serves to emphasize the dandyism of the pose. The gesture suggests that the overtones reverberating through the picture are delicate harmonics, lightly plucked at the neck of the guitar. Photo by Archivo Mas, courtesy of the Patrimonio Nacional, Palacio Real, Madrid.

plucked instruments was definitely drawing to a close in northern Europe. A typical sign of the times: the Honorable Roger North, circa 1700, recommends "the harpsichord for ladies rather than the lute; one reason is, it keeps the body in a better posture than the other, which tends to make them crooked."

The new-twanged quill-plucked harpsichord proved to be more convenient for playing aria accompaniments, and "hence, away all yee lutes and guittars, and make room for the fair consort basses!" (as North noted rather irritably). Within a generation the lute had virtually disappeared, while the guitar held its own mainly among amateurs, who tended to give it a bad name. The guitar, said the reverend English moralist Dr. John Brown in 1758, is "a trifling instrument in itself, and generally now taught in the most ignorant and trifling manner . . . while the theorbo and the lute, the noblest because the most expressive and pathetic of all accompaniments, are altogether laid aside. What is the reason of this? Because the guitar is a plaything for a child." Inevitably, fierce competition broke out between guitar-makers and harpsichord manufacturers. The eminent Dr. Charles Burney, the leading musical savant of eighteenth-century England, tells of some rather desperate infighting that followed a sudden surge in guitar sales—a boom so great "as nearly to break all the harpsichord and spinet-makers":

All the ladies disposed of their harpsichords at auction for one third of their price, or exchanged them for guitars; till old Kirkman, the harpsichord maker, after almost ruining himself with buying in his instruments, for better times, purchased likewise some cheap guitars and made a present of several to girls in milliners' shops, and to ballad singers, whom he had taught to accompany themselves, with a few chords and triplets, which soon made the ladies ashamed of their frivolous and vulgar taste, and return to the harpsichord.

This is the stuff of which fashions are still made in London, but the snobbery tactic would never have worked in Spain, where guitars remained the staff of musical life. "Here no one does anything but dance and play the guitar," reported Don Diego de Torres Villarroel (1693–1770) at midcentury. "Today Madrid has 4,000 more musicians [than in the days of Philip III]." In his memoirs,

(86) Watteau: study of a seated guitarist, again with a very high hand position. Photo by Ellebe, courtesy of the Musée de Rouen.

(87) Watteau: study of a standing guitarist. Photo courtesy of the National-museum, Stockholm.

(88) Watteau: study of a woman and a guitar. Photo courtesy
of the Rijksmuseum, Amsterdam.

The Remarkable Life of Don Diego, he indicates that playing the guitar was one of the local fine arts in which any young gentleman was expected to be conversant. At the University of Salamanca, in his youth,

My range of comic and eccentric songs I accompanied on the guitar. I danced trippingly and with an air all the Spanish dances, now with castanets, now again to the guitar, and in others showed my prowess over sword and buckler. . . . In the end I forgot my Latin, my textbooks, the miserable rudiments of logic I had acquired so stumblingly, a good part of my Christian doctrine and all the modesty and reserve my upbringing had given me. In exchange I turned out a notable dancer, a good torero, a tolerable musician, and in all a polished and daring rascal.

The guitar's indispensable position in Spanish affairs is nowhere summed up more succinctly than in *The Barber of Seville* by Beaumarchais, a playwright with the instincts of a documentarian, and one of the first French writers to see for himself what life was like on the other side of the Pyrenees:

COUNT: Figaro!
FIGARO: What is it?
COUNT: Your guitar—
FIGARO: I have forgotten my guitar! I am losing my wits.

As it happens, the greatest Spanish court composer of the century was an Italian, Domenico Scarlatti (1685–1757), who spent nearly forty years in Spain and Portugal. It was Scarlatti who would have made the ideal composer for Watteau's guitarists—Scarlatti the genius of the short attention span, who could elaborate a musical idea more brilliantly in two minutes than anyone else in twenty. Unfortunately, as far as we know, Scarlatti never got around to playing or writing for the guitar—"but surely no composer ever fell more deeply under its spell," writes his biographer Ralph Kirkpatrick. "Some of Scarlatti's wildest dissonances seem to imitate the sound of the hand striking the belly of the guitar, or the savage chords that at times almost threaten to rip the strings from the instrument. The very harmonic structure of many such passages that imitate the guitar seems to be determined by the guitar's open

[133]

(89) Watteau: drawing known as "Musicien pincant de la guitare."
Photo courtesy of the Musées de Rennes.

(90) Watteau: studies of three seated women, two of them playing the guitar. Photo courtesy of the Louvre, Paris.

(91) Watteau: studies of a guitarist. Photo courtesy of the Trustees of the British Museum.

strings and by its propensities for modal Spanish folk music."

When Luigi Boccherini arrived in Spain during the 1760's, he was exposed to these same violent influences, but they left a much less profound impression on his music. Boccherini (1743–1805) settled in Madrid as household composer to the king's brother, the Infante Don Luis, and to the Benavente-Osuna family; though a cellist by preference, he started writing for the guitar at the behest of his patron, the Marquis of Benavente, an enthusiastic amateur guitarist. It was on his account that Boccherini wrote his twelve quintets for two violins, guitar, viola, and cello—the first important chamber music-*cum*-guitar by a well-known composer (some of these quintets were afterward published in Paris with a second viola substituted for the guitar part). Guitar parts for the Marquis appear even in his orchestral scores, such as the *Symphony Concertante* for four violins, oboes, guitar, viola, horn, bassoon, cello, and bass.

In certain subtle ways Boccherini's non-guitar music is also *hispanizado,* as the Spanish say; scholars have pointed out that his minuets tend to sound like *seguidillas aminuetadas*—the "minuet-ized seguidillas" which were the local fashion. In one of his quartets he makes use of "the fandango which was played on the guitar by Padre Basilio," and a quintet entitled *Night Music of the Streets of Madrid* faithfully reproduces the sounds of dancing and merry-making, the songs of nocturnal serenaders, religious chants of the Rosario, street tunes, the strumming of guitars, and the march of the night watch. These things were so immutably Spanish that Boccherini felt they were not exportable. "This piece is absolutely useless and even ridiculous outside Spain," he explained to his French publishers, "because the audience cannot hope to understand its significance nor the performers play it as it should be played." Obviously, though he did not mind using it for an occasional joke or a "Ballet Espagnol," Boccherini never really warmed to Spanish folk music. As a composer he was of the classical persuasion—"Haydn's wife" was his nickname among the *cognoscenti*—and even after he had lived in Madrid for twenty years the "barbarities" of a barber's harmonies could still exasperate him. A British visitor, William Beck-

(92) Watteau's "Mezzetin": one of the three or four most famous guitar paintings in the world. Photo courtesy of the Metropolitan Museum of Art (Munsey Fund, 1934).

(93) A figure from the French Rococo theater, "Le Turc a La guitare," by Nicolas Lancret (1690–1743). Photo by Giraudon, courtesy of the Louvre, Paris.

ford, remembered afterward how incensed Boccherini had been when he saw the Englishman doing folk dances at a party to the accompaniment of furious strumming on Spanish guitars. It was December, 1787, and the scene was a ball given by a wealthy Portuguese in Madrid; Beckford writes that Boccherini stood by and watched his dancing "with the utmost contempt and dismay":

He said to me in a loud whisper: "If *you* dance and *they* play in this ridiculous manner, I shall never be able to introduce a decent style into our musical world here, which I flattered myself I was on the very point of doing. What possesses you? Is it the devil? Who could suppose that a reasonable being, an Englishman of all others, would have encouraged these inveterate barbarians in such absurdities. There's a chromatic scream! There's a passage! We have heard of robbing time; this is murdering it. What! Again! Why this is worse than a convulsive hiccup, or the last rattle in the throat of a dying malefactor. Give me the Turkish howlings in preference; they are not so obtrusive and impudent." So saying, he moved off with a *semi-seria* stride, and we danced on with redoubled delight and joy.

The "Padre Basilio" who managed, nevertheless, to win Boccherini's approval—at least for his fandangos—was not a character in *The Barber of Seville* but a Cistercian monk (originally named Miguel García) who had been called to the Escorial as organist to the king and music master to the queen. He was considered the best guitarist of the day; his rooms at the Escorial were usually crowded with aficionados, and groups of admirers would gather beneath his windows at night to hear him play. Among Padre Basilio's pupils were Dionisio Aguado, later a major virtuoso, and Don Manuel Godoy, the queen's favorite and virtual viceroy of Spain, whom Goya promptly caricatured as a guitarist in one of his *Caprichos*—a monkey guitarist, giving a recital before the king, who is thinly disguised as a donkey. The title: *Brabisimo!*

Goya's guitars are rarely instruments of pleasure, like Watteau's. Only the early *Majo de la Guitarra* (1780) conforms more or less to the standard conventions of the galante "seated figure with guitar." The rest of his guitars belong to ghosts and blind men— the last-rattle-in-the-throat guitars of which his friend Boccherini complained; guitars that scream chromatically instead of filling his pictures with soft sounds. As totems of a passionate and disordered Spain at once beloved and despaired of, they also symbolize man's eternal attempt to wring some comfort out of chaos. "All through the work of Goya, the theme of the guitar runs like a steady, unremitting accompaniment," writes the critic Edward Fenton. "In every mood that he created . . . there is always a guitar. To have left it out would have been like leaving out the hard Spanish sunlight."

Goya himself, before he became deaf as Beethoven, regarded the guitar, like a true Spaniard, as one of the necessities of life. "I do not require much in the way of furniture for my house," he once wrote to a friend who was arranging lodgings for him in Saragossa, where he had a commission to paint frescos for the Church of Our Lady of Pilar, "for I think that with a print of Our Lady of Pilar, a table, five chairs, a frying pan, a cask of wine and a *tiple* guitar, a roasting spit and an oil lamp, all else is superfluous." He kept on sketching guitarists long after he could no longer hear them play; one of his last drawings, made during the 1820's, is a marvelously rude, unsentimental sketch of a burly guitarist practicing his finger work (Plate 124).

It was in Goya's day that the Spanish guitar finally broke with its 250-year tradition of *cifras* and chord tablatures. At the very close of the century, in 1799, Fernando Ferandiere published his *Arte de tocar la Guitarra española por Música*—the first instruction manual to teach players how to read from notes rather than fingering symbols. His introduction explains some of the advantages to be gained thereby: "The guitar can play together with any of the instruments of the orchestra" if it can read from the same sheet of music; moreover, "it can easily imitate other instruments, such as flutes, trumpets or oboes, and has the ability to accompany singing as though it were a pianoforte." This sounds a new and ominous note in the literature of the guitar—a theme of instrumental transvestism which we shall have occasion to hear a great deal more about during the romantic era.

The guitar described in Ferandiere's book has seventeen frets and six courses of strings—five double, and a single chanterelle.

(94) Lancret: study of a guitarist. Photo by Rouault, courtesy of the Musée des Beaux
Arts, Valenciennes.

(95) Jean-Baptiste Greuze (1725–1805): study for the painting, "Un oiseleur accordant sa guitare" (A Bird-catcher Tuning his Guitar) of 1757. Photo courtesy of the Bibliothèque Nationale, Paris.

Many of the French guitar-makers of the same period, however, had already abandoned double courses in favor of single strings. This represented another important break with tradition. The double-string system reinforced the tone of the instrument, but since no two gut strings were ever of the same thickness, they had a tendency, when stopped, to be not quite in tune with each other. Dr. Burney tells of a strange Portuguese composer "in a very peculiar style," the Abate Costa, who was in the habit of stringing his guitar with not two but three strings to a course, and consequently had to devise a very complex solution to the problem of shifting microtones:

He wanted very much to correct the imperfections of the fingerboard of his guitar, which being strung with catgut, and having three strings to each tone, he found it frequently happen, that these strings, though perfectly in unison, when open, were out of tune when stopped, and this at some of the frets more than others. . . . Inventing a cheap and simple method of correcting the fingerboard . . . he placed longitudinally, under the upper covering, or veneer, as many rows of catgut strings as there were strings upon his instrument; then cutting through the ebony at each fret, and laying these under strings open, he placed under them little moveable bits of ebony, which rendered the chords upon his instrument equally perfect in all keys.

When the French cured these problems by eliminating double-stringing, they also launched the process of simplification which culminated in the plain, utterly functional Torres guitar of the 1850's. Some of the conservative builders, however, went on making double-course models well into the nineteenth century; many folk guitars, notably in Latin America, are still strung that way—for emphasis, as it were. Watteau's and Goya's guitars were narrower in the body, less incurved at the waist, and deeper in the chest than their descendants; by modern standards their tone was mellow but rather weak. The internal bracing system consisted merely of two to five bars running transversely across the belly; they served to keep the top straight and prevent the neck from pulling forward. It was only later that "fan bracing" or "fan barring" was introduced to distribute the vibrations of the strings, via the bridge, to the entire surface of the belly, rounding out the bass and enlarging the sound

[143]

of the whole instrument. The more expensive instruments had intricate three-dimensional rosettes and other elaborate ornamentation—a fleur de lys pattern covering the entire back, in one extreme case (Plate 224), or more generally, wood and mother-of-pearl inlays that ran around the top, the sound hole, and the edges of the fingerboard. The bridge was a simple bar of wood to which the strings were tied with a loop; there was no saddle, as there is in modern guitars. The pegging arrangements varied: most instruments had rear tuning pegs like the flamenco guitar, but violin-style pegs were still used occasionally. Fixed brass frets, of course, had replaced the tied frets of earlier epochs, but their number might vary from nine to seventeen.

It is beyond the scope of a social history to go much more deeply into the technical aspects of the instrument, but it may be useful at this point to include at least one technical description of a typical eighteenth-century guitar, if only to show the lengths to which one can go in cataloguing even the simplest example, and to indicate some of the complexities of modern organology. The following description is taken from an article by Terence Usher in the *Galpin Society Journal*, a professional publication by British organologists:

SPANISH GUITAR BY RAFAEL ROLDAN. Bears printed label: *Rafael Roldan me hizo en Malaga, Año de 1797*, the last figure of the date in ink.

Head, back and sides of rosewood. Flat rosewood fingerboard to 9th fret, remainder covered by extension of belly wood. Rosewood figure inlay on this extension, and similar inlays between bridge and end of guitar on belly. Ebony bridge (no saddle). Ivory nut. Eleven brass frets on fingerboard, five ebony frets on belly. Immature Spanish heel. Spanish head with six pegs on each side, and bridge with six pairs of string holes. Indicates six double strings, and is stage intermediate between five double strings and six single ones, giving a date to this fashion. Pearl diamond-shaped inlays in rosette round soundhole. Two transverse bars below belly, one above and one below the soundhole, as in the Cusworth guitar [a model previously described]. No sign of lateral or fan barring, or residues of glue from such bars. One must not, however, assume from this that fan barring was then unknown, as one finds modern guitars of Spanish luthiers which for cheapness were made with two transverse bars only. However, this Roldan is obviously of good quality and one would assume

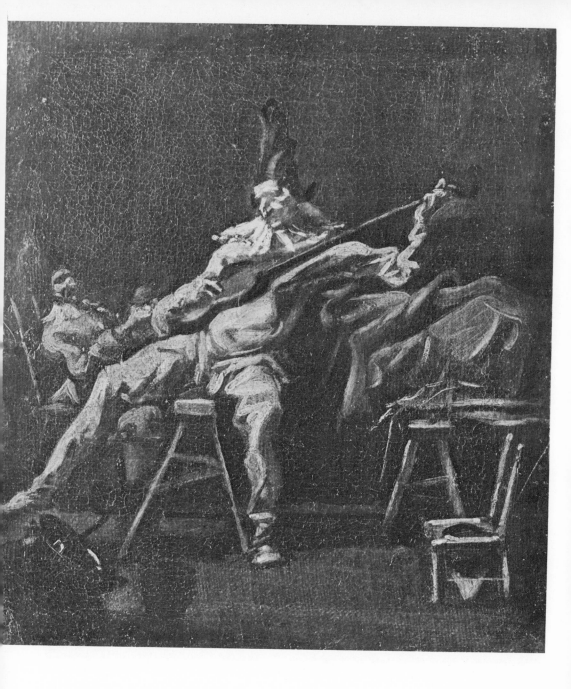

(96) "Pulcinella suonatore di chitarra" (The Guitar-playing Pulcinella) by
Alessandro Magnasco (c. 1677–1749). The last of the Baroque guitarists plays an
instrument with an implausibly long neck in an impossibly awkward position,
as befits the *commedia dell' arte*. Photo by Alinari, Florence.

[145]

(97) Jean-Honoré Fragonard (1732–1806): "La Guimard à la guitare,"
a portrait of the dancer Marie Madeleine Guimard.
Photo courtesy of the Bibliothèque Nationale, Paris.

(98) Portrait of Claude
Balbastre (1729–1799),
organist of the Church of
St. Roch, Paris. Miniature, on
ivory, by an unknown artist.
Photo by Giraudon, courtesy of
the Musée des Beaux Arts,
Dijon.

(99) Study of a seated guitarist
by an unknown eighteenth-
century artist. Photo courtesy of
the Bibliothèque Nationale,
Paris.

that the maker incorporated the then most advanced barring method. It probably comes from the transitional period when the new idea of lateral strutting had not been universally adopted in Spain.

DIMENSIONS:

Body length	17½ ″
Scale length	26 ″
Upper Bout	9 ″
Waist	6½ ″
Lower Bout	11 ″
Depth	4 ″
Fingerboard width	1¹⁵⁄₁₆″
Total number of frets	17

Back is flat. Table is slightly arched, by affixing a bridge with an arched base. Contrasting stringing round edge of belly and back, as in the Cusworth Hall guitar. Not in playable condition; tone cannot be estimated, but craftsmanship, wood qualities and thicknesses indicate that it will be of less volume of sound but far greater refinement than that of the Cusworth instrument.

The "invention" of the sixth string of the guitar is often attributed to a German instrument-maker, the Weimar luthier August Otto— a claim which is all the more difficult to believe because, up to that point, Germany had hardly figured as a guitar country at all. Indeed, the lute was so firmly entrenched in local affections that guitars had never been able to make much headway in central Europe. As Johann Mattheson wrote in his *Neu eröffnetes Orchester* (Hamburg, 1713):

> *Wir wollen . . . die platte Guitarren aber mit ihren Strump Strump den Spaniern gerne beim Knoblauch-Schmauss überlassen.*

The flat guitar with its strum, strum
We shall gladly leave to the garlic-eating Spaniards.

During most of the eighteenth century the German musical world was otherwise occupied: with Italian opera, the beginnings of the symphony orchestra, the harpsichord, the pianoforte. When the guitar finally appeared in Rococo drawing rooms it had the charm of sounding like an exotic novelty. "The instrument came to us from

(100) "The Guitar Player," a color aquatint by Jean François Janinet after
Nicolas Lavreince, or Lafrensen (1737–1807). Here, as in several previous examples,
the guitarist is left-handed, and the strings of her instrument have been reversed
so that the upper strings are bass strings. Apparently there were a good many
left-handed guitarists in eighteenth-century France. In many cases, however, the
picture shows a left-handed player merely because the design has been reversed in
the process of turning an original into a print or *contre-épreuve*.
Photo courtesy of the National Gallery of Art, Washington, D.C.

(101) Portrait of Caroline D'Arcy, Fourth Marchioness of Lothian (1778).
Though ascribed to Allan Ramsay, the picture is more probably by William Hoare
(1707–1799), another fashionable British portraitist. By this time the guitar
had become a standard fixture in society portraits; when not in the lady's hands,
it can often by found lying on a table or standing at her feet.
Photo courtesy of the National Gallery of Scotland, Edinburgh.

Italy," August Otto remembered. "In 1790 the Duchess Amalie of Weimar brought the first guitar from Italy to Weimar, and in those days it was regarded as a new instrument. Instantly it was warmly applauded on all sides. Court chamberlain von Einsidln commissioned me to copy the instrument for him. Then I had to do the same thing for many illustrious persons, and soon the guitar became known and appreciated in several larger towns—Dresden, Leipzig and Berlin."

Herr Otto claimed that he and a Dresden conductor first had the idea of adding the low E-string to the guitar, and this claim has been accepted at face value by many subsequent writers. Actually, of course, it was another of those inventions, like the telephone, that occur to different people in different places at the same time. Instrument-makers in the Mediterranean countries, with the precedent of the six-course vihuela to fall back on, had been experimenting with six-string guitars for nearly a century. Campion, in 1701, refers to *"la guitarre à cinq et à six cordes,"* and the Spanish composer Andrés de Sotos, in his *Arte para aprender* of 1764, addresses himself to guitars of four, five, or six courses. At any rate, to make things easier for both players and painters, the standard model of the 1800's had just six strings—three of gut, three of silk wound with silver wire.

Only the Russians were not entirely satisfied with this arrangement. During the 1790's a seven-string guitar was developed by a young virtuoso from Vilna, Andreas Ossipovitch Sichra (1772–1850), who went on to write a widely used method for the instrument. Smaller than the modern concert guitar, and tuned D-G-B-d-g-b-d', it became immensely popular in nineteenth-century Russia, especially among the gypsies. "It had a narrow waist and a detachable neck fitted with a screw to hold it in position," writes Vladimir Bobri, the Russian artist who founded the Society of the Classic Guitar when he came to America. "This feature was especially liked by the gypsy guitarists since it afforded a certain amount of play between the neck and the sound box, which permitted the guitarist to shake the guitar in both hands after striking a chord, producing a peculiar tone somewhat like that of a Hawaiian guitar."

[151]

In Italy, meanwhile, guitar developments had kept pace with those of France and Spain, though the lute held a preferred position for many years. One of the richest seventeenth-century collections is the four tablature books, *I quatro libri della Chitarra spagnola*, produced about 1630 by a composer named Foscarini who signed himself *L'Accademico Caliginoso detto il Furioso* (The Obscure Academician Called Mr. Furious). One of the first angry men of the Baroque, he vented his spleen in a series of remarkably elegant "*passacalli spagnoli variati, ciacone, follie, zarabande, arie diverse, toccate musicali, balleti, correnti volte, gagliarde, alemande . . .*" as the title page (Plate 59) carefully itemizes. At about the same time we hear a great deal about "La bell' Adriana," the beautiful harpist and guitar player Adriana Basile, who charmed the cardinals of Rome and the dukes of Mantua with the "graceful caresses" of her playing. She is said to have been the foremost virtuoso in all Italy—a rare distinction for a woman in that or any other century.

While Il Furioso and Adriana established the courtly Italian style that Corbetta brought to France and England, the "charlatans and saltimbanques who use it for strumming" were busy in the towns and villages, playing a less rarified kind of guitar music. Visitors to Italy came away with vivid impressions of the strolling musicians that Karel Dujardin liked to paint (Plates 80–81); the French critic François Raguenet, making his invidious *Comparison Between French and Italian Music* (1702) went so far as to say that the folk fiddlers and guitarists of the Piazza Navona, in Rome, "accompany their voices so justly that we seldom meet with much better music in our French [art] consorts." The same talented players were to be heard in Venice seventy years later when Dr. Burney arrived for a tour of inspection: "Upon the Piazza di San Marco I heard a great number of vagrant musicians, some in bands, accompanying one or two voices; sometimes a single voice and guitar, and sometimes two or three guitars together." Later he was fascinated by the guitar-playing peasants who came to Naples from Calabria just before Christmas, performing "a very singular species of music, as wild in modulation, and as different from that of all the rest of Europe, as the Scots."

(102) Portrait of Clothilde de France by François-Hubert Drouais (1727–1775).
Granddaughter of Louis XV and sister of Louis XVI, Clothilde was married
to a prince of Piedmont at sixteen and afterwards reigned briefly as Queen of
Sardinia. She was the last French princess to be married at Versailles. The picture
is dated "Salon 1775," the year of her wedding and of Drouais' death. Since she
tended to obesity—her nickname was "La gros Madame"—the painter has rendered
her features with a certain tolerant vagueness and lavished his full powers
of *trompe l'oeil* on her elaborately inlaid guitar.
Photo by Giraudon, courtesy of the Château de Versailles.

(103) "La leçon de musique" by Jean-Baptiste Hilair (1753–1822). Dated 1781,
less than a decade before the French Revolution, this is one of the last well-known
paintings in the Watteau-pastoral tradition. Photo courtesy
of the Archives Photographiques, Paris.

Chitarra Spagnola

Mandola

(104) Plate 51, "Chitarra Spagnola," from Filippo Bonanni's *Gabinetto Armonico* (The Showcase of Musical Instruments), published in its final form in Rome, 1722. The 150 illustrations for this sumptuous classic of organology were engraved by Arnold van Westerhout (1651–1725). According to Bonanni, the guitar is called "Spanish" because so many Spaniards use it, and he shows it in a woman's hands because ladies are particularly fond of it. He mentions two kinds of playing: beating it with the hand (rasgado) or plucking it with the fingers, "which produces a more suave, delicate sound." Five double courses of strings are shown, and the lady's hand position suggests a rhythmic rasgado, flamenco style. Collection of the author.

(105) Bonanni's "Mandola"—plate 53 of the *Gabinetto Armonico*—seems to be identical with the "vandola" mentioned by Carles y Amat in his treatise on the guitar. Most other sources define the mandora, alias mandola, as a small four-string version of the lute (from which the Neapolitan mandolin was derived). Bonanni's illustration, however, shows what is unmistakably a small guitar, which he describes as having only four strings, and as being related to the Eastern pandora and the rebec. Such confusion invariably arises when words of the rival "pandora" and "cithara" families are applied indiscriminately to several related species of stringed instruments. Collection of the author.

[155]

Somewhere between the splendid primitive art of the Neopolitan *pifferari* and the aristocratic counterpoint of the court of Mantua there was a vast middle ground consisting of *fiori* and canzonettas and other easy music likely to catch the ear of young ladies in the course of an evening's serenade. The preferred instrument for such affairs was not the big Spanish guitar but the smaller chitarra italiana, or chitarrino, usually tuned d-g-b-e'. Since everybody sang, and the guitar's function was simply to strum chords, various kinds of harmonic shorthand were devised—usually a crude alphabetic system, inexact but adequate to the purpose, which spelled out the chords and left it to the player to reel them off ad lib, whenever the song seemed to need one. With Sunday guitarists visibly multiplying everywhere, it was only natural that the European market for guitar music should soon be glutted with trivia of this kind, whose chief attraction was that anybody could play after a couple of hours of instruction.

"Nothing can be really more simple in itself than the guitar," boasted an English beginner's book toward the end of the century, by way of introducing a typical collection of salon ditties: If 'tis Joy to wound a lover, Blithe as the feather'd Songsters, Cupids Recruiting Serjeant, Moggy Lawther Variations, Mullony's Jig, I do as I will with my Swain, etc. The titles may have differed, but the style was the same wherever guitars were being played in salons or under balconies; these are the songs that are echoed in the society portraits of the Age of Reason, the musical equivalent of the ormolu and porcelain bibelots with which the age diverted itself. If the fourth Marchioness of Lothian could step out of her frame and begin to play her guitar (Plate 101), it would be *Believe My Sighs* or *Tho Prudence May Press Me* we could expect to hear, and the two musical ladies in Hilaire's *La leçon de musique* (1781), far from studying Mozart, are probably learning *La double entendre* (Plate 103).

By now the painted guitar, so brilliantly alive and resonant in Watteau's hands, has become something of a cliché. If not in the sitter's lap it will usually be found standing at her feet, lying on a table, or resting on a divan—the implication being that this lady,

[156]

(106) Bonanni's "Chitarrino diverso" covers a multitude of guitar sizes between the full-scale "spagnola" and the tiny "mandola." Bonanni's text explains that van Westerhout's purposely comic illustration represents a Neapolitan sailor on shore leave playing an Italian chitarrino of four to six strings, though the engraving itself clearly shows ten. "It is not ideal for harmonies, but it produces a bright, acute sound that pleases the senses of these rustic people." Collection of the author.

(107) Musical instruments in the *Presepe della Reggia*, the nativity scene of the royal palace of Caserta, Italy. The biblical shepherds, here represented as peasants of the Campania, play violin, mandolin, and guitar. This elaborately theatrical crèche is the work of several eighteenth-century sculptors: Matteo Bottiglieri, Nicola Ingaldi, Giuseppe Sanmartino, Giuseppe Gori, and Francesco Celebrano. Photo courtesy of the Ente Provinciale per il Turismo, Caserta.

Chitarrino diuerso

LIV

whatever her intellectual or other endowments, knows how to give pleasure when it is asked of her. For some painters the guitar itself becomes an obsession. In Drouais' portrait of Princess Clothilde de France (Plate 102), the guitar is much more expertly and lovingly depicted than the princess, with every last piece of marquetry work carefully painted in. Was it because the guitar sat still and Clothilde didn't, or because Drouais thought it more politic not to look too closely at "La gros Madame"?

In any case, the quintessential guitarist of the age is not a princess but a dancer, Marie Madeleine Guimard, who gazes so elegantly out of her portrait by Fragonard, *La Guimard à la guitare* (Plate 97). She was a woman of affairs and a self-made millionairess. Having begun as a dancer at the Paris Opéra, she was taken up in turn by the Russian Count Boutourbin, the Count of Rochefort, Benjamin de la Borde, and the Prince de Soubise, a man renowned for his generosity toward his mistresses. According to the tattle-tale *Mémoires secrets* of 1784, La Guimard was in the habit of giving three lavish suppers every week, at which she played hostess to an age: "One composed of gentlemen of the court and all sorts of important personages; another to which writers, painters and scholars had been invited to amuse this muse . . . and finally a third, to which she invited the most seductive, the most lascivious young women; suppers that were veritable orgies where lust and debauchery were heaped to overflowing."

In 1786, when she was forty-three, La Guimard was compelled—just in time—to sell her huge mansion, with its Fragonard décor and its private theater, where forbidden plays were performed. In three more years the whole princely world, of which she had represented the most enjoyable part, came crashing down around her ears. When Beaumarchais, a few years earlier, had applied for royal permission to stage a sequel to his *Barber of Seville*, Louis XVI had replied with one of his fits of temper. "Detestable!" he had cried when the manuscript of *The Marriage of Figaro* was read to him. "This play must never be given. The man mocks everything that should be respected in the government. The Bastille would have to be torn down before the presentation of this play could be anything

(108) The guitar in Spanish chamber music: a fascinating but unlikely combination of instruments from Pablo Minguet's *Modo de tañer todos los instrumentos mejores* (Method of Playing All the Best Instruments) published in Madrid, 1752. Photo courtesy of the Biblioteca Nacional, Madrid.

(109) Finger positions for stopping standard chords, from Minguet's treatise. Nonplaying fingers are indicated with a ring, as in Gaspar Sanz's method. Photo courtesy of the Biblioteca Nacional, Madrid.

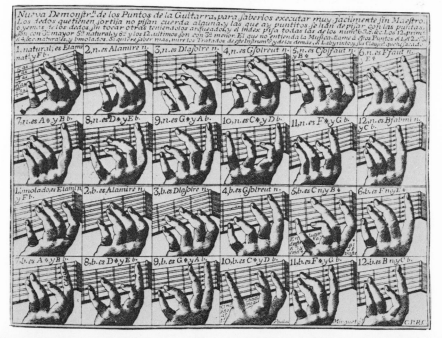

COPLAS

DE LA JOTA CON ESTRIVILLO, Y SEGVIDILLAS,
Coplas de la eſtopa, y otras diferentes cantatas,
nuevamente compueſtas en eſte
preſente año.

Y AGUILA ſoy del amor,
    que remontando mi buelo,
voy à vèr ſi encontraré
un Amante verdadero.
Eſtrivillo.
A los rayos del Sol me retiro
á vèr en què pàra mi amor tan querìdo
A los montes me voy con violencia,
antes que pierda mi amor la paciencia,

   2 Què pretendes alcanzar
gallarda imaginacion,
ſi tus alas ſon de cera,
y es ingrato el corazon?
Eſtrivillo.
Me quiſiera poner en clauſura
por no vèr los rayos dta hermoſura,

Me quiſiera ir peregrinando,
por no vèr deſdenes de quiẽ quiero tãto

   3 Mis ojos en vueſtra auſencia
ſon dos caudaloſos rios,
mi corazon en el pecho,
ſujeto en cadena, y grillos
   Eſtrivillo.
Priſionero ſe encuentra mi amor,
ſin ſaber la cauſa de tanto rigor:
La ſentencia me han dado de muerte,
tu eres la cauſa eſtàr deſta ſuerte,

   4 Què pincél avrà tan recio,
ſupueſto que Apeles ſea
el que le govierne, y riga,
para imitar tu belleza?

Eſtri.

(110) An eighteenth-century Spanish song-sheet with the texts of popular *jotas* and *seguidillas*. The coplas are as trivial as any modern pop-song lyric: "I'm going to see if I can find my true love," etc. Photo courtesy of the Instituto Municipal de Historia, Barcelona.

[160]

but dangerous folly." Now, when it had come out just as he had foreseen, the populace sang *"Ah ça ira, ça ira, ça ira"* instead of the old ditties, the aristocratic guitars were silenced, and their owners went to the guillotine. The rest of the story is told by the inventories of the revolutionary commission, established by the Committee of Public Safety, in charge of confiscating the possessions of those who had fled the country or been condemned to the scaffold. The entries —a few of them are given below—are dated according to the revolutionary calendar, which counted its years from the day the republic was proclaimed:

9 Prairial, Year II [29 May, 1794]: Confiscated from the Prince de Conti, three guitars and their cases, manufactured by Salomon.

1 Thermidor, Year II [19 July, 1794]. Confiscated from de la Borde, a guitar by Pierre Louvet, 1758.

13 Brumaire, Year III [3 November, 1794]. From Count (Lord) Kerby, a guitar by Saunier, appraised at 800 francs.

12 Frimaire, Year III [3 December, 1794]. From the Maison D'Heronville (condemned), a guitar without case, appraised at 6 francs.

28 Pluviose, Year III [17 February, 1795]. From the Marquise de Marbeuf (condemned) a guitar made by Guillaume of Paris in 1789, appraised at 100 francs. . . .

Viva el bayle Bolero.   **PRIMERA POSTURA.**   *Natural regocijo*
Pues es con gracia,   **EN LA ACCION DE DAR LA VUELTA**   *De nuestra España.*

(111) A guitar and a bandurria (the Spanish mandolin) play for a bolero danced at a *romeria*, or country excursion, near Madrid, c. 1800. "Long live the bolero because it has grace and is the natural delight of Spain," reads the accompanying text. Photo courtesy of the Biblioteca Nacional, Madrid.

(112) Spanish guitarist on an eighteenth-century Valencian plate. Photo by Archivo Mas, courtesy of the Mora Collection, Barcelona.

Chapter 6

Guitaromanie

I love the guitar for its harmony; it is my constant companion on all my travels.

—NICCOLO PAGANINI

T HE NINETEENTH-CENTURY romantics, who do a lot of traveling and like to make music out of doors, learn to prize the guitar for its portability and its elastic touch. The young Carl Maria von Weber and two of his Mannheim friends are often heard serenading after dinner, "strolling through the town with their guitars to rouse the sopranos of the opera with the sound of their strumming, and to sing them their latest songs."

Franz Schubert's principal possessions consist of "a few books, a guitar and a pipe"; friends who come to visit him in the mornings are accustomed to finding him still in bed, "singing newly composed songs to his guitar." Giuseppe Mazzini, the literary firebrand of the Italian *risorgimento*, goes cheerfully into exile carrying a guitar case: "I could live willingly all my life in a closed room if I only had with me my books and guitar."

Thomas Moore uses it to bring *Believe Me, If All Those Endearing Young Charms* to the English; the pianist Moscheles notes in his diary that he has heard Moore, along with Coleridge, at a party given by Sir Walter Scott's daughter, where "he sang his own poems, adapted to certain Irish melodies, harmonized and accompanied by

(113) Guitarist on an eighteenth-century Catalan tile. Photo courtesy of the Museo Municipal de Barcelona.

(114) In another tile of the same series, a stunt player performs with the guitar held behind his back. Photo courtesy of the Museo Municipal de Barcelona.

(115) Catalan majolica tile with guitarist-contortionist. Photo by
Archivo Mas, courtesy of the Mora Collection, Barcelona.

[165]

himself on the guitar." Lord Byron, knowing that his friend is an aficionado, writes to him from Italy, "The Carnival's coming, Oh Thomas Moore!"

> Masking and humming,
> Fifing and drumming,
> Guitaring and strumming,
> Oh Thomas Moore!

The woods are full of romantic poets with guitars. "I am surrounded by the coolness of a copse of chestnut trees," writes the twenty-one-year-old Theodor Körner, soon to lose his life in the Napoleonic Wars, "and the guitar that hangs behind me on the nearest tree occupies me in moments when I'm resting." When nights are warm and the moon is out, the author of *Lyre and Sword* takes to the road: "I always hang the guitar round my neck and ramble through the neighboring villages." At long last the German-speaking countries are discovering the pleasures of guitar-playing. "The Germans have known and played the cither or cister and the lute for a long time," asserts a Viennese journal at the turn of the century. "But the Spanish guitar has come to us only lately, by way of France." The arch-romantic storyteller E. T. A. Hoffmann has recorded the exact psychological instant when, as it were, the discovery was first made; in his short story *The Fermata* a young German musician, trained on the standard piano repertoire, suddenly encounters a breathtaking new sound that changes his whole *Weltanschauung:*

Lauretta said that she would sing. Teresina took up her guitar, tuned it, and struck a few chords. It was the first time I had ever heard that instrument, and the characteristic mysterious sounds of the trembling strings made a deep and remarkable impression on me. Lauretta began to sing very softly. . . . I felt that all the music within my own spirit, which had lain mute and sleeping all my life, had been awakened and enkindled, so that it could burst forth in strong and splendid flame. Ah, I had never before heard music; in all my nineteen years, I had never known what music was.

This story—one of the wittiest and most subtle of the *Tales of*

(116) "A Barber Serenading his Beloved" by Manuel de la Cruz (1750–1792). Barbers and blind beggars were *ex officio* guitarists in many parts of Spain. Photo by Archivo Mas, courtesy of the Museo Municipal, Madrid.

(117) "Blind Man Playing the Guitar" by Manuel de la Cruz. Photo by Archivo Mas, courtesy of the Museo Municipal, Madrid.

(118) Guitar behind bars: an illustration from the fourth (1732) edition of Alain René Le Sage's "Gil Blas." The guitarist is a Spanish cavalier whom Gil meets in prison, Don Gaston de Cogollos. He sings "a very touching ballad whose words express the cruelty and despair of a lady rejecting her lover." Photo courtesy of the Bibliothèque Nationale, Paris.

Hoffmann—was actually inspired by a painting he had seen at an 1814 art exhibition in Berlin, a canvas by Johann Erdmann Hummel now also known as *Die Fermate*, but originally entitled *Company in an Italian Inn* (Plate 138). Everything about this picture is purest German Biedermeier romanticism, and Hoffmann recognized it at once as a starting point for one of his marvelous grotesques: "Two Italian ladies are seated facing each other; one sings, the other plays a guitar—and between them stands an Abbé, who acts as music director. With his battuta raised, he is awaiting the moment when the Signora shall end the cadence with a long trill . . . then his hand will descend sharply, while the guitarist gaily dashes off the dominant chord."

Hoffmann's Berlin and Schubert's Vienna were undergoing their first attack of what the French called *la guitaromanie*—an all-embracing mania for the guitar that showed no signs of abating until the 1830's. Though a number of men also had a hand in it, it was very largely a feminine affair, as Werden's *Taschenbuch (Pocket Journal) für Freunde der Musik* pointed out in 1804:

Isn't it true that it can be found in the home of every even only moderately modern, attractive, affectionate, flirtatious, playful, pretty, exuberant, mischievous or even innocent, demure, respectable woman? And that every day new songs, choruses, romances, duets, trios, solos, sonatas, potpourris, chansons, contredanses, anglaises, waltzes, minuets, allemandes, and rondos, yes even concertos, are created, written, composed, produced, and arranged for guitar?

But from the professional guitarist's point of view this sudden popularity was not an unmixed blessing. Simon Molitor (1766–1848), one of the leading Viennese guitarists of the day, complained that "although it is already universal, it is still not well understood; indeed a very much misunderstood instrument":

The true connoisseur and lover of music sighs over the fact, as proof of the frivolity of our time, that we have taken up an instrument which is suitable only for accompanying trifles, and then only in a few keys, and with only the most commonplace chords. Sterner critics even condemn this instrument for encouraging the shallowest kind of tinkling, owing to the facility with which one can learn to produce these obvious chords,

[169]

and the thoughtlessness with which they are played. . . . These frivolities, these endless arpeggios of chords that submit to no rules, these artificial ornaments that are not really suited to the instrument though cultivated even by the better players, can only give the instrument a bad name among the cognoscenti.

Apparently unaware of Boccherini's existence, or of any of the other important guitar composers, Molitor claimed that he had never heard a work that did justice to the instrument. Though for many years a civil servant in the Austrian War Office, he devoted most of his energies to filling up what he felt were the gaps in the repertoire, and to imparting some musical dignity to this stepchild of Vienna's golden age. He composed solo sonatas, duets, trios, and concertos for guitar, hoping to make it as important in its field as the parvenu pianoforte, while "leading the bass and middle voices in such a way that the harmonic relationships correspond to what one otherwise expects from instruments whose very nature is harmonic."

The results, though historically interesting, are not quite as earth-shaking as he had hoped, but he did help to launch a lively school of Austro-German guitar music that produced, among other things, a lot of chamber music: Leonhard von Call's trios for flute, viola, and guitar; Anton Diabelli's *Serenades* for violin, viola, and guitar; Joseph Kreutzer's trio for flute, clarinet, and guitar; Wenzel Matiegka's *Notturno* for flute, viola, and guitar (which Schubert adapted into a quartet with cello); Weber's *Divertimento* for guitar and piano, Opus 38, and a great many more. These are minor works, belonging to what the Germans call *Musikantentum,* which might be translated as "fiddlers' music." Yet they seem well worth the effort of an occasional revival, if only as mementos of that, in retrospect, incredibly gentle and sensitive Germany, where Clemens Brentano could wander up and down the Rhine with his guitar, collecting folk songs for *Des Knaben Wunderhorn,* or Heinrich Laube walk all the way from Silesia to Halle, carrying a guitar on his back and not much besides. Like the sundials that stood in Biedermeier gardens among the lilac bushes, this music records only the sunny hours of German romanticism; a time when even Faust (in Nikolaus Lenau's version) was strumming the guitar.

(119) The Spanish guitar in the colonies, as seen by a critic: "The Dress and Manner of Living of the Spaniards in South America" by John Henry Fuseli (1741–1825). The lady's shocking deshabille represents another link in the tradition that associates the guitar with loose living. Collection of the author.

(120) The guitar in Spain during the epoch of Beaumarchais' "Figaro." In this detail from a painting by Antonio Carnicero (1748–1814) it finds a place in a fishing boat on a beach where the makings of a paella are being sold. Photo by Archivo Mas, Madrid private collection.

(121) "El Majo de la guitarra" by Lorenzo Baldissera Tiepolo (1736–1776), son of the better-known Giovanni Battista Tiepolo. This is one of the Madrid folk scenes which he painted in the 1770s for the Spanish court; the guitar is a small *requinto* with a short neck, a large head, and only six frets. A "majo" is a young gallant, a man-about-town. Photo by Archivo Mas, courtesy of the Patrimonio Nacional, Palacio Real, Madrid.

[173]

In England, meanwhile, the upper classes were caught up in their own outbreak of *guitaromanie* largely because (as the *Giulianiad* magazine asserted) Wellington's officers in the peninsular campaigns against Napoleon had acquired a taste for it:

Mixing, as did our warriors, with the people of Spain and Portugal; and domesticated as many of them were, and are to this day, with the families of those countries, it was only natural that they should have discovered the immense influence which the guitar there possessed, and have felt themselves, the witching power of its fascination. . . . How delightful must be the associations connected with this instrument to those who first heard its sound, and learnt its touch, amid the danger and terror of warfare, now that they can recall to their memories those days of chivalry and romance, by their own peaceful hearths in old England!

Beating swords into plowshares, the returned warriors also taught their wives and daughters how to play *The Soldier's Flask, La Sentinelle, Sans Argent Comptant, Oh! Cease, Love to Grieve Thee*, and all the rest of it. Far from endangering the posture of young ladies, the guitar was now held to be a salubrious employment for the weaker sex. "The instrument is so obedient to the expression of their feelings—it echoes their sportive gaiety, their little griefs, calm tranquility and noble and elevated thoughts, with such nice precision, that it would seem to be a natural appendage and true barometer of the state of their own fair bosoms."

Despite these affinities of form and feeling, virtually all the serious work on the guitar continued to be done by men. A whole generation of concert virtuosos, most of them from the Mediterranean countries, established a new image of the guitar as an instrument that could (in the words of the *Westminster Review*) "warble, or articulate, or sigh, or wail, or tremble, like the human voice under emotion."

The leading exponents of this "expressionist" school were the Spaniards Sor and Aguado, and the Italians Carulli, Carcassi, and Giuliani. The outstanding figure in the group, Fernando Sor (or Sors, as it was originally spelled) was the greatest guitarist of the romantic era. The son of a Catalan merchant, he was born in Barcelona—the date is in dispute, but it was probably February 17,

(122) "El Majo de la guitarra" by Goya's brother-in-law, Ramon Bayeu (1746–1793). Photo courtesy of the Museo del Prado, Madrid.

(123) "El Majo de la guitarra" by Francisco Goya (1746–1828); another major masterpiece of guitar painting, produced as a design for a tapestry in 1780. Photo courtesy of the Museo del Prado, Madrid.

(124) Goya: sketch known as "Man with guitar." An untitled black chalk drawing of the painter's last period, 1820–1828. Photo courtesy of the Museo del Prado, Madrid.

(125) Goya: "Brabisimo!" The thirty-eighth of *Los Caprichos* shows the simian prime minister of Spain, Don Manuel Godoy, in the act of playing the guitar for King Charles IV, here thinly disguised as a donkey. Photo courtesy of the New York Public Library.

(126) Goya: drawing for the
etching "Dios se lo pague a
usted" (God Will Reward You).
Goya turns two classic Spanish
symbols into a bitter allegory
of Spain at the mercy of
implacable forces, like a blind
man tossed by a bull.
Photo courtesy of the
Museo del Prado, Madrid.

(127) Goya: etching known as
"Blind Man Singing." Photo
courtesy of the National Gallery
of Art, Washington, D.C.
(Rosenwald Collection).

1778—and received a musical education at the choir school of the nearby monastery of Montserrat. When he left the monastery, where his voice had been trained but his guitar-playing suppressed, one of the sacristans pressed a gold coin into his hand. "At first I refused to accept it, but when he told me that it was a custom for each pupil to receive one of these coins, so that they could bring it to their family and buy a memento of their stay on the holy mountain, I accepted the money." Instead of taking it home, however, he used it to buy himself the long-desired guitar.

At eighteen Sor wrote an opera, *Telemachus on Calypso's Isle*, which was produced in Barcelona in 1797. ("Since the theater will be illuminated," read the announcement, "the price of tickets, boxes and opera glasses will be doubled.") On the strength of that early success he was taken to Madrid, where he enjoyed the patronage of Goya's Duchess of Alba and the Duke of Medinaceli, as well as of Queen Maria Louisa and the inescapable Don Manuel Godoy. Sor always cut a dashing figure, and when he was called into the army he was commissioned a lieutenant, then a captain, in the Cordovan volunteers. During the confused period of French occupation, he cast his lot with the puppet government of King Joseph Bonaparte and became police commissary of Jerez de la Frontera—for many Spanish intellectuals, Goya included, looked to the Bonapartes for the political reforms they had been denied under Charles IV. But when the French withdrew, defeated by Wellington and the Spanish guerrilla armies, Sor and many of the other *afrancesados* had no choice but to leave with them.

He never returned. After 1812 he lived in Paris for the most part, though he also paid extended visits to Britain and Russia. In France he won the admiration of Méhul, Cherubini, and Pleyel; the powerful critic Fétis was moved to call him "the Beethoven of the guitar." There were other flattering comparisons: after one of his concerts a Paris journal noted that "he charmed all Parisians by an instrument which might from its appearance have been taken for a guitar, but judging by its harmony must have been a complete orchestra enclosed in small compass. He ought to be called the Racine of the guitar." When Sor made his London debut in 1815 the effect "was at once magical and surprising," according to an English aficionado who described the concert some years later:

Nobody could credit that such effects could be produced on the *guitar!* Indeed, there was a sort of suppressed laughter when he first came forth before the audience, which, however, soon changed into the most unbounded admiration when he began to display his talents. London was, at that time, not without persons who *professed* to teach the guitar; and I know that several of these guitar-quacks went there "to *scoff*, but remained to pray!"

Sor was the first and only guitarist invited to perform with the London Philharmonic Society during the first hundred years of its existence; on March 24, 1817, he appeared as soloist in his own *Concertante for Spanish Guitar and Strings.* During the 1820's he went to Germany and then to Russia, where everyone was surprised to see him play with equal facility in all keys, though his guitar had one string less than the local (Sichra) model. He produced three of his ballets in Moscow. At the death of Czar Alexander I in 1825, Sor composed a funeral march for the Preobrazhensky Guards at the request of the new Czar Nicholas I. The Czarina Alexandra is said to have presented him with black pearls of immense value. After his return to France he worked indefatigably as a teacher and composer, but his last years were to be tragic ones. Both his wife and his daughter, Julia, whom he had been training as a harpist, died quite suddenly, within a short time of each other. Sor himself died after terrible suffering—he had cancer of the tongue—on July 8, 1839. He was buried in a friend's tomb in the Montmartre Cemetery, but since Sor's name was never inscribed on it, its location was not discovered until 1934.

If a complete catalogue of Sor's compositions were drawn up, it would probably run to more than 250 or 300 works ranging from salon pieces to complete operas. His best-known major scores were ballets—*Cendrillon (Cinderella)* and *Gil Blas*—and his happiest hours, apparently, were spent backstage at the Paris ballet with Taglioni and the other beautiful dancers of the epoch, whom he liked to shower with presents and flowers. Thanks to his dance instincts he was usually at his best composing waltzes, minuets, galops,

(128) Goya: "Nun Frightened by a Ghost." Wash drawing in sepia. Photo courtesy of the Metropolitan Museum of Art (Harris Brisbane Dick Fund, 1935).

boleros, and so on; for a French encyclopedia he wrote the first authoritative study of such Spanish dances as the bolero, *seguidilla, murciana,* and *sevillana.* In a more classical vein he wrote sonatas, fantasias, and sets of variations on themes by Mozart, Hummel, and Paisiello.

But Sor's crowning achievement is his *Méthode pour la guitare* of 1830—easily the most remarkable book on guitar technique ever written. It represents the fruit of forty years of experience. With his inquisitive, keenly analytical mind, Sor has taken guitar-playing apart like a clockwork and examined all of its component parts in meticulous detail: the finger and wrist positions of both hands, the position of the instrument and of the player's body, the "manner of setting the strings in vibration," all are carefully discussed and illustrated (Plates 145–148). He teaches the importance of a steady hand, intelligent fingering, well-constructed harmonies, and neatly played ornaments. "Even at the risk of contradicting established tradition I have written about the experiences and reflections which have enabled me to regulate my playing," he explains in the introduction. "I have neither followed precedents nor set up rules out of sheer caprice, but merely indicated the route which I myself have followed." The whole tone of Sor's book is a calculated affront to the professional guitar teachers of the day. He does not want to instruct the professors, Sor claims; what he wants to reach are the amateurs. "An amateur takes up the guitar as a form of relaxation from his work; he has studied other things, acquired useful sciences and learned to think for himself, preferring reason to authoritarian strictures. Therefore he can understand me better than someone who has devoted his whole life to studying music."

The real test of the pudding was to be found in Sor's guitar studies —*24 Very Easy Exercises,* Opus 35; *12 Etudes,* Opus 6 and 29; *24 Lessons,* Opus 31; *24 Pieces for Lessons,* Opus 44; and so on. His etudes are often successful in striking what Segovia calls "the right balance between the pedagogical purpose and the natural musical beauty." And yet, for all the things to be said in its favor, Sor's music has never really been a candidate for a serious revival. It lacks that certain indomitable element which distinguishes the great romantics

(129) "Prelude to a Concert" by Marguerite Gérard (c. 1761–1837).
She was Fragonard's sister-in-law, and painted several important studies of
guitarists and other musicians. Photo by Roger Viollet, Paris.

(130) "The Model" by Marguerite Gérard. One of the famous French paintings in the Hermitage Museum, Leningrad. Photo courtesy of the Hermitage.

(131) Robert Lefèvre: portrait of Pauline de Montel, Madame Duchambge
(c. 1776–1858). Born in Martinique, Madame Duchambge married a
French baron and became a well-known teacher of music and composer of
salon pieces. Photo courtesy of the Château de Versailles.

(132) The Ten of Hearts: design for a playing card by the German architect Karl Haller von Hallerstein (1774–1817). Photo courtesy of Toby Molenaar.

(133) "The Family of Lucien Bonaparte" by Jean Auguste Dominique Ingres (1780–1867). The instrument at left is the lyre guitar, an elegant variation much in vogue during the Napoleonic era, when everyone was trying to look as neoclassical as possible. The drawing was made in Rome, 1815. Photo courtesy of the Fogg Art Museum, Harvard University.

from those who are merely interesting. The English *Harmonicon* magazine once put its finger on the trouble without intending to: "M. Sor stands at a vast distance from all other guitarists. He is an excellent musician, a man of taste, and his command over an instrument, which in other hands is so limited in its means, is not only astonishing, but what is more important—always pleasing."

That puts the Sor problem in a nutshell; the ability to be "always pleasing" can also be considered a fatal flaw. Rather than "the Beethoven of the guitar"—too tall an order, in any case—he was really a sort of Czerny, the founding father of a "school of velocity" and the composer of occasional small masterpieces like the ones Segovia keeps in his repertoire.

While living in Paris during the 1820's, Sor received a visit from Dionisio Aguado, then the most brilliant guitarist in Spain, who had come to France for the express purpose of getting to know him. Aguado (1784–1849) had already published some of his virtuoso music; born in Madrid and educated as a Latinist and an expert in ancient manuscripts, he was famous both as a guitarist and as a paleographer to the Council of Castile. The two musicians hit it off instantly, and Sor composed *Los Dos Amigos* to celebrate and cement their friendship. (It is said that it was hard for them to play it, since each of them kept interrupting himself to listen to the other.) "I shall never be able to play like you," Sor is quoted as saying, to which Aguado replied with equal gallantry, "But I shall never be able to compose like you, or express such profound feelings."

There was, however, one great bone of contention between them. Aguado, following the method he had learned from Padre Basilio, played with his fingernails. Sor eschewed fingernails; he used only the fleshy part of the fingertips, except in his rare "oboe" effect, obtained by attacking the string near the bridge with bent fingers and short nails. "This is the only instance when I allow myself to use nails. I could never abide guitarists who play with their nails."

"When Aguado heard some of my works," Sor wrote, "he set himself to study them, and asked my advice on interpretation. . . . I ventured to suggest to him the disadvantages of using nails in playing my music, which was conceived in a spirit utterly unlike that of most contemporary guitarists. Some years later, when we saw each other again, he confessed that if he were able to start over again, he would play without nails." The only thing holding him back, Sor thought, was that fact that he had reached the age "when it is too difficult to alter the acquired habits of the fingers."

But Aguado, in an edition of his own *Método* published after Sor's death, tells an altogether different story. Apparently his eleventh-hour conversion had extended no further than the thumb. "After hearing my friend Sor, I decided not to use the thumb nail any longer, and am very glad to have done so, for playing with the flesh, when the thumb is not striking the string at a right angle, produces a vigorous and pleasing sound, which suits the bass part." On the other fingers, however, he was as firmly pro-nail as ever. "My long experience may allow me, I hope, to express my candid opinion in this matter," he writes, weighing his words with the care of a pale-ographer. "I prefer to play with the nails because, if properly used, the resulting sound is clear, metallic, and sweet [*limpio, metálico y dulce*]. . . . Used in the right way they enable very fast runs to be executed with great clarity."

In their great fingernail controversy, Sor and Aguado were merely adding a chapter to an endless debate that must have begun very early in plucked-string history. Emilio Pujol's treatise on *The Dilemma of Timbre on the Guitar* cites documentary evidence on this question going back as far as the citharists—and with the weight of opinion on the side of the fingertips. Athenaeus the Greek, for example, speaking of Epigonus: "He was one of the great masters of music; he plucked the strings with his fingers, not with a plec-trum." Albius Tibullus the Roman: "Plucking the strings softly with his fingers, he sang these words. . . ." Fuenllana, the Spanish vihuel-ist: "To strike with the nails is imperfection. . . . Only the finger, the living thing, can convey the intention of the spirit." Thomas Mace, the English lutenist: "The nail cannot draw so sweet a sound from a lute as the nibble end of the flesh can do," etc., etc. The whole issue has never been solved to everyone's satisfaction. Flamenco guitarists, for one, go right on using their nails—though they prefer striking the flat of the nail against the string, which was never

(134) Ingres: preliminary study for the "Slave with the guitar" (actually a tanbur) in the painting, "L'Odalisque à l'esclave." Photo by Resseguié, courtesy of the Musée Ingres, Montauban.

Aguado's way. In the present century Segovia's nails-*cum*-flesh method has prevailed, making the best of both possible worlds; modern classical guitarists, playing on nylon strings, use their fingertips in conjunction with carefully shaped nails, and the stroke involves a combination of both.

Despite their differences on this point, Sor and Aguado saw very much eye to eye on other problems of timbre, and both were equally concerned with improving the tone and volume of the guitar. Sor encouraged leading French and Spanish guitar-makers to produce lighter instruments for him, with top, ribs, and back made of very thin woods, supported by interior bracing that could withstand the tension of the strings. After his death these design principles were finally perfected and codified by the great luthier Antonio Torres.

Aguado, meanwhile, had come up with an invention of his own, which was supposed to revolutionize guitar-playing—the so-called tripodion or "Aguado Machine" (Plates 142–143), a three-legged stand with several attached clamps, which supported the guitar so that the player did not have to hold it in his lap. Aguado believed that this would eliminate the dampening effects of the conventional body hold, so that "the whole instrument can vibrate without interference." It also left him free "to use the physical strength of both hands to draw from the guitar all of its tonal resources." That meant he could break away from the tradition of playing with the pinky of the right hand stiffly braced against the top, or the bridge—a very awkward position, considered very good form at the time, which most guitar teachers did not discard for another eighty years. It is this static hand position, with the little finger fairly glued to the top, that can be seen on most of the great French guitar paintings as far as Manet, and in the dozens of popular lithographs and steel engravings that document the course of *la guitaromanie* in France (Plates 158–168).

It was not just a nineteenth-century affectation, however, modeled on the Victorian way of holding a teacup; early instances can be found in paintings of the sixteenth century, and lutenists have cultivated the same rigid habit. Thomas Mace, in *Musick's Monument* (1676), advises players to "set your Little Finger down upon the

(135) Ingres: portrait of Niccolò Paganini (1782–1840), the foremost violinist and also one of the greatest guitarists of his time. The original drawing is dated Rome, 1818; it was engraved by Luigi Calamatta in 1830, just before Paganini's triumphal debut in Paris. Collection of the author.

(136) Anonymous pencil drawing of Hector Berlioz (1803–1869) playing the guitar. This is the earliest of the known portraits of Berlioz, and the only one that shows him with the instrument he played best. For the guitar he received from Paganini and later donated to the Paris Conservatoire Museum, see plate 226. Photo courtesy of the Columbia University Library, New York.

(137) Gottlieb Schick (1779–1812): portrait of Karoline von Humboldt, daughter of the naturalist Wilhelm von Humboldt. Painted in Rome, 1809, the canvas was destroyed by fire at Schloss Tegel, Berlin, during World War II. Photo courtesy of the Bildarchiv (Handke), Staatsbibliothek, Berlin.

(138) "Company in an Italian Inn" by Johann Erdmann Hummel. The picture is also known as "Die Fermate," the title of a short story that E. T. A. Hoffmann wrote about it after seeing it displayed at a Berlin exhibition in 1814. "Two Italian ladies are seated facing each other; one sings, the other plays a guitar—and between them stands an Abbé, who acts as music director. . . ." See page 169. Photo courtesy of the Bayerische Staatsgemäldesammlungen, Munich.

Belly of the Lute, just under the Bridge. . . . It *steadies the Hand* and gives a *Certainty* to the *Grasp*." Aguado, taking a surprisingly modern view of the matter, decided that this certainty could be dispensed with as long as his disciples had the tripodion to steady their grasp; without the anchored finger, "the hand is more airy [*airosa*] and free to make any movement one likes."

Like most romantic virtuosos, Aguado thought of the guitar first in terms of tone color, and how it compared in that respect to the noblest of man's musical edifices on earth, the symphony orchestra:

I believe that the guitar has a particular character: soft, harmonious, melancholy; sometimes it borders on the majestic, though it cannot rival the grandeur of the harp or the piano. On the other hand it offers a delicate charm, and its sounds are capable of being modified and combined so as to give it a very mysterious character, well suited to song and expressiveness. . . . Of all the instruments in use today, it may be the best means of suggesting the illusion of an orchestra in miniature, with its various effects.

The Italian school of guitarists, which flourished at about the same time, shared this vision of an "orchestral" guitar, but in accordance with their *bel canto* reflexes they thought of it, usually, as a miniature operatic orchestra. The founder of the Italian guitar *risorgimento*, Ferdinando Carulli (1770–1841) was a Neapolitan who settled in Paris. He devised a guitar with four extra bass strings (the decacorde), wrote a popular *Method* that is still being reprinted, and turned out literally hundreds of works, issued in over 330 opus numbers. A typical sampling might include *The Storm (sonata sentimentale)*, the *Cossack* Variations, arias from *The Barber of Seville* for guitar and violin duet, *The Fall of Algiers (pièce historique)*, *The Amours of Venus and Adonis* for solo guitar, and *La Girafe à Paris*, Opus 306 *(Divertissement Africo-Français)*.

His successor Matteo Carcassi (1792–1853) was a Florentine who expanded Carulli's technique with a *Complete Method* for the guitar, which became the most widely used study guide of the nineteenth century. It, too, is still in print, and has outlasted Carcassi's operatic fantasies on *Zampa*, *William Tell*, and *Fra Diavolo*. The best known and most influential of the group was the Bolognese

(139) "The painter Friedrich Salathé playing the guitar," a pencil drawing by the Swiss artist Hieronymus Hess (1799–1850). Guitars were indispensable traveling companions for artists of the romantic movement, to which both Hess and Salathé (1793–1858) belonged. The drawing was made during their trip to Naples, c. 1820. Photo courtesy of the Kupferstichkabinett der Oeffentlichen Kunstsammlung, Basel.

(140) "Guitarist" by the Russian painter V. A. Tropinin (1776–1857). Dated about 1823, it shows a typical Russian seven-string guitar of the type developed by A. O. Sichra in the 1790s. Photo courtesy of the Tretiakov Museum, Moscow.

(141) "Luigi Lablache as Figaro" by Jean-Pierre Dantan (1800–1869). Lablache (1794–1858), one of the leading singers of his day, was famous for his superbly acted Figaro in *The Barber of Seville*. This 1831 caricature of him appeared in *Musée Dantan*, a book of wood engravings by Théodore Maurisset based on a hundred of Dantan's caricature statuettes. Photo courtesy of the New York Public Library.

(142) Portrait of Dionisio Aguado (1784–1849) from his *Nuevo Método para Guitarra*, published in Paris and Madrid, 1843. Here he uses his own invention, the tripodion, designed to eliminate the dampening effect of the player's body. Photo courtesy of the Biblioteca Nacional, Madrid.

(143) *Right*. Illustrations of the tripodion and of model hand positions from Aguado's method. Note that the little finger is used as a stabilizer, braced against the bridge.
Photo courtesy of the Biblioteca Nacional, Madrid.

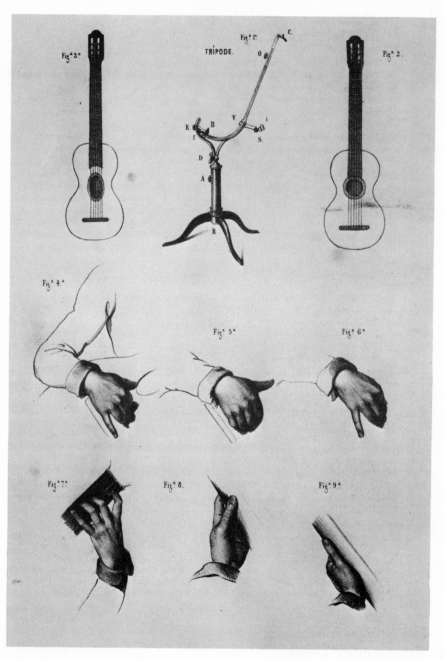

Mauro Giuliani (1781–1828). He lived for many years in Vienna, where he helped Beethoven introduce the *Battle Symphony* and took part in the *Nachtmusiken* performed at the Botanical Garden by such leading musicians as Hummel, Moscheles, and Mayseder. Besides potpourris, *ländler,* and a *Sonata Eroica* he wrote a *Practical Method* for guitar and perfected a design of his own, the so-called terz guitar, which was smaller than the usual and capable of being tuned a third *(terz)* higher. "Giuliani was the Paganini on his instrument," declared the English *Giulianiad* magazine, the first real fan magazine in the annals of music:

The tone of Giuliani was brought to the greatest possible perfection; in his hands the guitar became gifted with a power of expression at once pure, thrilling, and exquisite. He vocalized his adagios to a degree impossible to be imagined by those who never heard him—his melody in slow movements . . . was invested with a character, not only sustained and penetrating, yet of so earnest and pathetic a description, as to make it appear in reality the natural characteristic of the instrument. *In a word, he made the instrument sing* [their italics].

This slightly stunned reaction whenever someone happens to play the guitar really well is as repetitious as a broken record in nineteenth-century music criticism. Virtuosity on the guitar was rather like Dr. Johnson's dog walking on his hind legs; it was not so much how it was done, but one was surprised to find it done at all. José Maria de Ciebra, from Seville, is admired for his divine vibrato—"his guitar actually sobbed, wailed, and sighed."

The Bolognese Zani di Ferranti reveals equally astonishing gifts. "What Paganini is on the violin . . . Ferranti is on the guitar. . . . In his hands the guitar is no more the instrument you know—it becomes possessed of a voice and a soul." Trinitario Huerta, the guitarist and ex-army officer who composed the revolutionary *Himno de Riego* (a sort of Spanish *Marseillaise*) is hailed by Fétis in the *Revue Musicale* for having "raised the guitar to the sublime height that Paganini did the violin." Not to be outdone, Victor Hugo writes that in Huerta's hands "these are not strings that sigh; this is a voice, a true voice that sings, and speaks and weeps." Giulio Regondi, the author of yet another *Method,* turns his guitar into "quite another

(144) Portrait of Fernando Sor (1778–1839) by J. Goubaud,
engraved by M. N. Bate. Photo by Roger Viollet, Paris.

instrument than we have hitherto known it," as a Viennese critic observes. "He imitates by turn the violin, harp, mandolin and even piano so naturally that you must look at him to convince yourself of the illusion." Again, not unexpectedly, "Regondi is the very Paganini of the guitar. . . ."

The point of this persistent parallel is somewhat blunted by the fact that the guitar already had a Paganini—and no one else could possibly have asserted any claims to the title. Although he rose to fame on the violin, Paganini himself was also a formidable virtuoso on the guitar. Those who heard him on both instruments had difficulty deciding which of them he played better. According to an old legend which it would be a pity ever to disprove, he had spent several of his early years "in absolute retirement at the chateau of a lady of high rank, devoting much time to the study of the guitar, the lady's favorite instrument." The story is corroborated by a (posthumously published) piece of program music for two guitars, the *Duetto Amoroso* for lovers, dedicated to "a lady of high rank" and consisting of a rather cynical succession of nine episodes: Beginning, Entreaties, Consent, Timidity, Satisfaction *(Contentezza)*, Quarrel, Peace, Love Pledges, and Leave-taking. Paganini wrote almost as much music for guitar as for violin: virtually everything he published during his lifetime contains at least one guitar part. Among other things there are dozens of solo pieces and guitar duets for guitar and violin (in which the guitar makes off with the lion's share of the music), a group of trios for bowed instruments and guitar, and no less than fourteen quartets for guitar, violin, viola, and cello.

The Marchese Massimo d'Azeglio, an Italian statesman, tells in his memoirs how he and his friends, including Paganini and Rossini, disguised themselves as singing beggars for the Roman carnival of 1821. "Rossini and Paganini were to represent the orchestra, strumming on two guitars, and thought of dressing up as women. Rossini filled out, with great taste, his already ample contours, stuffing them with tow, and was a really inhuman thing! Paganini, straight as a door, and with his face which resembled the handle of his violin, appeared twice as dried-up and elongated as ever. I am not inventing it, we caused a furore. . . ."

(145) Sor's recommended playing position, as illustrated in his *Méthode pour guitare*, published in Paris, 1830. Like Aguado, he shows the little finger braced against the guitar. Photo courtesy of the Biblioteca Nacional, Madrid.

Hector Berlioz, who wrote *Harold in Italy* for Paganini, says in an essay about Paganini in Paris that whenever he grew tired of playing the violin, he would arrange a private séance so that he could enjoy his own string duets. "Choosing as partner a worthy German violinist, Monsieur Sina, he would take the guitar part and draw unheard-of effects from that instrument. And the two performers, Sina the unassuming violinist, and Paganini the incomparable guitarist, would thus spend together long *tête-à-tête* evenings to which no one, even the worthiest, ever won admittance."

Berlioz himself was a guitarist—not in Paganini's class, perhaps, but from all accounts a remarkable player. He was the first important symphonic composer who was not at the same time a virtuoso on some more exalted instrument, such as the violin or the piano, and this singular deficiency was to have important consequences for the development of his orchestral style. As a boy in provincial France he learned to play only the guitar, the flageolet, and the flute—"the flute, the guitar and the flageolet!!! These are the only instruments I play, but they seem to me by no means contemptible." He does not regret never having become a great pianist. Berlioz says: "When I consider the appalling number of miserable platitudes to which the piano has given birth, which would never have seen the light had their authors been confined to pen and paper, I feel grateful to the happy chance which forced me to compose freely and in silence, and has thus delivered me from the tyranny of the fingers, so dangerous to thought. . . ."

Everything that Berlioz composed is conditioned by the fact that he was not subject to the tyranny of piano habits. The way he spaces out his orchestral chords, the way his phrases are shaped and his rhythms change reveal a fresh, flexible mind that has been trained in the school of the guitar rather than the boxed-in formulas of keyboard harmony. The famous *idée fixe* of the *Symphonie Fantastique*, for example, is the kind of tune that might have slipped out as he was noodling on the flageolet, and its fragile harmonic setting is something that would occur only to a guitarist. Actually, Berlioz wrote for the guitar only very sparingly, notably in Mephisto's Serenade from the early *Eight Scenes from Faust*, in a chorus for

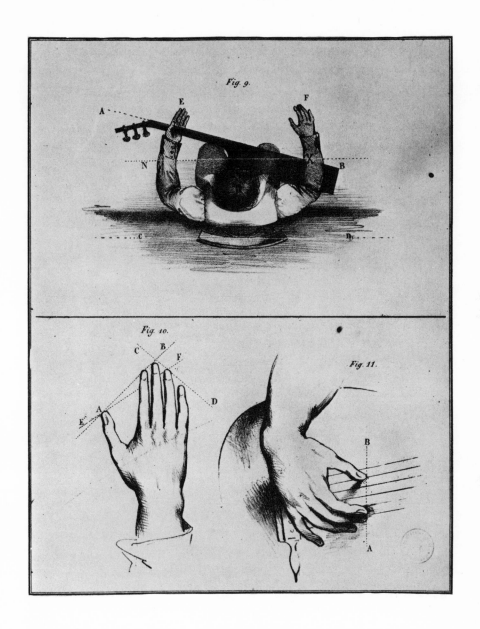

(146) Body and hand positions from Sor's *Méthode*.
Photo courtesy of the Biblioteca Nacional, Madrid.

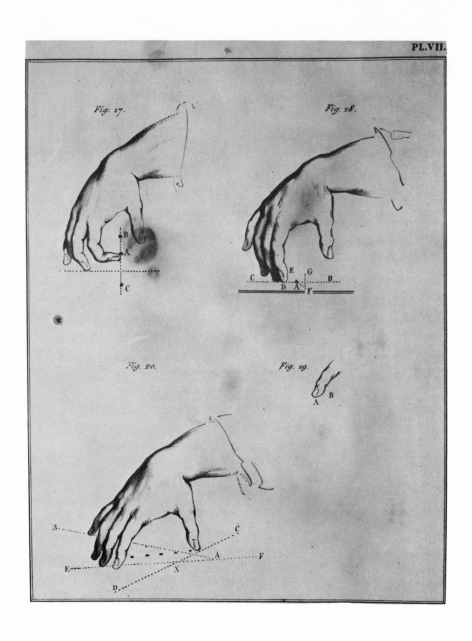

(147) Examples for the hands and fingers from Sor's *Méthode.*
Photo courtesy of the Biblioteca Nacional, Madrid.

Benvenuto Cellini and in the Sicilian drinking song from *Béatrice et Bénédict,* which calls for the unlikely combination of guitars, trumpets, and a tambourine. Yet the guitar played a much larger role in his musical life than this brief list would suggest. As a student in Paris, Berlioz gave guitar lessons when the money from home ran out; as a young composer "my wretched voice and paltry guitar were often requisitioned," and when he became bored in Italy as a Rome Prize winner, he would go walking in the mountains of the Abruzzi, guitar in hand, "strolling along, shouting or singing, careless as to where I should sleep."

Sometimes he would amuse the peasants along the way by playing saltarellos till his fingers burned. "I make them happy with my guitar," he wrote to a friend in September, 1831. "Before I came they only danced to the tambour de basque, and they are delighted with this melodious instrument." In his *Memoirs* he recalls that when he was alone with his guitar in the mountains he would remember long-forgotten passages from Virgil's *Aeneid:*

Then, improvising a strange recitative to a still stranger harmony, I would sing the death of Pallas, the despair of the good Evander, of his horse Ethon, unharnessed and with flowing mane and falling tears, following the young warrior's corpse to its last resting-place; of the terror of good King Latinus; the siege of Latium, which once stood on the ground beneath my feet; Amata's sad end, and the cruel death of Lavinia's noble lover. This combination of memories, poetry and music used to work me into the most incredible state of excitement; and the triple intoxication generally culminated in torrents of tears.

This is as fine a picture as any we possess of the musical creative process as the romantics understood it. On these hot afternoons above Subiaco he was laying the groundwork for his great Virgilian music drama, *The Trojans.* And he was not exaggerating when he wrote that the whole of the *Aeneid* had come pouring out of the soundhole of his guitar. His friend Ernest Legouvé, the French playwright, has described in his *Souvenirs* what it was like when Berlioz suddenly decided to make music for him in the author's Paris apartment:

[205]

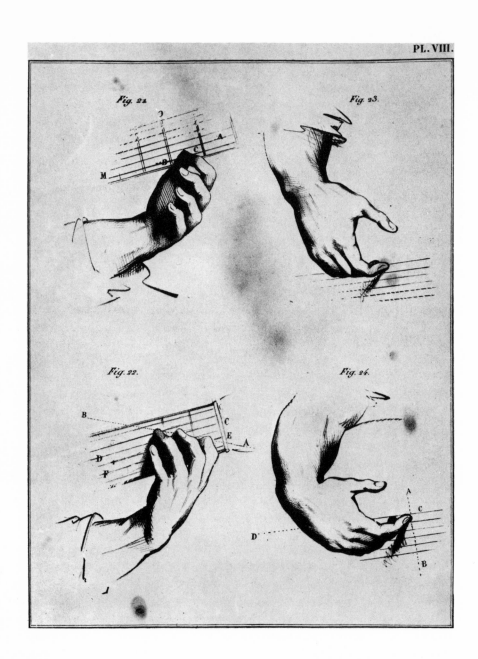

(148) Correct positions for stopping and striking the strings according to Sor's *Méthode*. Photo courtesy of the Biblioteca Nacional, Madrid.

But how to make music? I had no piano in my flat, and even if I had, what good would it have done? Berlioz played only with one finger. Fortunately there was one triumphant resource left to us: the guitar. The guitar embodied all instruments for him, and he was very good at it. So he took the guitar and began to sing. What? Boleros, songs, dance-tunes? He did the finale of the second act of *La Vestale!* He sang every-thing—the high priest, the vestals, Julia—all the characters, all the parts! Unfortunately he did not have a voice. No matter; he made one. Thanks to a method of singing with a closed mouth which he used with extraordi-nary skill, thanks to the passion and musical genius that animated him, he drew from his chest, his throat, and his guitar unknown sounds, piercing lamentations, which—occasionally mingled with cries of admiration and enthusiasm, even eloquent commentaries—united to produce a total effect that was such an incredible whirlwind of verve and passion that no per-formance of this opera has moved me, transported me, so much as did this singer without a voice, and his guitar.

The hereditary enemy of this kind of music-making was the grand piano. A nineteenth-century piano was not so much an instrument as a vested interest, as immobile as a piece of real estate. It was a triumph of mechanical engineering—a thing of levers and bolts and hammers utterly insensitive to the difference between being struck by a maiden's finger or the end of an umbrella. "The pianoforte!" exclaims Berlioz in 1855. "At the bare thought of this terrible instru-ment I feel a shudder run through my scalp; my feet burn; in writing its name I come upon volcanic ground. You see, you do not know what pianos are, or piano-dealers, piano-makers, piano-players, the protectors and protectresses of piano-makers. God preserve you from ever knowing it!" Against this massive machine and its minions a small, hand-plucked box can make little headway.

Various guitar "improvements" and alternatives were tried and found wanting: the githarfe, combining harp and guitar; the tasten-gitarre, sporting a set of keys; the guitare d'amour, played with a bow; the lyre-guitar, shaped like a Greek cithara—a form on which, in turn, H. P. Möller of Copenhagen based his patented mechanical lyre-guitar (it sounded almost like a piano). But not even a mechani-cal guitar could rekindle the imagination of a public that had sold its soul for the tactile thrill of running its fingertips over the lustrous ivory of a piano keyboard, so cool to the touch, so ingenious in its science. In the world of Charles Dickens and Queen Victoria the guitar lost its right to be regarded as a serious pursuit; by the time of *David Copperfield* (1849) it had become a mere bagatelle, the butt of bad jokes and the plaything of daft young lovers at bourgeois picnics:

. . . they wanted Dora to sing. Red Whisker would have got the guitar-case out of the carriage, but Dora told him nobody knew where it was but I. So Red Whisker was done for in a moment; and *I* got it, and *I* unlocked it, and *I* took the guitar out, and *I* sat by her, and *I* held her handkerchief and gloves, and *I* drank in every note of her dear voice, and she sang to *me* who loved her, and all the others might applaud as much as they liked, but they had nothing to do with it!

At mid-century, then, when nearly all the young romantics have gone on to an even better world, and the long night of "late romanticism" descends on the rest, Dora's "glorified instrument, resembling a guitar" is once more driven from the company of serious musicians and relegated to the saltimbanques and garlic eaters. One of the French trade magazines even publishes its obituary. "The race of Patagonians, of which some gigantic remains are still sometimes found in Tierra del Fuego, have disappeared from the surface of the earth," writes Henri Blanchard in the *Gazette Musicale*. "The same is true of guitar players. What is a guitar player among the incessantly growing population of instrumentalists? An atom, a nonentity . . . a fifth wheel on the wagon." And he goes on to relate the story of an Italian guitarist who has come to Bordeaux to give a recital. After the concert one of the local dignitaries walks up to him and says: "An astonishing performance, admirable, what richness of harmony, what purity of style! What clarity in those inextricable difficulties. What a beautiful talent!—but Sir, what a waste of time!"

(149) Portrait of Matteo Carcassi (1792–1853) by Jules David. Photo courtesy of the Bibliothèque Nationale, Paris.

(150) Portrait of Ferdinando Carulli (1770–1840): a lithograph by Paigel and Laduvoix, Paris. Photo courtesy of the Biblioteca Nacional, Madrid.

MAURO GIULIANI.

(151) Portrait of Mauro
Giuliani (1781–1828) by
Stubenrauch, engraved by
Jügel. Photo courtesy of the
New York Public Library
(Muller Collection).

(152) Portrait of the Viennese
guitarist Simon Molitor
(1766–1848) by Maurus and
John. Photo courtesy of the
New York Public Library
(Muller Collection).

Chapter 7

Wine Cups of Daybreak

Are you not scared by seeing that the gypsies are more attractive to us than the apostles?

—RALPH WALDO EMERSON

IN THE EPOCH of the grand piano the best place to find guitars is their native country, and it is to Spain that the itinerant poets and composers now come, impelled by an awakening interest in folklore, to observe the guitar in its natural habitat for the first time. After Washington Irving had demonstrated how easy it was to set up housekeeping in the Alhambra, and Frederic Chopin and George Sand had spent a winter on Mallorca, nearly the whole of literary and Left Bank Paris came trooping after them: Prosper Merimée, Alexandre Dumas, Franz Liszt, Théophile Gautier, Jules Verne, Edouard Manet, Gustave Doré, Constantin Guys—they found the music of Spain immeasurably exciting because it was unlike anything else to be heard in Europe. "The sound of the bolero bursts out in the loneliest places and on the darkest nights," Sand wrote in her travel notes. "There isn't a peasant who doesn't own a guitar and who doesn't play it at all hours."

When the aristocratic Michael Glinka, founder of the Russian nationalist school, paid a visit to Andalucía at mid-century, he spent hours and days listening to the fandangos of one Francisco Rodriguez, El Murciano (the Man from Murcia), reputedly the finest guitar in Granada. "This Murciano was a simple, untutored person who traded in wine at his own tavern," Glinka later noted in his memoirs. "He played the guitar with uncommon skill, however, and with great precision." These were dangerous times in Spain, beset by a wave of uprisings and civil wars, but the guitar was a staff of life, a kind of safe-conduct for its bearer, whether royalist or revolutionary; by ancient tradition one doesn't shoot a man with a guitar, at least not until one has heard him play. Even life in a prison could be made tolerable with a guitar. "There is no prison like Toro," explained the lady jailkeeper to that remarkable English traveler George Borrow. "I learned there to play on the guitar. An Andalucían cavalier taught me to touch the guitar and sing *a la Gitana*. Poor fellow, he was my first *novio*. Juanito, bring me the guitar, that I may play this gentleman a tune of Andalucía":

The carcelera had a fine voice, and touched the favorite instrument of the Spaniards in a truly masterly manner. I remained listening to her performance for nearly an hour, when I retired to my apartment and my repose. I believe that she continued playing and singing during the greater part of the night, for as I occasionally awoke I could still hear her; and, even in my slumbers, the strings were ringing in my ears.

Spain is a dancing country, and there were guitars wherever there was dancing—which is to say, everywhere but in the northern provinces, where Basque flutes and Gallegan bagpipes do most of the work. The simplest village dance orchestra might consist of a guitar and tambourine, with the dancers wielding castanets, but often there were two guitars and a bandurria (the flat-backed Spanish mandolin), or combinations of bass and treble guitars. "You see music done to a turn on every kind of guitar," Cervantes had already observed, and indeed a village festival or a *feria* in town would draw guitars of every imaginable shape and size, including half a dozen recognizable subspecies. The *bajo de la uña*, for example, was a bass guitar with a large body, short neck, and eight strings, played with a plectrum resembling the *uña del perro* (dog's nail)—and hence the name. The requinto was a small six-string guitar turned a fifth higher than usual, to B-e-a-d'-f#'-b'. The tiple, tible and timple were treble guitars tuned even higher, to a'-d'-g'-c^2-e^2; it survives today as the

(153) Portrait of Catherina Josepha Pelzer (1821–1895) by Charles Bauquiet. Daughter of the guitarist Ferdinand Pelzer, she was a child prodigy and afterwards the leading guitar teacher of Victorian London. The lithograph is dated 1853, the year before her marriage to the flutist Sidney Pratten. Photo courtesy of the New York Public Library (Muller Collection).

(154) Portrait of Giulio Regondi in 1841, by the Viennese lithographer Josef Kriehuber. Photo courtesy of the New York Public Library (Muller Collection).

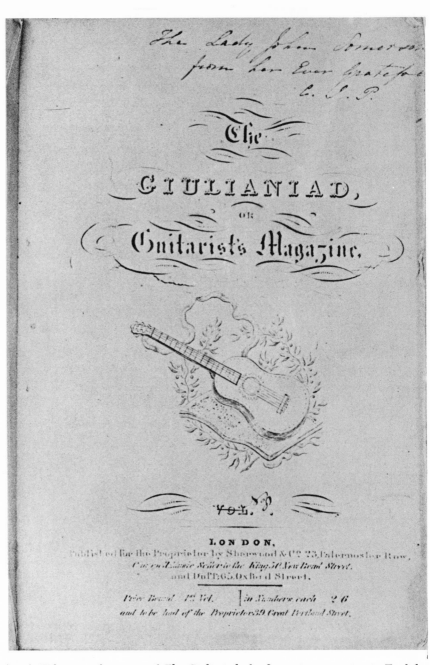

(155) Title page of an issue of *The Giulianiad*, the first guitar magazine in English. Named in honor of Giuliani, it was published in London by Ferdinand Pelzer during the early 1830s. This copy bears Catherina Josepha Pelzer's dedication to her patroness, the Lady John Somerset, who helped launch her teaching career in London. Collection of the author.

(156) Portrait of the ballerina Carolina Angiolini Pitrot by Andrea Appiani
(1817–1865). An outstanding example of the many Italian theater portraits with
guitar. Photo courtesy of the Quadreria dell' Ambrosiana, Milan.

(157) Portrait of Elizabeth, Lady Wallscourt (1805–1877) by Sir Thomas Lawrence (1769–1830). This steel engraving by George H. Phillips, published in 1836, helped make it one of the best-known portraits of its day. Collection of the author.

Hawaiian tipple, which is defined as an oversized ukelele. The char-ango was a small guitar with five strings, a vaulted back and very bright sound; the guitarron a bass guitar with off-board strings; the octavilla a Valencian six-course double-strung guitar with metal strings. Pajandi was the gypsy's guitar, literally "the thing that is touched, or played upon," but in common gypsy jargon the word is *sonanta*, derived from the Indian Manipuri lute, *sananta*.

It was the Andalucían gypsy who turned the primitive rasp of the sonanta into the dazzling flamenco sound that is instantly recognized the world over as the heartbeat of Spain. Yet historically flamenco is not a gypsy invention but rather a continuation of the most ancient music of Andalucía, a compound of Moorish, Byzantine, Jewish, Iberian and all the other potent cultures the Mediterranean is heir to. The seeds of flamenco may lie in Roman Spain; its present course was decided in the fifteenth century, when the gypsies inherited the "oriental" music of Andalucía from the Moors and Jews who were being expelled from the country. In their folk-song researches at the other end of Europe, Zoltán Kodály and Béla Bartók made the dis-covery that the oldest and most beautiful folk songs have a way of slipping down to the lowest rungs of the social ladder, where they end up as "beggars' songs." By a very similar process, the old melis-matic chants of Granada were reduced to the status of an under-ground music at a time when the gypsies were the outcasts of Spanish society. Yet these were the vestiges of Ziryab's royal art, and of the songs that had been played and sung by slave girls in the patios of Moorish Malaga. One can still hear traces of that legacy when the *cante jondo* is sung—a certain sensuous curve of the vocal line and a nonchalant wandering of the voice that George Sand once described as "smoke from a ship's funnel carried away and rocked by the breeze."

What remained, too, of the older traditions were the whiplash dance rhythms the poet Martial had already admired in the dancing girls of Roman Cadiz, and the minstrel habit of composing instant verses about everything and anything. "The musician composes at the stretch of his voice, whilst his fingers tug at the guitar," Borrow noted in the 1830's, as he was setting down a meticulous record of

[217]

the *cante* he heard "in the midst of a circle of these singular people, dancing and singing their wild music." He was the first of the great English aficionados of flamenco and the bullfight, and unlike those who came after him he could speak the gypsy language fluently, so that he could understand the full fury and sardonic humor of the primitive *cante jondo*. Borrow writes in *The Zincali:*

The themes of this poetry are the various incidents of Gitáno life— cattle-stealing, prison adventures, assassination, revenge, with allusions to the peculiar customs of the race of Roma. Here we behold a swine running down a hill, calling to the Gypsy to steal him, which he will most assuredly accomplish by means of his intoxicating *drao* [poison] —a gypsy reclining sick on the prison floor, beseeches his wife to intercede with the alcayde for the removal of the chain whose weight is bursting his body—the moon arises, and two Gypsies, who are about to steal a steed, perceive a Spaniard and instantly flee. Sometimes expressions of wild power and romantic interest occur. The swarthy lover threatens to slay his betrothed, even *at the feet of Jesus,* should she prove unfaithful. And another hopes to bear away a beauty of Spanish race, by the magic sound of a word of Romanny whispered in her ear at the window.

No one knows for certain how the word *flamenco* came to be applied to this fierce and bitter art. Some historians trace it to the Flemings who accompanied the Hapsburg Emperor Charles V when he came to Spain in the sixteenth century. Others have proposed derivations from the Arabic *felag-mengo* (fugitive peasant) or *fel-lah-mango* (singing laborer). The most reasonable explanation, however, takes it back to its most obvious root, *flama* or flame. In the underworld jargon of eighteenth-century Andalucía, someone *flamenco* was a dazzler, a flaming youth, a swaggerer. The word *gitano*, on the other hand, had the connotations of a curse after centuries of gypsy persecution. (It is still an expletive a mason will use if he hits his thumb with a hammer.) The upshot was that, when gypsy music came into its own as a distinctive, even admirable style, it was called *flamenco* in order to avoid the stigma of *gitano* and also because it was usually performed in public by the haughtiest, most flamboyant gypsies.

It is not merely a metaphor to say that this extraordinary alloy of

(158) "L'Accord Parfait en Amour" (Love's Perfect Harmony). An example of urban folk art at the beginning of the Romantic era, published by the Paris printseller Codoni. Photo courtesy of the Bibliothèque Nationale, Paris.

(159) An anonymous engraver's vision of a French lady guitarist in an Empire gown. By mid-century, "lady guitarist" had become one of the most overworked clichés of the graphic arts. Photo courtesy of the Bibliothèque Nationale, Paris.

Charmante Gabrielle,
Percé de mille dards.

(160) "Charmante Gabrielle" by Jean-Henri Marlet (1770–1847). Faint echoes
of Watteau, translated into a new industrial medium by Count Lasteyrie du Saillant,
who ran one of the first lithographic workshops in France.
Photo courtesy of the Bibliothèque Nationale, Paris.

[220]

musical and poetic elements received its characteristic shape and temper from the gypsy blacksmiths for which Andalucía was famous. One of the fundamental forms of flamenco is the *martinete,* or hammer song, sung by a man in a forge, and punctuated by the beat of hammer meeting iron:

Fragua, yunque y martillo	Forge, anvil and hammer
rompen los metales;	shatter these metals;
el juramento que yo a ti te he hecho	the oath I swore to you—
no lo rompe nadie.	no one can break it.

Many of the so-called primitive forms of flamenco were occupational in origin: the *serranas* of mountaineers and smugglers, the *cantes de trilla* of wheat threshers, *nanas* of mothers rocking their babies to sleep, *caleseras* of buggy drivers, *carceleras* of prisoners in jail. Some are religious, like the passionate *saeta* (arrow of song) addressed to the Virgin during Holy Week. Many of the rest were dance and song patterns associated with certain cities: the *sevillanas* of Seville, *granaínas* of Granada, *malagueñas* of Malaga, *murcianas* of Murcia, and so on. But it was not until the first *cafés cantante* opened their doors, in the 1840's, that the flamenco musician turned into a professional entertainer. What had been campfire music for centuries suddenly found itself on stage, illuminated by footlights. The new circumstances heightened its style without reducing its savagery. The French composer Emanuel Chabrier, a Parisian to the fingertips, was slightly overwhelmed to discover, in the *cafés cantante,* a way of life predicated on two guitars, a cask of manzanilla sherry, and five or six dancing women "wriggling about like intoxicated snakes." After a run of nights watching the *malagueñas, soledas,* and *zapateados,* he wrote from Granada to a friend at home:

If you saw them wiggling their behinds, swaying their hips and writhing their bodies you wouldn't want to be off in a hurry. At Malaga things got so hot that I had to take my wife away; that was a bit too much. . . . This is the scene: one or two women begin dancing, two droll fellows scrape away something on tinny guitars, and five or six women bawl out in a screamingly funny voice triplets which are impossible to note down, for they keep changing the tune. . . . You hear syllables, words, porta-

(161) The guitar in the nursery: "Dors mon petit amour" (Sleep my little love) by St.-Ange Chaselat (1813–1880). Photo courtesy of the Bibliothèque Nationale, Paris.

(162) "Léocadie," a product of the print factory of Dembour & Gaugel in Metz, 1843. The words of her song convey her sentiments: "while he's gone I'll sing of the bonds of memory . . ." Photo courtesy of the Bibliothèque Nationale, Paris.

mentos, and then they begin clapping and beating out the six eighth-notes, accentuating the third and the sixth! And then the shouts of "Anda! Anda! La Salud! eso es la Mariquita! gracia, nacionidad; Baila, la chiquilla! Anda! Anda! Consuelo! Olé, la Lola! olé la Carmen! que gracia, que elegancia!"—all this designed to excite the young dancing girls; it's staggering, it's indescribable.

The flamenco guitar sounds "tinny" to foreign ears because it is smaller and lighter than the classical Spanish guitar; cypress is used for the back and sides instead of rosewood, and the head is kept very light for balance, since the flamenco style of playing requires that the instrument be held nearly upright, resting on the right thigh. For that reason many flamenco players still prefer the old-fashioned wooden pegs to the heavier roller pegs on "machine heads." The metallic quality of the tone is heightened still further when flamenco guitarists clamp on a *cejuela* (*capotasto*), as they often do, shortening the strings to make certain chord patterns easier to play, and increasing the surface tension of the sound. Since the invention of celluloid the Andalucían guitar has also acquired plastic guard plates—anathema to the classical player—designed to protect the wood against the drum taps and a thousand natural shocks that turn it into a veritable percussion instrument.

In the older forms of flamenco the guitar usually played a subordinate role and was supposed to limit itself to marking the rhythm and following the song. "It is a foundation for the voice and should be subject to the will of the singer," as Federico García Lorca explained in one of his lectures on the subject. "But since the personality of the guitarist is as deeply involved as that of the singer, he too must sing out, and thus *falsetas* [guitar improvisations] are born—sometimes, when sincere, of extraordinary beauty, but in many cases false, foolish and full of pointless Italianisms, especially when performed by one of the so-called virtuosos. . . . Some guitarists, like the magnificent Niño de Huelva, let themselves be carried away by the voice of their surging blood, yet without departing from the pure line and without presuming to display their virtuosity— precisely because they are the real virtuosos."

Evidently the great tocaores of the nineteenth century—men like

[224]

(163) The French lady guitarist as seen by a lady artist, Josephine Decomberousse, who was active as a copper engraver in Lyons during the 1820s. Photo courtesy of the Bibliothèque Nationale, Paris.

(164) "Les Charmes de la Musique" by Jules David (1808–1892), painter-lithographer known for his music covers and portraits of musicians. Photo courtesy of the Bibliothèque Nationale, Paris.

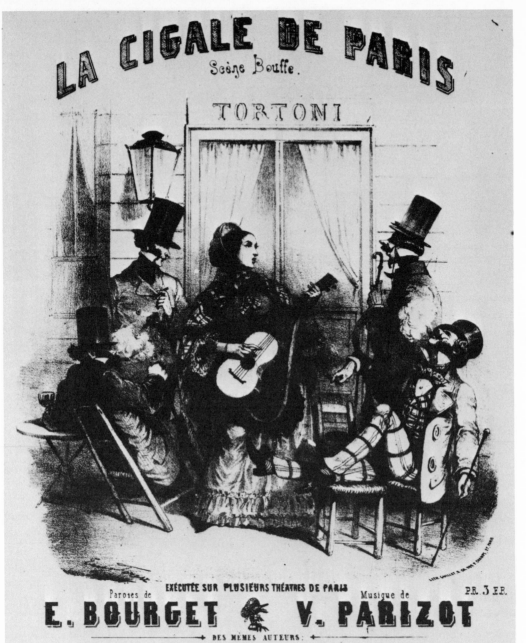

(165) Cover illustration by E. Forest for "La Cigale de Paris" (The Cicada of Paris), a vaudeville sketch about the affairs of a street singer. Photo courtesy of the Bibliothèque Nationale, Paris.

Paco el Barbero (The Barber), El Maestro Patiño and Habichuela (Kidney Bean)—were not only able to play dazzling falsetas but could sing or dance all the cantes and bailes for which they played. Within the present framework of flamenco there are perhaps fifty distinct ways of singing and thirty styles of dancing—*alegrías, caracoles, polos, soleares, zambras,* and so forth. There are also thirty-odd kinds of solo playing, but the guitarist who appears only as a soloist is a relatively recent development, viewed with suspicion by aficionados like Lorca, who knew flamenco before it was commercialized.

The concert soloists had their beginning in the *cafés cantante,* where they had to devise increasingly flashy ways of holding the audience's attention—playing behind their backs or over their heads, wearing gloves or socks on one or both hands, and setting new speed records for tapping, thumbing, and strumming their guitars. Though such tricks are now passé, further circus elements were added when flamenco moved from the cafés into the nightclubs and theaters.

"The grave, hieratic melody of yesterday," wrote Manuel de Falla in 1922, "has degenerated into the ridiculous flamenco style of today, in which those elements which once constituted its glory and its ancient title of nobility have been adulterated and modernized." But despite Falla's gloomy prognosis—he was looking back nostalgically to that golden age which the true aficionado always places a generation or two prior to his own—the art of flamenco has proven much more durable than anyone suspected. The twentieth century, in fact, has produced a steady succession of important tacaores whose work has expanded the technical resources of flamenco without sacrificing its inherent strength and austerity—among them Ramón Montoya, Javier Molina, Niño Ricardo, Paco Lucena, Perico el del Lunar, Luis Maravilla, Sabicas, Carlos Montoya, and Mario Escudero, to mention only a few of the better-known names. And there is a whole new generation of musicians who are devoting themselves to flamenco with the same intensity and respect for tradition which they might otherwise bring to the bullfight.

It is only the most gifted and dedicated of these guitarists who can hope to master the ardent, profoundly elusive idiom known as *toque jondo* (literally, deep playing)—the *siguiriyas* and *soleares*, *cañas* and *serranas* that constitute the inner core of flamenco, the music that has to "come up through the soles of the feet," as an old gypsy guitarist once defined it. "The toque jondo has no rivals in Europe," Falla pointed out. "The harmonic effects produced *unconsciously* by our guitarists are one of the miracles of natural art." To Lorca, whose poetry is full of images of toque jondo, the flamenco guitar sounds as though it had "the sighs of lost souls escaping through its round mouth." And in the poem "La Guitarra" he speaks of it as a *corazón malherido por cinco espadas:*

Empieza el llanto	The lament
de la guitarra.	of the guitar begins.
Se rompen las copas	The wine cups of daybreak
de la madrugada.	are shattered.
Empieza el llanto	The lament
de la guitarra.	of the guitar begins.
Es inútil callarla.	It is useless to silence it.
Es imposible	It is impossible
callarla.	to silence it.
Llora monótona	It weeps monotonously
como llora el agua,	as the water weeps,
como llora el viento	as the wind weeps
sobre la nevada.	over the snowfall.
Es imposible	It is impossible
callarla.	to silence it.
Llora por cosas	It weeps for things
lejanas.	far away.
Arena del Sur caliente	Sand of the warm south
que pide camelias blancas.	asking for white camellias.
Llora flecha sin blanco,	It weeps arrow without target,
la tarde sin mañana,	evening without morning,
y el primer pájaro muerto	and the first dead bird
sobre la rama.	upon the branch.
¡Oh guitarra!	Oh, guitar!
Corazón malherido	Heart grievously wounded
por cinco espadas.	by five swords.

Chapter 8

The Guitar
in America

Yes, we three were so happy, my wife, my guitar and me.
—BIG BILL BROONZY

T HERE is one other guitar that shatters the wine cups of daybreak—the blues guitar of the American Negro. Though they may seem far removed from each other in geography and tradition, there is, in fact, a tenuous historical connection between the two. The West African Negroes who were brought to America in slave ships were accustomed to playing many of the same plucked instruments as the Moors north of the Sahara, as well as variants of the guitar and rebec introduced by Portuguese mariners as early as the fifteenth century—instruments known locally as rabekin, ramki, ramakienjo, or raamakie. An eighteenth-century French explorer, François Le Vaillant, describes an African rabouquin as "a triangular piece of board with three strings made of intestines, supported by a bridge, which may be stretched at pleasure by means of pegs, like those of our instruments in Europe; it is indeed nothing else than a guitar with three strings." On American plantations the African exiles were usually forbidden to play their tribal drums (for fear of slave insurrections), but they were encouraged to go on making and playing their own stringed instruments.

Thomas Jefferson writes of the slaves in his *Notes on Virginia:*

"The instrument proper to them is the Banjar, which they brought hither from Africa, and which is the original of the guitar, its chords [strings] being precisely the four lower chords of the guitar." This skin-covered gourd instrument was the West African bania, soon to become better known as the banjo, and henceforth indispensable to a dozen kinds of American music. ("Cindy got religon, she's had it once before, but when she hears my old banjo, she's the first one on the floor.") Jefferson may have been correct in supposing a relationship between the banjo and the guitar, but one is certainly not descended from the other; according to the best available evidence, both are collateral descendants of the ancient lute.

In America, where musical integration is a continuous process going back to colonial times, the banjo player from Africa meets the guitar player from Europe, and the result is that instruments as well as styles are exchanged. The white forty-niner goes off to California with the banjo on his knee, and the black singer ("In music they are generally more gifted than the whites," Jefferson observed) addresses his cante jondo to the guitar: "Sometimes I feel like nothin'; sometimes th'owed away; Then I get my git-tar and play the blues all day."

The history of a specifically American music begins precisely at the point where the European-trained musician first becomes aware of the African-trained musician and makes an attempt to imitate him. A typical case in point is that of the German oboist and bass player Gottlieb Graupner, who ran a music store in Boston during the 1790's, and is generally credited with having written the first "minstrel" song. During a visit to Charleston, South Carolina, where he had been engaged to play an oboe concerto, Graupner happened to overhear a group of blacks singing to a banjo. Fascinated by the sound, he bought a banjo from them, learned—to their delight—how to play it, and jotted down some of their songs. After returning to Boston, he composed a vocal and banjo number, *The Gay Negro Boy*, which was inserted in a play called *Oroonoko*, produced at the Federal Street Theater in December, 1799.

Since that time virtually all the important European musicians who have come to America and been exposed to Negro folk music

[230]

(166) Episode from "Les Étudiants de Paris" by Paul Gavarni (1804–1866). A university student is bargaining with a dealer for a guitar: "It's worth fourteen francs." "Tra la la la; my needs are those of a simple bachelor. I'll give you three-fifty." "We're far from being in accord, dear fellow." "So is this old twanger of yours, old man." Collection of the author.

(167) "The Duet," 1836, by the Dutch painter Cornelis Buys:
a bourgeois variation on the traditional "Hausmusik" theme.
Photo courtesy of the Haags Gemeentemuseum, The Hague.

La Sérénade?

Litho de Mantoux, rue du Paon N°

(168) On this and the next page lithographs from Charles de Marescot's *La Guitaromanie,* a collection of teaching pieces for beginners. Marescot's illustrations document the guitar mania of Paris at mid-century: "The Serenade," a summer entertainment involving four guitars and a mandolin; "The Concert," in which the recitalist plays an *air varié;* "La Guitaromanie," reinforcements to be seen arriving at the door; "The Pleasures of Winter," in nightcap and dishabille; and "Discussion between the Carullists and the Molinists"—followers of two rival guitar masters, Ferdinando Carulli and François Molino. Photos courtesy of the Bibliothèque Nationale, Paris.

Litho de Mantoux r. du Paon N°

L'Air Varié

have responded to what George Washington Cable called "the dark inspiration . . . of the banjo's thump and thrum." When Antonín Dvořák taught composition in America during the 1890's he declared unequivocally (and with extraordinary intuition) that "the future of music in this country must be founded on what are called the Negro melodies." As early as the 1840's the Viennese-Parisian pianist and composer Henri Herz had come to very much the same conclusion. Herz writes in *Mes Voyages en Amérique:*

The banjo is the favorite instrument of the Negroes in the United States, just as the marimba is of the Negroes in Brazil. It is a kind of guitar with a long neck, which gives out solemn, resonant and harmonious notes. Negroes are very appreciative of music, and their souls are far from being closed to the beauties of poetry. A collection of their songs has been made, and a study of it reveals an uncommon tenderness and a rigorous observance of the laws of rhythm, that elemental core of all music, so well known to everyone and yet so difficult to explain. From time to time, while listening to Negro banjo players, I have pondered the mysterious law of rhythm which seems to be a universal law, since rhythm is a coordinated movement, and movement is life, and life fills the universe.

The guitar, being easier to make and manage, gradually superceded the banjo among Southern Negroes. Since many instruments were homemade, there was no clear dividing line between them in any case; we hear of four-string cheese-box banjos and four-string soapbox guitars that must have sounded just about identical. "When I was about ten years old," remembered the magnificent blues singer Big Bill Broonzy (1893–1958), "I made a fiddle out of a cigar box, a guitar out of goods boxes for my buddy Louis Carter, and we would play for the white people's picnics." And another great blues singer, Muddy Waters, told Paul Oliver about his childhood: "All the kids made they own git-tars. Made mine out of a box and bit of stick for a neck. Couldn't do much with it, but you know, that's how you learn." Makeshift though they may have been, these were the instruments that ultimately transformed the sound and rhythm of popular music in the Western world.

It was only gradually that the guitar became an essential part of white singing styles and the *Top of Old Smokey* school of folk music.

[235]

(169) "The Street Singer" by Honoré Daumier, a master drawing in black chalk, c. 1845. Photo courtesy of the City Art Museum of St. Louis.

(170) "The Guitarist" by Edouard Manet, dated 1860. Always immensely successful with the public, this picture provoked the first critical and popular reaction to Manet's work when it was exhibited in the 1861 Salon. People rarely notice that in this, one of the most famous of all guitar paintings, the player is left-handed. His hand position is quite modern and relaxed, and he appears to be strumming in D major. Photo courtesy of the Metropolitan Museum of Art, New York (gift of William Church Osborn, 1949).

Historically the guitar is a latecomer to the English folk song, and the standard accompaniments that are now played to *The Foggy Dew* and such are merely modern additions to Elizabethan originals. The British ballads that form the substratum of American folk song were traditionally sung unaccompanied, and "not only without gestures but with the greatest restraint in the matter of expression," according to the pioneer song-hunter Cecil Sharp. "Indeed, the folk singer will usually close his eyes and observe an impassive demeanor throughout his performance." On the American frontier these same songs first acquired accompaniments on instruments like the dulcimer (introduced by German settlers) and the parson's fiddle. Guitars appeared on the scene from three directions: the Eastern cities that followed London trends in drawing-room music; the Spanish Southwest, where there were few adobes without a guitar; and the Negro South.

Colonial and Revolutionary America was well supplied with English-made guitars. We know that Benjamin Franklin was a guitarist; so was Francis Hopkinson, another signer of the Declaration of Independence, who composed songs and became first civilian head of the U.S. Navy. About 1768 he writes in a letter to his fiancée, Ann Borden of Bordentown: "My Dear Nancy: This morning I wrote the enclosed Song which I shall set to music & play for you on the Guitar when I visit you next." The wealthy planters of Virginia also played in the English style. "When we returned about Candle-light," writes the colonial diarist Philip Vickers Fithian, in one of those flashes of description that can illuminate an era, "we found Mrs. Carter in the yard seeing to the Roosting of her Poultry; and the Colonel in the Parlour tuning his Guitar." In Philadelphia, meanwhile, Mr. Henri Capron performed his own *Sonata Guitarre* at a concert and advertised in the program:

Mr. Capron respectfully informs the public that he instructs ladies and gentlemen in the art of singing and playing on the Spanish and English guitars, recording the most approved method of the finest masters in Europe. . . . His terms are one guinea for eight lessons and one guinea entrance—the entrance to be dispensed with if the person applying to him has received previous instruction from another master. At two

[238]

(171) Manet: "The Street Singer." Etching, 1860.
Photo courtesy of the New York Public Library.

(172) "The Music Lesson" by Manet, dated 1870. In typical nineteenth-century
fashion, the lesson involves bracing the little finger against the top of the guitar.
Styles of guitar-making had changed since "The Guitarist" was painted;
the instrument shown here is a sort of Torres model, with wide roller pegs.
Photo by Bulloz, Paris.

(173) "Girl Playing the Guitar"—originally known as "Girl in a Reverie"—by Gustave Courbet. The artist did this pencil drawing of his sister Zelie Courbet in his native Ornans, near Besançon, in 1847. Photo courtesy of the Fogg Art Museum, Harvard University (bequest of Grenville L. Winthrop).

lessons per week he engages to perfect any person, possessing a tolerable ear, in the space of six months. The guitar, from the late improvement which it has received, being so portable and so easily kept in order, is now considered not only as a desirable but as a fashionable instrument. . . .

The first guitar manual published in North America, the *Complete Instructor for the Spanish and English Guitar, Harp, Lute and Lyre,* was brought out in 1820 by J. Siegling of Charleston, South Carolina. It was followed, in due course, by *The American Guitarist,* Ryan's *True Guitar Instructor,* Winner's *Primary School for the Guitar,* and others. A number of American guitarists—many of French or Spanish background—earned considerable reputations during the nineteenth century; among them William Bateman, Charles de Janon, Luis T. Romero, William Foden, Manuel Y. Ferrer, Clarence L. Partee, Charles James Dorb, and Zarh M. Bickford. But it was the anonymous legion of country guitarists who accounted for the westward expansion of twang; settlers who packed their guitars on Conestoga wagons and sailors who shipped theirs around the Horn. On the Western plains, in the days of the long cattle drives, a guitar was more useful than a six-gun, and many cowboys found it advisable to pack both. The traditional night-herding song is a perfect illustration of Jacques Dalcroze's theory about the relationship of rhythm to body movement (eurhythmics); the cowboy sang to keep himself awake and to quiet the restless cattle as he circled the herd, adjusting his rhythm to the swinging gait of the horse and tossing in a soothing refrain of cattle calls:

> Whoopee ti yi yo, git along little dogies,
> It's your misfortune and none of my own,
> Whoopee ti yi yo, git along little dogies,
> For you know Wyoming will be your new home.

From Texas to California, guitars of the open range frequently had direct Spanish antecedents. Mexican settlers in the northernmost parts of what had been Nueva España were still playing the old vihuelas when the first Anglo-Saxon intruders pushed into that region. It was the Spanish who had brought the first guitars to the Western Hemisphere; the only plucked instrument indigenous to the

New World had been the mouth-bow used by some tribes of Indians. Spanish missionaries, who lost little time converting the Indians to Christianity, also took the guitar situation in hand. In his book *The English American* (1648) Thomas Gage describes his travels in Spanish America during the 1620's and 1630's, and mentions visiting a Franciscan monastery at Guacocingo, a town near Mexico City where there were five hundred Indians and one hundred Spaniards. The monks entertained him gallantly, Gage writes,

and made shew onto us of the dexterity of their Indians in music. . . . Their greatest glory and boasting to us was the education which they had given to some children of the town, especially such as served them in their cloister, whom they had brought up to dancing after the Spanish fashion at the sound of the guitarra. After this a dozen of them (the biggest not being above 14 years of age) performed excellently for our better entertainment that night. . . .

In a short time the guitar became as ubiquitous in Spanish America as ever it had been in the mother country, for it suited the Indians quite as much as the conquistadores. In Brazil, too, it quickly established itself as the most popular instrument—both in the form of the six-string urban violão (vihuela) and the peasant viola, which may have anywhere from four to fourteen strings (usually ten) strung in pairs. A lively trade in imported music and musicians soon sprang up in the major Latin American cities. In Buenos Aires, for example, the Philharmonic Society programs of the 1820's included such chamber music items as a *Quartet for Guitars and Piano* by Haydn (an arrangement, obviously) and a *Quartet for Guitars* by Carulli; soon afterward the works of Sor and Aguado were introduced to the Argentine capital.

In Mexico, where Spanish cuttings were successfully grafted onto the root stock of Indian music, guitars formed the backbone of folk ensembles like the famous mariachi bands of Jalisco, which consisted of a large five-course guitar, a treble guitar, two violins, and a five-octave harp (clarinet and trumpet were later additions). The Mexican folk ballads knows as *corridos* (from *correr*, to run, because the song runs on indefinitely without a change) were sung at fairs and fiestas to guitar accompaniments—sometimes by women selling

(174) "The Guitar Player" by Courbet: a self-portrait in romantic costume,
painted in 1844. Of the five canvases which he submitted to the Paris Salon of 1845,
this was the only one accepted. Courbet came from a musical family and liked
to think of himself as a musician, occasionally composing songs to his guitar.
Photo courtesy of Mrs. Walter Wood Hitesman, New York.

(175) "Pagans the guitar player and Auguste De Gas" by Edgar Degas:
painted 1868–1869 as a memorial to his father, and as a tribute to the Spanish
opera singer Lorenzo Pagans, often a guest in Degas' home. In this and the
next picture a painter focuses for the first time on someone in the act of listening
to a guitar rather than merely playing it; the implication of music in the room serves
to establish an extraordinary relationship between the two figures. Photo by Bulloz,
courtesy of the Louvre (Musée du Jeu de Paume), Paris.

(176) "The Father of Degas listening to Pagans": Degas' second treatment of
this theme, painted about 1870, was one of his favorite works and used to hang
in his bedroom. The earlier picture shows the elaborate marquetry inlay of
Pagans' guitar; a traditional but pointless form of decoration which the guitar-maker
Torres eliminated when he began to redesign the instrument. Here Degas himself
simplifies its pattern with a few strokes of the brush, so that all diagonal movements
in the painting converge on the father, though he is the smaller figure.
Photo courtesy of the Museum of Fine Arts, Boston (bequest of John T. Spaulding).

[245]

(177) "Woman Playing the Guitar," 1897, by Auguste Renoir. One of Renoir's innumerable larger-than-life women plays a guitar of the French type, which has ebony running only halfway down the fingerboard. Photo, Bulloz, Paris.

(178) "Woman with Guitar," 1818–1819, is one of Renoir's last works, painted when he was seventy-seven. Here the guitar has become merely the memory of a form, but Renoir is still vitally concerned with the form of woman: "Un sein, c'est rond, c'est chaud." Photo by A. J. Wyatt, courtesy of the Philadelphia Museum of Art.

colored broadsides containing the texts of the day's favorite ballads. Many of the same traditions maintained themselves in the territory of New Mexico even after it became part of the United States in 1846 (later to be divided into the states of New Mexico and Arizona and a portion of Colorado). Guitars supplied the indispensable accompaniment for both the songs and dances of the region. "For the typical Spanish dance, the guitar and fiddle are used, and curiously enough, the fiddler is usually blind," writes Alice Corbin in her foreword to *Spanish Folk Songs of New Mexico,* which deals with local customs at the beginning of the twentieth century. "When you see a man with a guitar leading a blind man with a fiddle, you know that a dance or a wedding or a christening is about to occur somewhere."

The New Mexican *bihuela,* however, made itself heard only in the Southwest; in most other regions of American folk music it was the Negro influence that proved to be decisive. The same Southern hillbillies who now seem as inseparable from their guitars as Siamese twins were still singing to their dulcimers, or without accompaniment, early in the 1900's. "Negroes introduced the guitar and the blues into the hills some time after the turn of the century," writes Alan Lomax in *The Folk Songs of North America,* "so recently in fact that the most complex of hillbilly guitar styles is still called 'nigger pickin.'"

The Negro blues guitar fascinated hillbilly ears for precisely the same reasons that the subsequent American jazz and pop styles have taken the whole world by storm: its rhythmic ingenuity ("two centuries ahead of Europe," as W. E. Ward once wrote of African music) and its marvelously flexible harmony. Rooted in African music, and growing out of Mississippi Delta field hollers and work songs, the blues deliberately avoided the very square, European major-minor tonality, which is utterly foreign to the African tradition. To escape from the too-rigid diatonic scale, the blues guitar had first to be converted into something like a bania, capable of keeping the "blue notes" (third and seventh of the scale) hovering with twanging microtones between major and minor. This was accomplished with the simplest of devices: a bottle neck, or a metal slide or pocket

COSTUME ESPAGNOL.

(Bolero.)

(179) "Bolero" by Joaquín Becquer (1805–1841), leading folklore painter of Seville, was turned into a popular lithograph by the French artist Achille Devéria (1800–1857). Photo courtesy of the Bibliothèque Nationale, Paris.

knife, applied to the neck with the left hand. By "teasing the box with a knife," as it was called, the blues singer made his guitar just as elastic as the jazz trumpeter who modified his instrument with various muting gadgets that stretched or compressed the tone. The blues singer Son House, in the account of his early years quoted earlier, recalled how the dwoinging of a guitar teased with a bottle had started him off on his career in the 1920's:

This boy, Willie Wilson, had a thing on his finger like a small medicine bottle, and he was zinging it, you know. I said, "Jesus! Wonder what's that he's playing?" I knew that guitars hadn't usually been sounding like that. So I eases up close enough to look and I see what he has on his finger. "Sounds good!" I said. "Jesus! I like that!" And from there I got the idea and said, "I believe I want to play one of them things." So I bought an old piece of guitar from a fella named Frank Hopkins. I gave him a dollar-and-a-half for it. It was nearly all to pieces, but I didn't know the difference. The back was all broken in, but I got it from him and began to try to play. It didn't have but five strings on it, though. So I showed it to Willie Wilson and explained to him what I wanted to do. I wanted to learn to play. He said, "Well, you'll never learn this way. You need another string. Takes six strings. It's all busted in the back, too. Tell you what I'll do. I'll see if I can fix it up for you." So he got some tape and stuff and taped it all up and got a string and put that on and then he tuned it. He tuned it in Spanish to make it easier for me to start. Then he showed me a couple of chords. I got me an old bottle. Cut my finger a couple of times trying to fix the thing like his, but finally I started zinging, too.

House, who became one of the major blues recording artists of the 1930's, afterward liked to tease his box with a piece of metal tubing and to play with what he called the "cross Spanish" tuning, e-b-é-g#-b-e². A similar blues tuning is the one used by Skip James—e-b-e-g-b-e²—which he called "cross note" because "the major and minor cross during the music." For blues singers like House and James there was something tactile and responsive about the guitar that a piano could never hope to reach with an eighty-eight-note span. "The sight and feel of his music box in his hands lit up those homeless stretches of his spirit," remembered Woody

(180) "Dance of the Gypsies" by Joaquín Dominguez Becquer (1819–1879). The dancers move around the hats thrown at their feet without touching them; the accompaniment consists of singing, two guitars, castanets and hand-clapping. Photo by Archivo Mas, courtesy of the Patrimonio Nacional, Palacio Real, Madrid.

(181) "Gypsy Musicians on the Outskirts of Granada" by Gustave Doré (1832–1883). Accompanying the writer Charles Davillier on an extended tour of Spain in 1862, Doré made drawings for a series of articles in a travel magazine, *Le Tour du Monde*, which were later published in book form. In Granada, Davillier wrote, "We encountered a family of nomad musicians, barefoot, with a guitar slung on a bandolier. A young woman with a sweet, melancholy expression held a child in her arms. These poor people had come on foot way from Guadix to Granada." Photo courtesy of the New York Public Library.

(182) "El Jaleo" by John Singer Sargent. Completed in 1882, when he was
twenty-six, it was based on sketches that Sargent had made during a trip
to Spain three years earlier. Like Courbet he was knowledgeable about music.
During his trip, which took him on horseback through the mountains of Andalucia,
he jotted down folksongs for a friend's collection. But he reported afterward that
most of the songs he had heard were "dismal, restless chants" that he had
found impossible to put on paper. "Jaleo" in this context is not so much a form of
dance as the whole sonic ambiance of a gypsy *zambra*, with its vocal uproar,
hand-clapping, and the grating of flamenco guitars. Photo courtesy of the
Isabella Stewart Gardner Museum, Boston.

(183) Sargent: "The Musicians," one of the studies for "El Jaleo." Photo courtesy of the Fogg Art Museum, Harvard University (Grenville L. Winthrop bequest).

[253]

Guthrie about Leadbelly, the self-proclaimed king of all the twelve-string guitar players in the world.

The circumstance that the guitar could "articulate, or sigh, or wail, or tremble, like the human voice under emotion" made it the ideal blues instrument. Of Charley Patton, the earliest major figure mentioned in Samuel Charters' history *The Bluesmen*, a fellow musician reported: "He used to play the guitar and he'd make the guitar say, 'Lord have mercy, Lord have mercy, Lord have mercy, pray, brother, pray, save poor me.' Now that's what Charley Patton'd make the guitar say." Indeed, long before the white churches began to consider the possibility of revitalizing their liturgy with the guitar, it had already emerged as the mainstay of certain black gospel sects, who brought the instrument back into a church setting for the first time since the days when angels with vihuelas frequented the Belens of Spanish cathedrals. Brother John Sellers explains:

The Holy Roller Church—you know they call them Sanctified Holy Rollers—well this is the church that I belong to where we play the tambourines and the guitars and the horns. And the reason we play these instruments is because we get it from the 150th psalm of David, you know: "Praise the Lord with the handclapping, with the shakin' of cymbals, with the tambourines and the guitars."

There was another old Spanish custom that was revived in the new world of the blues guitar: "Up town in New Orleans they had a lot of country guitar players used to come to town and sit around and in barber shops you know, and play," the ragtime pianist Charles Love told Paul Oliver (*Conversation with the Blues*). "They hear [bands] playing and they sit around in the barber shops and if they catch the piece they pick it out on the guitar." In such eminently musical circumstances it was only natural that the guitar should have played a prominent role in the genesis of jazz, especially at those historic "$1.50 a couple" picnics, held on the outskirts of New Orleans, where some of the first jazz was blown.

But the acoustic guitar was never really loud enough to hold its own against such stentorian partners as the trumpet, cornet, trombone, and clarinet, which commanded a decisive majority in the early jazz band. The very sensitivity and expressiveness that were

[254]

(184) "Lady at a Desk" by Amasa Hewins, a nineteenth-century American primitive
with a fine sense for the proper positioning of a guitar in space.
Photo courtesy of the Wadsworth Atheneum, Hartford.

(185) The guitar in America: Portrait of Mrs. Samuel Boyd (Sophia Eleanor Keyser)
by an unknown painter of the nineteenth-century American school. Mrs. Boyd
has hold of a C Major chord, but the fact that her thumb is crooked over the edge
of the neck marks her as an extremely amateur guitarist. Photo courtesy of
the Frick Art Reference Library, New York (collection of W. Fenwick Keyser).

[256]

(186) "Home Ranch" by Thomas Eakins. Painted in 1888, when Eakins was
forty-four, it conveys something of a guitaristic paradox: a rough-and-ready
pioneer type playing in a refined salon style—someone has taught him to brace his
little finger against the top. Photo courtesy of the Philadelphia Museum of Art.

its great advantage for the blues—a personal, painful, introverted form of folk art—made the guitar less than ideal for jazz, which was essentially music for extroverts and virtuosos. Soon the guitar was being out-shouted in the rhythm section by the banjo and the piano. Although there were a number of pioneers in the field, like Lonnie Johnson, who became famous "thumping a guitar" with Charlie Creath's band on the Mississippi riverboats, the first jazz-man to elevate the guitar to an independent status was Eddie Lang (1903–1933), who founded a melodic "single string" style (*punteado* as opposed to *rasgado*, in the older terminology) fusing jazz with the Italian popular guitar.

Both Eddie Condon and Freddie Green distinguished themselves in the medium during the 1930's—Green, according to Nat Hentoff, being the "*echt* rhythm guitar"—but it was not until the advent of Charlie Christian and, almost simultaneously, the emergence of the electric guitar, that the jazz guitar finally came of age. Christian's life was tragically short: born in Dallas in 1919, he grew up in Oklahoma City, began playing professionally in his teens, joined Benny Goodman's band at twenty, and died of tuberculosis at twenty-three, in 1942. Yet there was time for him to revolutionize the technique of the jazz guitar and—at after-hours sessions at Minton's Playhouse, Harlem, with Dizzy Gillespie, Charlie Parker, Thelonius Monk, *et al*—to help launch the nervous, electrically charged new style, which he himself christened "be-bop."

He had begun on an acoustic plectrum guitar, producing a sound just able to hold up its end of the more refined jazz conversations. But in 1937 he was introduced to the electric guitar by Eddie Durham, a trombonist and arranger as well as a guitarist. "He [Christian] had big eyes to sound like a saxophone," Durham later remembered, "and I showed him how, by using down strokes, we could get a sharper tone, and how, on a downstroke only, the player could get a more legato effect while the strings were bouncing back as the hand was on its way back up." To realize his ambition of sounding like a saxophone, Christian handled the sharp, whining sonorities of the electric guitar primarily as a melody instrument, playing with extraordinary freedom and imagination. He is admired,

(187) "The Old Guitarist" by Pablo Picasso, 1903. An early, blue-period statement of a recurrent theme in Picasso's work. Photo courtesy of the Art Institute of Chicago.

(188) "Harlequin with Guitar," a Picasso drawing of 1916, belongs to the same period as the famous Picasso drop-curtain for Satie's ballet *Parade,* in which a bullfighter plays a guitar. The drawing bears the artist's inscription to the sculptor Jacques Lipchitz. Photo courtesy of Sebastian Junyer, Barcelona.

(189) "Gitarrenspieler" by Emil Nolde, an India-ink drawing dated 1920. German Expressionists rarely show the guitar, which has remained very much a symbol of the Mediterranean tradition in European art. Photo courtesy of Sotheby & Co., London.

too, for his arcane sense of harmony—for basing his improvisations not merely on the standard chord progressions of his themes, but on altered chords and passing notes deftly slipped in between the lines. His few treasured recordings constitute the great divide of the jazz guitar: there is the guitar before Christian and the guitar after Christian, and they sound virtually like two different instruments.

The post-Christian era has produced a spate of notable guitarists, including Wes Montgomery, Barney Kessel, Kenny Burrell, Jim Hall, Jimmy Raney, Johnny Smith, Tal Farlow, Herb Ellis, Charlie Byrd and Laurindo Almeida (who doubles in classics). Montgomery, who used a lightning-swift thumb instead of a plectrum, ranked as the leading jazz guitarist of the 1960's; he died, suddenly and far too prematurely, in 1968 at the age of 45. With electric amplification, jazz guitarists have now been playing louder than anyone else in the band for thirty years—with the predictable result that the instrument has become far more assertive in character, and now fills as important a musical role as the saxophone, clarinet, or piano.

Yet oddly enough there has been no really commanding avant-garde figure since Christian. In fact, the only other guitarist to have earned that rather too loosely applied jazz adjective "great" was the improbable Django Reinhardt (1910–1953)—a European, an outsider even in his own country, a Belgian-born French gypsy with no discernible connection to the jazz tradition. As if those were not enough strikes against him, Reinhardt also lost the use of two fingers of his left hand, but he worked his way around that problem with a brilliantly resourceful style. Modeled on Eddie Lang's single-string technique, his playing also reflected gypsy influences, though of the Central European rather than the Spanish flamenco variety. His famous Quintet of the Hot Club de France, made up entirely of strings (three guitars, violin, and bass), was easily the best of all European jazz groups, precisely because it was never intended to produce an *ersatz*-American sound. Reinhardt took up the electric guitar only after World War II, when he came briefly to the United States to play with Duke Ellington. Like Christian, he won a place in the jazz hagiography largely through his recordings, which have exerted an immense posthumous influence; significantly, the most successful piece by John Lewis and the Modern Jazz Quartet is named *Django* in his honor.

"The artist is like a millionaire," Jean Cocteau once said. "He travels ahead in a private car. The public follows behind in a bus." On the American guitar scene it is the jazz virtuoso who travels ahead with his "personalized" guitar (special tunings, gadgets, strings, individually cut-away designs, etc.) and the great mass of grass-roots guitarists who follow behind with truckloads of production-line models suitable for hillbilly, rock and roll, rockabilly, western swing, Bluegrass, rhythm and blues, authentic folk, commerical folk, plain commercial, and plain folk; trying to define all the current categories would be like determining how many angels can dance on the head of a gittern. Obviously this is a genuinely popular phenomenon, charged not only with musical but also with psychological, libidinous overtones. The titles of some of the LP albums of the 1960's reveal, quite unconsciously, the extent to which this universal twang reflects the inner concerns of the American psyche: *Guitars on the Go, Frantic Guitars, Guitar Freakout, Tuff Guitar, Twangsville, Funky 12-String Guitar, 50 Guitars in Love, Gin-Mill Guitar, Guitars Anyone?, Solid Gold Guitar, The Guitar That Changed The World. . . .*

But the guitar in Amerca plays only a supporting role in most cases. For folk singers and the country-and-western people, for example, the instrument is as much a badge of office as anything else, and the ability to strum a few modest chords is usually regarded as quite sufficient. Anything more guitaristic than that would smack of commercialism and the despised artifices of the professional arranger. As the North Carolina folk singer Frank Proffitt once said about the virtuosity of Earl Scruggs, the world's greatest Bluegrass banjo picker: "I'd like to be able to do it, and then not do it." For folk singers like Joan Baez, Bob Dylan, Odetta, Simon and Garfunkel, Burl Ives, and Richard Dyer-Bennett, it isn't so much what they play that counts as the fact that they play it themselves. "I can testify under oath, of course, that the guitar never betrays a singer who knows his guitar," Carl Sandburg once wrote

(190) "Guitar and Clarinet" by Juan Gris, 1920. The Cubists took the guitar out
of the luthier's hands and transformed it into the most versatile of shapes.
To follow up their innumerable guitar variations, however, would go far beyond
the scope of this book. Gris' typically subdued, simplified study here stands for the
whole spectrum of paintings and collages by men like Braque and Picasso,
who developed a new philosophy of art in their still lifes with guitar.
Photo courtesy of the Oeffentliche Kunstsammlung, Basel.

[263]

(191) Jacques Villon (1875–1963): "Musicians in a Bistro." An etching in the tradition of Manet's "The Street Singer," produced just before World War I, as Villon was moving away from cubism toward his "vision pyramidale." Photo courtesy of the New York Public Library.

(192) "Jazz Mexican," by Raoul Dufy, an indefatigable painter of musical subjects on both sides of the Atlantic. Here the huge bass guitar, or guitarron, is combined with string bass, violin, saxophone, trumpet, and drums—a distinctly Mexican mixture of instruments. Photo by Giraudon, Paris.

Raoul Dufy

in *The Guitar Review*, drawing on his own experience as an uncertain but unabashed Sunday guitarist:

When you have practiced your song to where you have some degree of loving understanding of your song—and when you have practiced your guitar chords (adding any little interspersals you choose to design as decor) till you feel they are a genuine help rather than a hindrance to your singing, the result when presented to a crowded house may fail to bring tumults of applause but it will not bring you into contumely, contempt or bad repute.

The genuine Arkansas traveler and folk balladeer, moreover, is quite satisfied to be an under-achiever on the guitar; that is why folk music often brings out the best in people but the worst in guitars. "I learned that I could plunk along on *Birmingham Jail* in the key of, say, G and get by plumb and dandy with only one chord change in the whole song, up to D and back to greasy G," said Woody Guthrie. "I've pounded out *Ida Red, Old Judge Parker Take Your Shackles Offa Me* for as high as thirty or forty minutes with no more than two chords—D to A, D to A, and D to A—ten blue jillion times through a square dance. Lots of the old full-blooded fiddlers will toss you off from his platform if you go to getting too fancy with your chording."

At that rather humble level of proficiency, the guitar has served innumerable causes in American politics. It has been a factor to be reckoned with in Southern elections ever since the days when "Kissin' Jim" Folsom won the governorship of Alabama by demonstrating, to the voters' satisfaction, his ability to head up a vocal and guitar trio. In the early years of the century it played a significant role in the "Wobbly" labor movement, when the folk singer Joe Hill hit on the idea of teaching aural history to members of the IWW:

> Some time ago when Uncle Sam he
>   had a war with Spain,
> And many of the boys in blue were
>   in the battle slain,

(193) "The Song of the Poet" by Peppino Mangravite, 1944. The erstwhile
instrument of courts and kings, having returned to the people and become the
folk guitar, now symbolizes all the brave virtues of the vanished frontier.
Photo courtesy of the Art Institute of Chicago (Friends of American Art Collection).

(194) Jacques Lipchitz: "Man with Guitar," 1925. Photo by Adolph Studly, courtesy of the Marlborough-Gerson Gallery, New York.

(195) Flamenco guitarist Quiqui Pororro, c. 1880.

(196) Flamenco dancer Pastora Imperio, by Julio Romero de Torres.
Photo courtesy of the Ministry of Education, Madrid.

(197) Flamenco dancer Juana "La Macarrona" in the 1920s; at left the young guitarist El Niño Ricardo, who became the leading *tocaor* of the century.

Not all were killed by bullets though,
    no, not by any means,
The biggest part that died were killed
    by Armour's Pork and Beans.

Although Hill was put out of action when he was executed on trumped-up charges by the state of Utah in 1915, the protest song has remained very much a part of liberal and radical movements in the United States ever since, from *I Don't Want Your Millions, Mister* to *We Shall Overcome*. Curiously enough it is the urban rather than the rural areas that are most susceptible to musical appeals; in Greenwich Village it is not unusual to see political meetings where not only are guitars present on the platform but half the audience expresses its solidarity by bringing along guitars of its own. Even the hippies, normally so reluctant to appear *engagé* in anything, have taken over this part of the American political tradition. "Last week the hippies were in full flower," reported *Time* magazine on July 7, 1967. "In New York City, they brought their tambourines and guitars to the aid of dog owners protesting the leash laws in Greenwich Village's Washington Square Park, chanting 'What is *dog* spelled backward?' "

On the other hand, several tidy capitalist fortunes have been made the same way, and Joan Baez is probably mistaken when she insists, "There's never been a good Republican singer." The guitar has given many young men destined to be millionaires their first boost onto the economic escalator of limitless upward mobility. According to the *Reader's Digest*, a hod carrier named Don Wilson and his building foreman, Bob Bogle, parlayed a guitar quartet called The Ventures into a $25 million enterprise that produces guitars, teaching methods, and record albums. One of the first to discover this precipitous path to success was the cowboy star Roy Rogers, whose life story, as told in a studio biography headlined FROM GUITAR TO SILVER SCREEN, had the makings of a new Horatio Alger legend:

As a small boy, Roy bought his first guitar at a Cincinnati hockshop for three dollars. As he grew, he mastered a flock of cowboy songs, and on

Saturday nights doubled as square dance caller and master of ceremonies. . . . Roy went to Hollywood and began appearing in bit parts and small radio shows—always featuring his guitar. On a tip he heard in a hat store that Republic Studio was testing for a new cowboy star, Roy rushed to the studio. But he failed to get an audition. However, he melted into a crowd of extras and poured through the gates with them. He found little trouble playing one of his favorite numbers, *Tumblin' Tumbleweeds,* for a group of executives. That did it. Music put him to the top in one little number. He was signed immediately, became a star in his first picture and has now [1948] starred in some 75 other western pictures. . . . "Music makes our family rich and our life happy," the Rogers all say.

It has been estimated by *Hi-Fi Stereo Review* that 40 percent of the recordings sold in America are in the country-and-western category; the best-known country-and-western singer, Eddy Arnold ($500,000 a year), is said to be a shoo-in for (Democratic) governor of Tennessee anytime he chooses to run. Defined by Robert Shelton as "one of our bedrock popular forms," country-and-western as a musical industry has grown into a giant spreading chestnut from a few modest acorns planted in the 1920's by Fiddlin' John Carson, the Carter Family, and the yodeling brakeman Jimmie Rodgers, who sold so many records that he could buy himself a guitar entirely covered with mother-of-pearl. The "high and lonesome sound" of this blues-descended music with thirty-five million fans has long accounted for a major share of the mail-order guitars sold by Sears and Montgomery Ward. But the champion guitar-setting pacer of the industry was the young Elvis Presley, whose swiveling hips and flashing plectrum led the nation's great march on the electric guitar. Seen in musicological perspective, Presley represents one of the main terminal points in the blues-country-and-western-rockabilly line of development. The simple, homespun tale of his boyhood in Tupelo, Mississippi, as told by the RCA Victor press department, might be, like Roy Rogers', the story of any typical American hometown guitarist, except that it ends with the boy selling thirty or forty million records:

From the time he was knee-high to a hound dog Elvis sang a lot, around home and at church with his parents, and at school. While still in the fifth

(198) Francisco Tarrega (standing, with beard)
and members of the Bilbao Guitar Society.

(199) James Joyce in Zurich, 1915. "At home Joyce impressed Weiss with his
fine, pleasant voice, but scandalized him by a totally unacceptable accompaniment,
played at that time on a guitar, and later on an old upright piano." (Richard Ellmann)
Photo by and courtesy of Ottocaro Weiss.

grade at Tupelo he won first prize in a singing contest at the Tri-State Fair, and he was still small fry when his dad bought him a $12.95 guitar which became the boy's most prized and, as it turned out, his most fateful possession. He taught himself the basic chords on the guitar, spent hours by the radio or phonograph learning songs he liked, and soon he was lugging his guitar to school to entertain the kids during lunch hour and, frequently, at school assemblies.

The musical wheel finally came full circle when Presley's guitar went back across the Atlantic and became the basis of the so-called Mersey Beat created by the Beatles, who wedded their own British music-hall tradition to the Afro-American twang of the blues. The Beatles originally came on singing like very young and energetic angels flapping wing-shaped guitars, with a sound already remarkable for its dark timbre and strong basses. They required no less than three solid-body electrics to make themselves heard above the surrounding percussion: lead guitar, rhythm guitar, and bass guitar. In later recordings—"we got bored with twelve bars all the time, so we tried to get into something else," Paul McCartney explained—they dabbled in jangling harps and harpsichords, Indian sitars, cocks crowing, dogs barking, French horn obbligatos, baroque trumpets, random noises, and a forty-two-man symphony orchestra. But the immutable pillars of the Beatle style, and of beat groups as a whole, have always been guitars, even when they sound like wobbling oboes.

These Anglo-Ozark instruments, of course, are no longer guitars in the sense that Watteau or Vermeer would recognize. Amoebic in shape and electronically amplified to raise their janizary twang to the nth power, they have discarded their ancient sound chest in favor of such things as patented reverberation intensity control units, mute levers, chrome-plated tuning keys, nickle-plated silver frets, and celluloid-bound oval fingerboards. It is understandable that attempts are being made to expel these instruments from the community of true guitars, particularly since their various brand names—Panther II, Dreadnaught, Maurauder, Spitfire, Hurricane, etc.— all suggest that they really belong in the airplane or auto-racing category. Indeed, French electric guitarists have borrowed the

[274]

(200) Miguel Llobet in a portrait by Lopez Mezquita.
Photo courtesy of the Museo Provincial de Bellas Artes, Granada.

(201) Andrés Segovia in the 1920s.

(202) Segovia in 1955. Photo by Walter Bursten, New York.

phrase *mettre toute la sauce* (to pour on all the decibels) from the vocabulary of Le Mans.

"IT'S NEW, IT'S BIG, IT'S LOUD, IT'S EXPENSIVE, IT WORKS" proclaims a typical manufacturer in a brochure that is certain to raise the hackles of the organologists. Those who still hope to avert an irreparable schism in the ranks of the guitarists can only cite the learned Juan Bermudo's dictum (propounded in the 1550's) that as times change, music and musical instruments are bound to change with them: *Y como la música con el tiempo se mudare, mudaronse con ella los instrumentos.*

Sooner or later, however, the electrics will have to split off from the phylum and acquire a proper name of their own. Some of the latest Hawaiian-inspired designs no longer exhibit even the rudiments of an incurved waist or the feminine contours that have always been an essential prerequisite for guitars. Instead they look rather like a sewing machine on its own stand—long, horizontal, zitherlike "necks" with eight to sixteen strings, eight knee pedals for changing the tuning, and stereo amplification, at prices between $1,000 and $2,000. One such steel "guitar" is described as:

Solid one-piece cast dural necks mounted on English sycamore bodies finished in lustre polyestre. Knuckle action roller bridge lever with pedal mechanism operated by steel rods. Pedals can be pre-set to raise or lower strings. Each pedal controls up to three strings. Generous section foot plates in cast dural. De luxe leatherette covered plywood case is fully plush lined and holds both the instrument and the special satchel for the detachable tubular steel legs.

When a guitar has to have detachable steel legs to support it, it can no longer, under any circumstances, be classified as one. That way, in fact, lies the piano, at the bare thought of which one feels a shudder run through one's amplifier. Surely we must look elsewhere for the apotheosis of the guitar.

Chapter 9

Six
Maids Dancing

A Riddle: Six maids dancing at the cross-road circle; three
of flesh and three of silver. Yesterday's dreams they seek, but
they are held in the embraces of a golden polypheme. . . .
—FEDERICO GARCÍA LORCA

ON CANVAS and in the sketchbooks of the French painters
the guitar enjoyed a series of spectacular successes during
the latter part of the nineteenth century. The new wave
began with Daumier's drawings and Courbet's romantic self-portrait
with guitar, shown in the Salon of 1845, and reached its first crest
with Edouard Manet's *The Guitarist*, which excited a storm of controversy at the Salon of 1860. Manet had posed a Spanish model in
Andalucían costume singing to his own accompaniment on the
guitar, and had painted him in a manner reminiscent of Velásquez.
"*Caramba!*" wrote Théophile Gautier in the *Moniteur universal*.
"Here is a *Guitarero**** who hasn't stepped out of a comic opera, and
who would cut a poor figure in a romantic lithograph. But Velásquez would have given him a friendly wink, and Goya would have
asked him for a light for his *papelito*. How heartily he plucks away
at his guitar! We can almost hear him."

* This word, which is so often applied to French paintings of Spanish guitarists, is both misspelled and a misnomer. In Spanish a *guitarrero* is a guitar-
maker; a *guitarrista* a guitar-player.

(203) Carl Sandburg with his bell-shaped folk guitar.
Photo courtesy of Culver Pictures.

(204) Narciso Yepes with his ten-string guitar. Photo by Gyenes, Madrid.

The echoes of that persuasive guitarero can be seen reverberating through the whole Impressionist era and its aftermath: in Manet's own *Music Lesson*, for example, in the pictures that Degas painted of his father listening to the guitarist Pagans, and in Renoir's various women-with-guitar. Gradually the forms of both the guitars and the women become diffuse and difficult to recognize, but not until Picasso and the Cubists put the instrument on the chopping block does the guitar pass from figure painting to the still life, and then out of the picture altogether (Plates 170–190).

The Manet-Degas epoch is auspicious in the history of the guitar for another reason; it coincides with the flowering of Antonio Torres (1817–1892), the great Spanish luthier who is revered as the Stradivarius of the guitar. Drawing on the best of the designs that had gone before, Torres established the size and proportions of the body as well as of the fingerboard, standardized the length of the strings (650 mm.) and developed new patterns of fan-barring to produce a more resonant top. His best instruments are magnificently simple, without the elaborate inlays and encrustations that had been in fashion for two hundred years; they are noted for their easy action, a mellow tone, and an elegance of form that has never been surpassed.

But although great instruments were being made, and pictures being painted, these were lean years, in fact, for the concert guitar, which had never recovered the ground it had lost to the piano. "The guitar is but little used now in England, though at one time it was very fashionable," reported Sir John Stainer in his musical dictionary of 1898, adding that it was valuable chiefly as "a portable means of accompaniment." To its few remaining partisans, it seemed as though the symphony orchestra and the concert grand had divided the musical world between them and left nothing for anyone else. Even in Spain only students, peasants, and gypsies were supposed to play the guitar, for as Segovia was told disparagingly when he was a boy, "People know of Sarasate, and of a great German pianist who was in Granada just a while ago. But what guitar player has become famous outside the tavern?"

The first classical guitarist to break out of this dreary cul-de-sac

(205) Julian Bream. Photo courtesy of RCA Victor Records.

was Francisco Tárrega (1854–1909), an almost legendary virtuoso who overcame tremendous handicaps in order to rehabilitate the *guitarra de concierto*. He came from humble circumstances; his father was a watchman in Villareal, his mother the doorkeeper of a convent. As a child he was pushed into a polluted stream by a vicious nursemaid and nearly drowned. As a result of the incident, he contracted a severe eye infection that left him with chronic ophthalmia and seriously impaired his sight. After working in a rope factory as a boy, he learned to play piano from a blind pianist and guitar from a blind guitarist. To support himself after leaving home he took to playing in the streets and cafés; once, a famous bandit whom he entertained in his mountain hideout rewarded him with a gold coin. At last, settling in Barcelona, he acquired well-to-do pupils and patrons, one of whom presented him with a superb Torres guitar.

In his biography of Tárrega, Emilio Pujol relates that the young guitarist fell in love with one of his pupils, a girl named Clemencia, with whom he gave duet recitals. But Clemencia took liberties with music; in the middle of a concert she once cheated on a difficult passage, winking at him as she did so. "I would have preferred a knife blade in my heart," Tarrega told her afterward, and broke off the affair: he was a stickler in such matters.

By 1880 the newspapers were referring to him as "the Sarasate of the guitar." He made an exploratory trip to England, where he appeared with Catherina Josepha Pelzer, the leading Victorian guitarist (Plate 153). But London did not agree with him: "I couldn't stand the English rigidity, nor the language, which I don't speak, nor the climate, nor the fog."

Tárrrega reawakened the dormant possibilities of the classic guitar by writing a new romantic repertoire for it, including his own etudes, preludes, and waltzes, and over a hundred transcriptions of Beethoven, Chopin, Schumann, Bach. When he played them in public the critics responded with their customary stock of clichés. "In his hands," reported *Ilustración Española* after a Madrid concert in 1883,

[284]

(206) John Williams, with Eugene Ormandy and members of the
Philadelphia Orchestra. Photo courtesy of Columbia Records.

the guitar cries and laughs. Sometimes he takes away his right hand and only plays with his left so that he can smoke and play at the same time [Tárrega was accustomed to smoking a cigarrillo while playing]. Sometimes it seemed to us as if we were hearing a harp, and sometimes a whole orchestra of bandurrias. When he played a jota we seemed to hear the words of the coplas; no doubt he has a duende, a familiar spirit, that sings within the guitar.

Tárrega's pupils revered him not only as "the spiritual Phoenix of the guitar" but as an utterly selfless friend and artist. He seems never to have made the slightest attempt to exploit his reputation by becoming a touring virtuoso, despite his admirers' attempts to lure him abroad. He was much happier playing for his friends than performing on a stage. Pujol, himself a pupil of Tárrega, describes him as a man oblivious of everything but an obsession with the guitar:

Every morning after getting dressed, Tárrega lights a cigarrillo, takes his guitar and sits down on his small working chair, in a corner of the dining room. Adjusting the tuning, he stretches his fingers by caressing the strings with improvised harmonies. . . . Breakfast interrupts the monologue, while the guitar rests on the Maestro's knees. After this, without any further preamble, to work! A matchbox on the table holds up the pocket watch that measures to a second the duration of each exercise: chromatic scales, diatonics, in thirds, in sixths. . . . Another hour of arpeggios, the same time for runs and trills and one or more hours for difficult positions or rebellious passages. . . . Thus passes the morning. After lunch, once more the guitar, but the work is different. The complete works of Schumann for the piano are on the table. . . . Tárrega skims through them, stops at a page, and tries it on the guitar to see if it will lend itself to transcription. . . . Every day, toward evening, some intimate friends and aficionados come to hear him play. . . . Then at night, after dinner, when everybody is asleep in the house, Tárrega plays for himself. This is the moment when the guitar and the artist are one. How many hours pass like this?

During Tárrega's lifetime the whole of Spanish music sprang to life again after lying fallow for a century. Suddenly there was a new generation of composers who could interpret Spain to the outside

(207) Laurindo Almeida. Photo courtesy of Capitol Records.

world in its own idiom—Isaac Albéniz (1860–1909), Enrique Granados (1867–1916), and Manuel de Falla (1876–1946). All of them admired the guitar as aficionados, but only Albéniz grew up playing the guitar as well as the piano. A friend, the painter Octave Maus, remembered him during his student days in Brussels as "a little black man, bearded, squat, who arrived from Spain in 1880 or 1881; in the folds of his cape, which was proudly draped over his body, he hid an enormous guitar. In the intimacy of the studios and salons of friends, he sang. Leaning on a table or on the arm of a chair, his eyes wrinkled with laughter, his fingers nimbly plucked the chords; he evoked on those unforgettable evenings the Spain of the dance, of love and joy. And often the concert was continued in the nocturnal streets with serenades and Andalucían songs."

Albéniz went on to become one of the great pianists of the century, but like Scarlatti before him he wrote for the keyboard as though it were a guitar. In *El Albaicín* of the *Iberia Suite*, for example, he re-created "the deafening sounds of a guitar that laments in the night," as Debussy once described it. Many of his works are eminently well suited to guitar transcription; as he himself observed when he heard one of them performed by Tárrega on the guitar: "This is precisely as I had conceived it!"

Granados, too, wrote some of his keyboard pieces and the sparse piano accompaniments to his songs almost as if they were guitar music. But it was Falla, the greatest composer of modern Spain, who pursued this tendency to its logical conclusion by writing for symphony orchestra as though it were a giant guitar—in *Nights in the Gardens of Spain, El Amor Brujo,* and *The Three-Cornered Hat,* among others. He introduced a flamenco guitarist on stage in his opera *La Vida Breve* and—more important—composed one of the great twentieth-century masterpieces for guitar, the *Hommage à Debussy,* which was published after his friend's death in the *Revue Musicale's* memorial supplement, *Le Tombeau de Debussy.* It is Falla's only solo work for that most Spanish of instruments, but it sums up, in one magnificently concise statement, all of the guitar's protean possibilities for modern harmony. For Falla this was "the instrument that has always hung at the Spanish hearth," as he wrote

[288]

(208) Carlos Montoya. Photo courtesy of RCA Victor Records.

in his introduction to Pujol's *Escuela Razonada de la Guitarra*, the great textbook and compendium of the Tárrega method:

It is a marvelous instrument, as austere as it is rich in sound, and which, now powerfully, now gently, takes possession of the soul. It concentrates within itself the essential values of many noble instruments of the past, and has acquired these values as a great inheritance without losing those native qualities which it owes, through its origin, to the people themselves.

After Tárrega's death in 1909, at the age of fifty-seven, his work was carried on by a circle of gifted pupils, including not only Pujol but also Miguel Llobet, Daniel Fortea, and Alberto Obregón. Llobet was known for many years as the most elegant guitarist in Spain; he gave concerts throughout Europe as well as the United States and South America, but he died in Barcelona during the Spanish Civil War, at the height of his career.

Tárrega, Llobet, Pujol, and half a dozen others are the reason why the modern guitar revival did not have to spring fully armed from the forehead of Andrés Segovia, as is sometimes assumed. But it remained for Segovia to reap what the others had sown, and to establish a sovereign place for the guitar in the twentieth century's arsenal of new and exciting sounds. Born in Linares in southern Spain on February 28, 1890, Segovia came north too late to have the benefit of Tárrega's teaching. He is, in fact, as completely self-taught as it is possible for a musician to be, and by his own account, "as I had to fight the opposition of my family there was no question of a teacher, a school, or any other of the usual methods of instruction." He taught himself how to play from methods and etudes, including Tárrega's; he plays Tárrega's music superlatively well, and he sees himself as pursuing the same fundamental goal—of expanding the horizons and repertoire of the guitar. "I have imposed on myself the duty of following the example of Saint Francisco Tárrega, who lived and suffered for his beloved instrument without hoping for profit or glory," Segovia told Manuel Ramirez, when the famous Madrid guitar-maker made him a present of his first great concert guitar. That momentous occasion is described in Segovia's autobiography (pub-

(209) Simon and Garfunkel. Photo courtesy of Columbia Records.

lished in irregular installments in the *Guitar Review*) as an ecstatic experience, a case of love at first sight followed by immediate consummation:

I looked at it for a long time before awakening its resonances. The grace of its curves, the old gold of its fine-grained pine top, the delicately worked ornamentation around the exactly placed sound-hole; the neck stemming straight and slim from the austere bust with its back and sides of palosanto, and ending in a small and dainty head; in short, all of its features, all the lines and highlights of its graceful body, penetrated my heart as deeply as the features of a woman who, predestined by heaven, suddenly appears before a man to become his beloved companion.

My whole being was seized by an indescribable happiness as I began to play the guitar. Its inner qualities proved no less perfect than its outward appearance. For its tone was deep and sweet in the bass notes, diaphanous and vibrant in the higher ones. And its accent, the soul of its voice, was noble and persuasive. I forgot everything but the guitar. . . .

What Segovia calls his "real debut" took place that same year, 1916, at the Ateneo, the most important concert hall in Madrid. Within a few years, playing a rapidly expanding repertoire of original guitar music and transcriptions ranging from Bach to Albéniz, he had become one of the best-known musicians of Spain and Latin America. His debut in Paris, 1924, at the concert hall of the Conservatoire, was attended by a capacity audience. Paul Dukas, Manuel de Falla, Albert Roussel, Joaquín Nin, and the philosopher Miguel de Unamuno heard him from Madame Debussy's box. From then on, he made annual tours of Europe that took him to England, Italy, Germany, Hungary, and the Soviet Union. In 1928 he made his first concert appearance in New York, followed by tours of Japan, the Philippines, China, and Indonesia. The Spanish Civil War forced him to give up his home in Barcelona, and during World War II he confined his activities to the Americas, where—especially in Uruguay and Mexico—he helped launch local revivals of the classic guitar. Resuming his world tours after the war, he has followed an immensely active routine as a concert artist and as a teacher of annual master classes at Santiago de Compostela, the Academia Chigiana in Sienna, and the University of California at Berkeley—a

(210) The old cowhand's guitar. Photo courtesy of Oak Publications.

(211) Big Bill Broonzy. Photo courtesy of Culver Pictures.

(212) Bob Dylan. Photo courtesy of Columbia Records.

typically jet-age agenda for an itinerant modern classicist with homes in New York, Geneva, Madrid, and Granada.

"Segovia is the Cortot of the guitar," writes the French critic Bernard Gavoty. It might be more accurate—to use this overworked formula for the last time—to call him the Landowska of the guitar, for like the rediscoverer of the harpsichord he has become the proprietor of certain vast tracts of musical estate. The twenty-odd LP records that he has made for Decca merely sketch in the outlines of Segovia's domain: it includes vihuelists like Milán and Mudarra, the elegant music of Visée, romantic pieces by Sor and Paganini, and works by contemporary composers like Joaquín Rodrigo and Heitor Villa-Lobos. His transcriptions of Handel and Bach have long since ceased to horrify the purists, for it is now generally conceded that a work like the immense Bach *Chaconne* sounds far more natural on the guitar than it ever did on the solo violin. When he made his debut in Paris, Roussel presented him with a virtuoso concert piece —it was called *Segovia*—and since then he has encouraged many other composers to think in terms of the guitar, including Alexandre Tansman, Federico Moreno Torroba, Manuel Ponce, and Mario Castelnuovo-Tedesco. In effect, a whole branch of musical literature has been created, like Joan Manén's *Fantasia-Sonata*, especially "*por y para Andrés Segovia.*"

Like most other virtuosos of his generation, Segovia has little use for avant-garde experimentalism of the sort represented by Pierre Boulez's *Le Marteau sans maître* (for alto, flute, viola, vibraphone, xylorim, guitar, and percussion) or Mauricio Kagel's *Sonant* (for guitar, electric guitar, harp, string bass, and percussion). "I love order and clarity and balance," he explains, to justify the traditionalism of his repertoire. At the same time, his presence and example have opened the doors for guitar virtuosos of all persuasions—some of them already established artists in the field, and others representing the post-Webern generation: the Venezuelan Alirio Diaz, the Italian Oscar Ghiglia, the American Stanley Silverman, the Austrian Karl Scheit, the Cuban José Rey de la Torre. There is the brilliant young Australian, John Williams, whom Segovia has called "a prince of the guitar," and who has introduced the music of the English

(213) Marlon Brando in Tennessee Williams' *The Fugitive Kind.*
Photo courtesy of Culver Pictures.

(214) Elvis Presley. Photo courtesy of Culver Pictures.

(215) The Beatles. Photo courtesy of Capitol Records.

modernist Stephen Dodgson. And, of course, the phenomenal English-man Julian Bream, who plays everything from Renaissance lute music to the latest Benjamin Britten variations or Malcolm Arnold's elegy for Django Reinhardt, whom he regards as one of his great idols. Many of the important guitarists of the younger generation have been taught or, as the saying goes, "guided" by Segovia; in any case, it was he who established the criteria by which every new guitarist must be measured, and he who accustomed international audiences to the idea that one could spend two hours in a concert hall listening to a man plucking six strings dancing above a box.

Segovia and his children do not play like an orchestra of ban-durrias; his instrument moans not, neither does it wail. It is at all times nothing more nor less than a transcendently well-played guitar —an honest and affecting sound because it is a beautifully hand-made thing, in which the left hand always knows what the right hand is doing. And that, in the last analysis, is the point and purpose of the whole art of the Apollonian twang.

(216) Jimi Hendrix, chewing on a guitar. Photo by Henry Grossman, New York.

(217) Huddie Ledbetter ("Leadbelly"). Photo by W. Eugene Smith,
courtesy of Oak Publications.

(218) Woody Guthrie. Photo courtesy of Folkways Records.

(219) Coptic "guitar," fourth to eighth century A.D., from the excavations at Qarara, Egypt. Photo courtesy of the Aegyptologisches Institut, Heidelberg University.

(220) English medieval gittern, perhaps originally of the fourteenth century. All the violin features of the instrument, however, including the tailpiece, finger board and sound board, are anachronisms which have been added by some subsequent restorer. Since the silver plate covering the peg box bears the arms of Queen Elizabeth I and her favorite, the Earl of Leicester, probably belonged to one of them. Photo courtesy of the Trustees of the British Museum.

(221) Spanish vihuela from the monastery of Guadalupe, Estremadura. Photo by Bulloz, courtesy of the Musée Jacquemart-André, Paris.

(222) Front and back views of a twin guitar by Alexander Voboam. Paris,
1696. Photo courtesy of the Kunthistorisches Museum, Vienna.

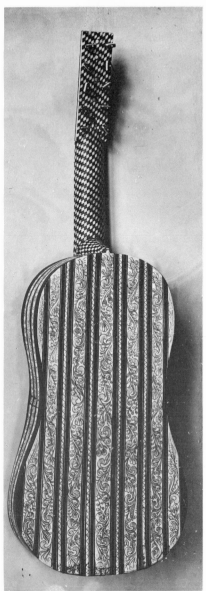

(223) Front and rear views of an Italian guitar by the eighteenth-century luthier, Jakob Stadler. Photo courtesy of the Kunthistorisches Museum, Vienna.

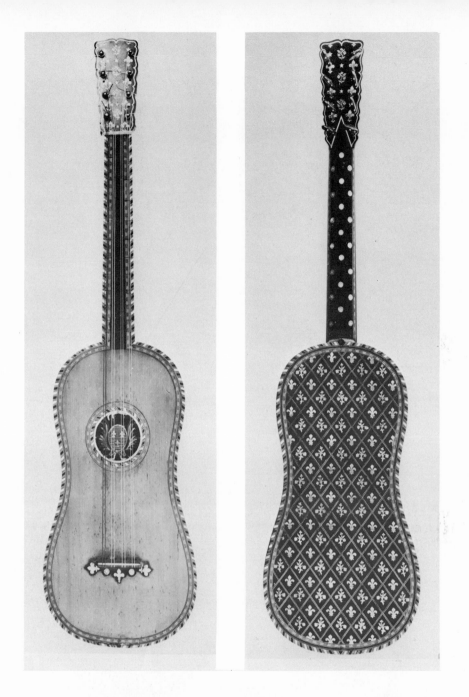

(224) Guitar signed Boivin "A la guitare royale," rue Tiquetonne, Paris, 1743.
Photo courtesy of the Musée Instrumental du Conservatoire
National de Musique, Paris.

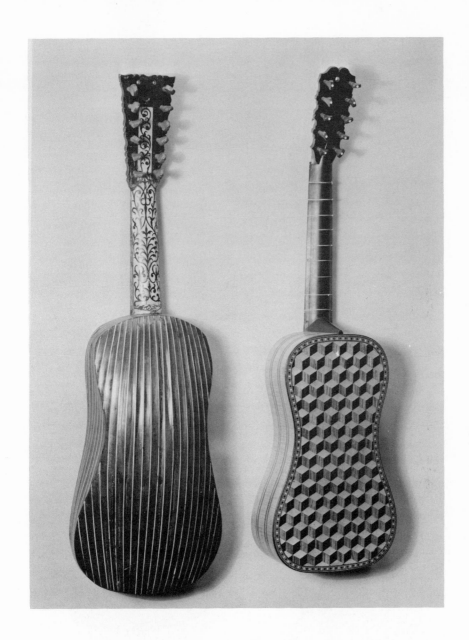

(225) Front and back views of a French guitar made by Guillaume in 1770, and an Italian chitarra battente of the seventeenth century. Photo courtesy of the Metropolitan Museum of Art (gift of Joseph W. Drexel, 1889).

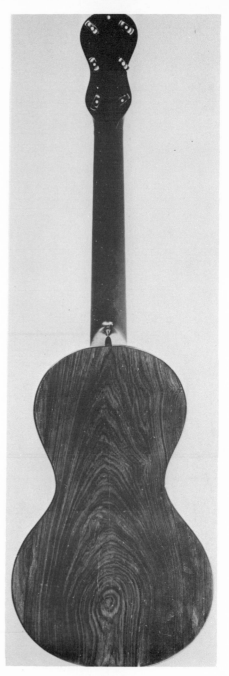

(226) The guitar that Paganini gave to Berlioz. Made by Grobert, Paris, it bears the signatures of both composers. Photo courtesy of the Musée Instrumental du Conservatoire National de Musique, Paris.

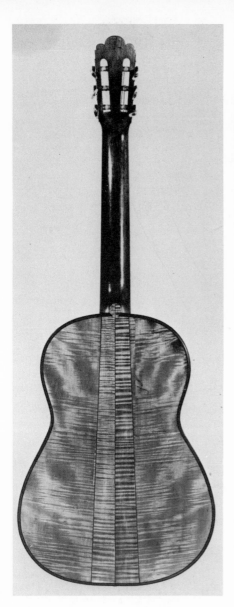

(227) Guitar by Antonio Torres, Seville, 1883. Photo courtesy of Musée Instrumental du Conservatoire National du Musique, Paris.

Notes

Sources of quotations not fully identified within the text.
Numbers given are for the last line of the quotation.

PAGE LINE

5 1 M. Praetorius: *Syntagma musicum*. Vol. II *De organographia*, Wolfenbüttel, 1619, Part 1—"Quinterna."

5 12 Percy Bysshe Shelley: "With a Guitar."

5 16 Quoted in *B.M.G.* ("Banjo, Mandolin, Guitar"), London, July, 1960, p. 285.

17 23 Arthur Loesser: *Men Women and Pianos*, N.Y., 1954, p. 430.

17 35 New York *Post*, July 5, 1967, p. 58.

22 13 Quoted in Samuel Charters: *The Bluesmen*, N.Y., 1967, p. 38.

22 17 Jacques Barzun: *Music in American Life*, N.Y., 1956, p. 70.

22 30 Quoted in *B.M.G.*, July, 1962, p. 301.

25 4 *Ibid.*, March, 1966, p. 199.

25 10 *Middle English Dictionary*, edited by Sherman M. Kuhn and John Reidy, Ann Arbor, 1963—"Giterne."

25 31 *Newsweek*, Oct. 9, 1967, pp. 46–47.

30 3 Bernard Gavoty: *Andres Segovia*, Geneva, 1955, p. 17.

35 8 Robert Graves: *The Greek Myths*, London, 1955, Vol. I, p. 64.

35 17 *Ibid.*, p. 65.

38 10 Quoted in Hortense Panum: *The Stringed Instruments of the Middle Ages*, London, c. 1920, p. 31.

38 14 Plutarch: *De Musica*, chapter 6. Quoted in *ibid.*, p. 31.

41   11   *A New English Dictionary on Historical Principles*, edited by James A. H. Murray, Oxford, 1893, Vol. II–"Cithara."

41   28   Boethius: *De institutione musica*, Book I. Translated in Oliver Strunk: *Source Readings in Music History*, N.Y., 1950, pp. 81–82.

45   33   Francis W. Galpin: *The Music of the Sumerians*, Cambridge, 1937, *passim*.

46   25   Ernst Biernath: *Die Gitarre seit dem III. Jahrtausend vor Christus*, Berlin, 1907, pp. 21–22.

48   15   Hans Hickmann: *Aegypten* (Musikgeschichte in Bildern, Band II, Lieferung 1), Leipzig, c. 1961, p. 82.

51   29   Ovid: *Fasti*, Book V, verse 104.

55   1   Henry George Farmer: *A History of Arabian Music*, London, 1929, *passim*.

55   12   H. G. Farmer: *Islam* (Musikgeschichte in Bildern, Band III, Lieferung 2), Leipzig (c. 1966), p. 98.

55   21   H. G. Farmer: *The Influence of Music, from Arabic Sources*, London, 1926, p. 22.

56   4   Julian Ribera: *Music in Ancient Arabia and Spain*. Translated E. Hague and M. Leffingwell, Stanford, 1929, p. 101.

58   20   *Ibid.*, pp. 115–116.

58   34   *Ibid.*, p. 116.

61   9   Quoted in Biernath, *op. cit.*, p. 116.

62   8   Quoted in John Stevens: *Music and Poetry in the Early Tudor Court*, London, 1961, p. 270.

67   2   Emanuel Winternitz: *Musical Instruments and their Symbolism in Western Art*, London, 1967, pp. 57–65.

67   23   John Wycliffe: *Leaven Pharisees*, chapter 9. Quoted in Kuhn and Reidy, *op. cit.*, "Giterne."

67   33   Chaucer: *Canterbury Tales*, "The Miller's Tale."

69   8   Ramón Menéndez Pidal: *Poesía juglaresca y juglares*, Madrid, 1924, p. 376. Translated in Gilbert Chase: *The Music of Spain*, N.Y., 1959, p. 35.

69   19   *Les deux Menèstriers*, Bodleian Library, Oxford. Quoted in Howard D. McKinney and W. R. Anderson: *Music in History*, N.Y., 1940, p. 170.

70   13   Karl Geiringer: "Der Instrumentenname 'Quinterne' und die mittelalterlichen Bezeichnungen der Gitarre, Mandola und Colascione." *Archiv für Musikwissenschaft* (1924), Vol. VI, pp. 103–117.

70   29   Juan Ruiz, archpriest of Hita: *Libro de buen amor*. Edited by J. Cejada y Franca, Madrid, 1913, copla 1228.

72   15   Quoted in Benito Vidal Revvelta: *La guitarra*, Madrid, 1962, p. 7.

72   26   Cf. Walter Starkie: *Spain: A Musician's Journey through Time and Space*, Geneva, 1958; and J. B. Trend: *Luis Milan and the Vihuelistas*, London, 1925.

PAGE	LINE	
72	33	Francis Galpin: *Old English Instruments of Music*, London, 1965, p. 218.
75	6	Juan Bermudo: *Declaración de instrumentos musicales*, Osuna, 1555, chapter LXV.
75	17	Henry George Farmer: *Historical Facts for the Arabian Influence*, London, n.d., pp. 154–155.
75	32	Bermudo, *op. cit.*, chapter XXXVI.
78	12	Quoted in Felipe Pedrell: *Cancionero musical popular español*. Barcelona, 1958, Vol. II, p. 92.
78	23	Luys Zapata: *Miscelanea*. In *Memorial histórico español*, Real Academia de la Historia, Madrid, Vol. XI (1859), p. 95.
81	5	Cristobal de Villalon: *Camparación entre lo antiguo y lo presente*, 1539. Quoted in José Subirá: *Historia de la música española e hispanoamericana*, Barcelona, 1953, p. 291.
82	1	Thomas Heywood: *The English Traveler* (1633) in *Dramatic Works*, London, 1874, Vol. IV, p. 29.
82	13	Quoted in Chase, *op. cit.*, p. 59.
82	16	Alonso Mudarra: *Tres libros de Música en cifras para vihuela*, Seville, 1546. Edited by Emilio Pujol, Barcelona, 1949, *passim*.
86	2	Enríquez de Valderrábano: *Libro de música de vihuela intitulado Silva de Sirenas*, Valladolid, 1547. Edited by Emilio Pujol, Barcelona, 1965, p. 12.
86	14	*Ibid.*, p. 24.
86	15	*Ibid.*, p. 12.
91	8	Anonymous: *La manière de'entoucher les lucs et guiternes*, Poitiers, 1556. Quoted in Daniel Heartz: "Parisian Music Publishing under Henry II," *Musical Quarterly*, Oct., 1960, p. 460.
94	6	Heartz, *op. cit.*, p. 466.
94	27	Quoted in Pierre Trichet: *Traité des instruments*, c. 1630. Edited by François Lesure in *Annales musicologiques*, III and IV, Paris, 1955–56 (p. 217, Vol. IV).
96	2	Robert Laneham: *Captain Cox, his Ballads and Books, or Robert Laneham's Letter* (1548–49). Edited by Frederick J. Furnivall, London, 1871, pp. 59–60.
96	25	Nicholas Udall: *Ralph Roister Doister* in *Representative English Comedies*, edited by Charles Mills Gayley, London, 1903, Vol. I, p. 131.
96	30	Ben Jonson: *The Gypsies Metamorphosed*, in W. W. Grey: *Jonson's Masque of Gypsies*, London, 1952, p. 124.
98	2	John Crowne: *Sir Courtly Nice*, in *Dramatic Works*, London, 1874, Vol. III, p. 276.
98	14	Quoted in Emilio Pujol: "La guitare," article in *Encyclopédie de la musique* (A. Lavignac and L. de la Laurencie), Paris, 1927, p. 2004.

PAGE   LINE

98   17   *Ibid.*, p. 2004.

98   31   Quoted in Subirá, *op. cit.*, p. 427.

102   12   Quoted in Trend, *op. cit.*, p. 30.

102   33   Juan Carles y Amat: *Guitarra españla y vándola*, Gerona, 1639. Facsimile edition, n.d. (c. 1960), p. 4.

105   18   *Ibid.*, pp. 23–24.

106   7   S. de Covarrubias: *Tesoro de la lengua Castellana o española*, Madrid, 1674–"Vihuela." Translation quoted in *B.M.G.*, Sept., 1959, p. 291.

106   33   Trichet, *op. cit.*, Vol. IV, pp. 216–219.

109   2   Adolphe Boschot: *Portraits de musiciens*, Paris, 1947, Vol. II, p. 134.

109   5   Johann Mattheson: *Neu-eröffnetes Orchester*, Hamburg, 1713, para. 14. Reprinted in Julius Schlosser: *Die Sammlung Alter Musikinstrumente*, Vienna, 1920, p. 47.

109   37   Cf. Richard Keith, "La Guitare Royale," in *Recherches sur la musique française classique*, VI, Paris, 1966, p. 75.

112   9   Boschot, *op. cit.*, p. 135.

112   26   *Ibid.*, p. 134.

112   28   Richard Keith, "The Guitar in the Courts of Louis XIV and Charles II," in *Guitar Review*, No. 26, June, 1962, p. 5.

112   30   Maria Rita Brondi: *Il liuto e la chitarra*, Turin, 1926, p. 102.

115   3   Francisque Corbett: *La guitarre royalle* (I), Paris, 1671, "Advis au lecteur."

115   25   Anthony Hamilton: *Memoirs of Count Grammont*. Edited by Sir Walter Scott, London, 1905, p. 204.

118   15   *Ibid.*, pp. 204–205.

118   25   Corbett, *op. cit.*

118   37   Cf. Sir Frederick Bridge: *Samuel Pepys Lover of Musique*, London, 1903, pp. 78–79.

120   15   Quoted in Pujol, *op. cit.*, p. 2008.

124   5   Edmund Hildebrandt: *Antoine Watteau*, Berlin, 1922, pp. 28–29.

127   28   Gaspar Sanz: *Instrucción de música sobre la guitarra española*, Saragossa, 1674. Facsimile edition published by Instituto Fernando el Católico, Saragossa, 1952, p. LXI.

127   35   J. Ricart Matas: *Refranero internacional de la música y de la danza*, Barcelona, 1950, p. 201.

130   5   *Roger North on Music*, edited by John Wilson, London, 1959, p. 16.

130   8   *Ibid.*, p. 248.

130   17   John Brown: *An Estimate of the Measures and Principles of the Times*, Vol. II, 1758. Quoted in Loesser, *op. cit.*, p. 217.

130   30   Abraham Rees: *The Cyclopaedia*, London, 1819–"Guitarra." Quoted in Loesser, *op. cit.*, p. 218.

PAGE	LINE	
130	36	Quoted in Subirá, *op. cit.*, p. 612.
133	12	Diego de Torres Villaroel: *The Remarkable Life of Don Diego*, translated by William C. Atkinson, London, 1958, pp. 72–73.
133	21	Beaumarchais: *The Barber of Seville*, Act I.
136	1	Ralph Kirkpatrick: *Domenico Scarlatti*, Princeton, 1953, p. 205.
136	30	Letter from Madrid, July 10, 1797. Quoted in Germaine de Rothschild: *Luigi Roccherini*, London, 1965, p. 122.
139	118	William Beckford: *Italy, with Sketches of Spain and Portugal*, London, 1834, Vol. II. Quoted in Rothschild, *op. cit.*, p. 58.
140	8	Edward Fenton: "Goya and the Guitar," *Guitar Review*, No. 14, 1952, p. 2.
140	16	Letter to Martin Zapater, July, 1784. Quoted in Domingo Prat: *Diccionario biográfico, bibliográfico, historico, critico, de guitarras, guitarristas, guitarreros*, Buenos Aires, 1933, p. 156.
140	31	Fernando Ferandiere: *Arte de tocar la guitarra española por música*, Madrid, 1799, p. 1.
143	21	Charles Burney: *The Present State of Music in Germany, the Netherlands, etc.*, London, 1773, Vol. I, pp. 284–285.
148	18	Terence Usher: "The Spanish Guitar in the Nineteenth and Twentieth Centuries," *Galpin Society Journal*, No. 9 (June, 1956), pp. 10–11.
148	28	Matheson, *op. cit.*, para. 17.
151	8	Fritz Buek: *Die Gitarre und ihre Meister*, Berlin, 1926, p. 8.
151	36	Vladimir Bobri, "Gypsies and Gypsy Choruses of Old Russia," *Guitar Review*, No. 20, 1956, p. 26.
152	14	Brondi, *op. cit.*, p. 97.
152	32	Charles Burney: *An 18th Century Musical Tour in France and Italy*, edited by Percy Scholes, London, 1959, p. 255.
156	17	Anonymous: *A Pocket Book for the Guitar*, London, Longman, Lukey & Broderip, n.d. (c. 1795), p. 1.
158	24	Quoted in Edmond Pilon and Frédéric Saisset: *Les fêtes en Europe au XVIIIe siècle*, Paris n.d. (c. 1945), p. 173.
161	1	Jeanne Louise de Campan: *Memories*. Quoted in Marvin Carlson: *The Theatre of the French Revolution*, Ithaca, N.Y., 1966, p. 2.
161	21	Antonio Bartolommeo Bruni: *Un inventaire sous la terreur*. Edited by J. Gallay, Paris, 1890, *passim*.
163	7	Max Maria von Weber: *Carl Maria von Weber*, Leipzig, 1864, Vol. I, p. 188.
163	11	Quoted in Philip J. Bone: *The Guitar and Mandolin*, London, 1954, pp. 317–318.
163	14	Brondi, *op. cit.*, p. 161; translated in Bone, *op. cit.*, p. 229.
166	1	Ignatz Moscheles: *Recent Music and Musicians*, N.Y., 1879, p. 199.
166	7	Lord Byron: "To Thomas Moore."

PAGE	LINE	
166	15	Emil Engel: "Der Dichter und die Gitarre II, Theodor Körner," *Die Gitarre*, Vol. II, No. 5, p. 24.
166	20	Julius Adolph Werder and Wilhelm Schneider: *Taschenbuch für Freunde der Musik*, Vienna, 1804. Quoted in Joseph Zuth: *Simon Molitor und die Wiener Gitarristic (um 1800)*, Vienna, c. 1919, p. 7.
166	34	E. T. A. Hoffmann: *Tales of Hoffmann*, edited by Christopher Lazare, N.Y., 1946, p. 301.
169	12	*Ibid.*, p. 295 (with changes based on the original German text).
169	25	Quoted in Adolf Koczirz: "Die Wiener Gitarristic vor Giuliani," *Die Gitarre*, Vol. II, No. 8, p. 81.
170	5	Zuth, *op. cit.*, p. 7.
170	16	*Ibid.*, p. 8.
174	13	*The Giulianiad, or Guitarist's Magazine*, London, 1833. (As least eight volumes were issued, in which certain text materials seem to have been repeated.) Vol, 8, p. 18.
174	23	*Ibid.*, p. 39.
174	30	*Ibid.*, p. 19.
179	8	Manuel Rocamora: *Fernando Sor*, Barcelona, 1957, p. 32.
179	13	*Ibid.*, p. 39.
179	30	Bone, *op. cit.*, p. 335.
179	36	*Ibid.*, p. 338.
180	9	*The Giulianiad, op. cit.*, p. 27.
182	21	Fernando Sor: *Méthode pour la guitare*, Paris, 1830, pp. 1–2.
182	28	*Ibid.*, p. 5.
182	34	Quoted in liner notes, "Andrés Segovia, Masters of the Guitar," Decca Record DL 9794.
187	6	*The Harmonicon*, Feb., 1831. Quoted in Bone, *op. cit.*, p. 338.
187	25	Rocamora, *op. cit.*, p. 78.
188	5	Sor, *op. cit.*, p. 16. Cf. Emilio Pujol: *El dilema del sonido en la guitarra*, Buenos Aires, 1960, pp. 43–47.
188	19	Dionisio Aguado: *Nuevo método para guitarra*, Paris, n.d. (c. 1846), chapter VII, p. 7.
188	33	Pujol: *El dilema, op. cit.*, pp. 40–42.
190	22	Aguado, *op. cit.*, p. 4.
194	2	Thomas Mace: *Musick's Moment*, London, 1676, p. 73.
194	6	Aguado, *op. cit.*, p. 5.
194	17	*Ibid.*, p. 7.
198	18	*The Giulianiad, op. cit.*, p. 7.
198	25	Bone, *op. cit.*, p. 79.
198	29	*Ibid.*, p. 114.
198	33	*Ibid.*, p. 173.
198	35	Prat, *op. cit.*, p. 163.
200	5	Bone, *op. cit.*, p. 293.

PAGE	LINE	
200	15	W. H. Husk: "Paganini," in Grove's *Dictionary of Music and Musicians*, First Edition, London, 1880.
200	36	Massimo d'Azeglio: *I miei ricordi*, Turin, 1866, p. 223.
202	9	Hector Berlioz: *Les soirées de l'orchestre*, Paris, 1854, p. 217.
202	18	Berlioz: *Memoirs*, translated by R. and E. Holmes, annotated and revised by Ernest Newman, N.Y., 1932, p. 13.
202	25	*Ibid.*, p. 14.
205	7	*Ibid.*, p. 137.
205	10	*Ibid.*, p. 145.
205	15	*Hector Berlioz: A Selection from his Letters*, edited by Humphrey Searle, London, 1966, p. 43.
205	26	Berlioz: *Memoirs, op. cit.*, pp. 145–146.
207	16	Ernest Legouvé: *Soixante ans de souvenirs*, Paris, 1886, Vol. I, pp. 294–295.
207	28	Berlioz: *Musical Grotesques*, in *Hector Berlioz: Selections from his Letters and Aesthetic, Humorous and Satirical Writings*, translated by William F. Apthorp, N.Y., 1879, p. 307.
208	13	Charles Dickens: *David Copperfield*, London, 1927, p. 451.
208	25	Henri Blanchard, "Les guitaristes." *Revue et Gazette Musicale de Paris*, IX, 1842, pp. 395–396.
211	15	George Sand: *Un hiver a Majorque*, Palma de Mallorca, 1953, p. 61.
212	4	Mikhail Ivanovich Glinka: *Memoirs*, translated by Richard B. Mudge, Norman, Okla., 1963, pp. 199–200.
212	20	George Borrow: *The Bible in Spain*, London, 1906, pp. 199–200.
212	28	Quoted in José Antonio de Donostia and Juan Torres: "Instrumentos de musica popular española," in *Anuario Musical*, Vol. I, Barcelona, 1946, p. 130.
217	21	Zoltán Kodály: *Folk Music of Hungary*, London, 1960, p. 22.
217	30	Sand, *op. cit.*, pp. 165–166.
218	2	G. Borrow: *The Zincali*, London, 1841, Vol. II, p. 8.
218	19	*Ibid.*, p. 5.
218	28	Cf. Julian Pemartin: *El cante Flamenco*, Madrid, 1966, pp. 98–100.
221	9	Quoted in Rafael Manzano: *Cante jondo*, Barcelona, n.d. (c. 1960), p. 18.
224	6	Yvonne Tienot: *Chabrier*, Paris, 1965, pp. 43–44. English translation in Edward Lockspeiser: *The Literary Clef*, London, 1958, pp. 72–73.
224	35	Federico García Lorca: *Obras completas*, Madrid, 1965, p. 60.
227	22	Manuel de Falla: *Escritos sobre musica y musicos*, Buenos Aires, 1950, pp. 130–131.
228	4	García Lorca, *op. cit.*, p. 110.
228	7	Falla, *op. cit.*, pp. 138–139.

PAGE	LINE	
228	37	Lorca: "Grafico de la petenera: Las seis cuerdas."
229	15	Quoted in Charters, *op. cit.*, p. 20.
230	3	Quoted in Gilbert Chase: *America's Music*, N.Y., 1955, p. 67.
230	17	*Ibid.*, p. 66.
235	2	George W. Cable: *The Dance in Place Congo*. Quoted in Lydia Parrish: *Slave Songs of the Georgia Sea Islands*, N.Y., 1942, p. 42.
235	19	Henri Herz: *My Travels in America*, translated by Henry Bertram Hill, Madison, Wis., 1963, pp. 75–76.
235	28	William Broonzy and Yannick Bruynoghe: *Big Bill Blues*, N.Y., 1964, p. 34.
235	32	Paul Oliver: *Conversation with the Blues*, London, 1965, p. 49.
238	9	Cecil Sharp: *English Folk Songs*, London, 1920, p. xii.
238	23	Clinton Simpson: "Some Early American Guitarists," *Guitar Review*, No. 23, June, 1959, p. 16.
238	28	*Ibid.*
241	4	*Ibid.*
241	29	Margaret Larkin: *Singing Cowboy*, N.Y., 1963, p. 104.
242	15	Thomas Gage: *The English American, A New Survey of the West Indies*, (1648). Edited by A. P. Newton, London, 1928, p. 53.
248	13	Mary Van Stone: *Spanish Folk Songs of New Mexico*, Chicago, 1926.
248	23	Alan Lomax: *The Folk Songs of North America*, London, 1960, p. 276.
248	27	Quoted in Parrish, *op. cit.*, p. 19.
250	26	Quoted in Charters, *op. cit.*, pp. 60–61.
250	32	*Ibid.*, p. 74.
250	36	Woody Guthrie: *American Folksong*, N.Y., 1947, p. 10.
254	10	Charters, *op. cit.*, p. 37.
254	21	Oliver, *op. cit.*, p. 169.
254	28	*Ibid.*, p. 77.
258	14	Letter to the author, Feb., 1967.
258	33	Quoted in Chris Spedding: "Charlie Christian," *B.M.G.*, Aug., 1964, pp. 366–367.
262	4	Quoted in Lawrence Malkin: "Goodbye to All What?", *Queen*, London, Jan. 5, 1966, p. 39.
262	31	*Time*, Nov. 23, 1962, p. 60.
265	9	Carl Sandburg: "Confession," *Guitar Review*, No. 12, 1951, p. 18.
265	21	Quoted in Jerry Silverman: *The Folksinger's Guitar Guide*, N.Y., 1962, p. 6.
271	4	Irwin Silber: "Fan the Flames," *Sing Out!*, N.Y., April-May, 1966, p. 39.
271	20	*Time, op. cit.*, p. 60.
271	29	Virginia Kelly: "Loud the Twang of the Guitar," *Reader's Digest*, Jan., 1967, p. 143.

PAGE	LINE	
272	11	*Music,* May-June, 1948, p. 15.
272	17	Robert Shelton: "A Basic Library of Country & Western Music," *Hi-Fi/Stereo Review,* Jan., 1968, p. 61.
274	7	RCA Victor Records Press Release, 1961.
274	18	Quoted in *Georgia Straight,* Vancouver, B.C., Aug. 11, 1967, p. 6.
278	3	Quoted in Shirley Fleming: "The Guitar on the Go," *High Fidelity,* July, 1966, p. 41.
278	26	Advertisement in *B.M.G.,* Sept., 1967, p. 409.
279	15	*Moniteur universel,* July 3, 1861. Quoted in George Heard Hamilton: *Manet and His Critics,* New Haven, 1954, p. 25.
282	28	Stainer and Barrett: *Dictionary of Musical Terms,* London, 1898— "Guitar."
282	35	Andrés Segovia: "The Guitar and Myself; Part One," translated by Eithne Golden, *Guitar Review,* No. 4, 1947, p. 2.
284	21	Emilio Pujol: *Tárrega,* Lisbon, 1960, p. 75.
284	28	*Ibid.,* p. 76.
286	7	*Ibid.,* p. 90.
286	9	*Ibid.,* p. 94.
286	33	*Ibid.,* pp. 156–157.
288	13	Octave Maus: *Trente Années de Lutte pour L'art,* Brussels, 1926, p. 21.
288	18	Claude Debussy in *S.I.M.,* Bulletin, Dec. 1, 1913. Quoted in Henri Collet: "Albeniz et Granados," Paris, 1948, p. 157.
288	21	Pujol: *Tárrega, op. cit.,* p. 104.
290	8	Manuel de Falla: Letter from Granada, Dec., 1933; foreword to Emilio Pujol: *Escuela razonada de la guitarra,* Buenos Aires, 1956.
290	26	Segovia, *op. cit.,* p. 1.
290	33	Segovia: "The Guitar and Myself; Madrid," translated by E. Golden, *Guitar Review,* No. 8, 1949, p. 31.
292	16	*Ibid.,* p. 30.
296	3	Gavoty, *op. cit.,* p. 10.
296	28	*Ibid.,* p. 17.

Bibliography

Abreu, Antonio, *Escuela para tocar con perfección la guitarra*, Salamanca, 1799.

Agricola, Martin, *Musica Instrumentalis Deutsch*, Wittemberg, 1528; reprint, Leipzig, 1896.

Aguado, Dionisio, *Nuevo método para guitarra*, Paris, c. 1843.

Alvarenga, Oneyda, *Música popular brasileña*, Buenos Aires, 1947.

Alver, Alfred W., "The Golden Age of the Guitar," *Chesterian*, vol. II, 1929.

Anglés, Higinio, *Gloriosa contribución de España a la historia de la música universal*, Madrid, 1948.

——, *La música de las Cantigas de Santa María del rey Alfonso el Sabio*, Barcelona, 1943.

——, *La música en la corte de Carlos V.*, Barcelona, 1944.

——, *La música en la España de Fernando el Santo y de Alfonso el Sabio*, Madrid, 1943.

——, *La música española desde la edad media hasta nuestros días*, Barcelona, 1941.

Anglés, Higinio and Subirá, José, *Catálogo musical de la Biblioteca Nacional de Madrid*, Barcelona, 1943–51.

Anon., *La maniere de'entoucher les lucs et guiternes* (Poitiers, 1556); in *Nouveau Musiciana*, Paris, 1890.

Azpiazu, J. de, *The Guitar and Guitarists from the Beginning to the Present Day*, London, 1960.

Baines, Anthony, ed., *Musical Instruments through the Ages*, London, 1961.

Bal y Gay, Jesús, *Fuenllana y la transcripción de la música de los vihuelistas*, Mexico, 1949.

Barzun, Jacques, *Berlioz and the Romantic Century*, New York, 1950.

——, *Music in American Life*, New York, 1956.

Beck, Sydney and Roth, Elizabeth E., *Music in Prints*, New York, 1965.

Behn, Friedrich, *Musikleben im Altertum und Frühen Mittelalter*, Stuttgart, 1954.

——, "Die Laute im Altertum und frühen Mittelalter," *Zeitschrift für Musikwissenschaft*, Nov., 1918.

Berlioz, Hector, *Evenings with the Orchestra*, trans. Barzun, Jacques, New York, 1956.

——, *Grand traité d'instrumentation et d'orchestration modernes*, Paris, 1844.

——, *Les grotesques de la musique*, Paris, 1859.

——, *Mémoires*, Paris, 1870.

——, *Memoirs*, trans. Holmes, Rachel and Eleanor, New York, 1932.

——, *A Selection from His Letters*, Searle, Humphrey, ed., London, 1966.

——, *Selections from His Letters, and Aesthetic, Humorous, and Satirical Writings*, trans. Apthorp, William F., New York, 1879.

——, *Les soirées de l'orchestre*, Paris, 1854.

——, *A Treatise on Modern Instrumentation and Orchestration*, London, 1856.

Bermudo, Juan, *Declaración de instrumentos musicales*, Osuna, 1555.

Bessaraboff, Nicholas, *Ancient European Musical Instruments*, Boston, 1941.

Bickford, Vahdah Olcott, *Olcott-Bickford Method for the Guitar*, Boston, 1921.

Biernath, Ernst, *Die Guitarre seit dem III. Jahrtausend vor Christus*, Berlin, 1907.

Blanchard, Henri, "Les Guitaristes," *Revue et Gazette Musicale de Paris*, Paris, 1842.

B.M.G. ("Banjo, Mandolin, Guitar" monthly: "The oldest established and most widely read fretted instrument magazine in the world"), London, 1902–

Boetticher, Wolfgang, and Hickmann, Hans, "Gitarre," *Die Musik in Geschichte und Gegenwart*, Blume, F. ed., Kassel and Basel, 1949.

Bonanni, Filippo, *Gabinetto Armonico*, Rome, 1722.

——, *The Showcase of Musical Instruments*, New York, 1964.

Bone, Philip James, *The Guitar and Mandolin*, London, 1954.

Borrow, George, *The Bible in Spain*, London, 1906.

——, *The Zincali; or, an Account of the Gypsies of Spain*, London, 1841.

Boschot, Adolphe, *Portraits de musiciens*, Paris, 1947.

Bradford, Perry, *Born with the Blues*, New York, 1965.

Bragard, Roger and De Hen, Ferdinand J., *Musikinstrumente aus zwei Jahrtausenden*, Stuttgart, 1967.

Branzoli, Giuseppe, *Ricerche sullo studio del liuto*, Rome, 1889.

Bream, Julian, "How to Write for the Guitar," *The Score & IMA Magazine*, no. 19, London, March, 1957.

Brizeño, Luis de, *Método muy facilísimo para aprender a tañer la guitarra a lo español*, Paris, 1626.

Brondi, Maria Rita, *Il liuto e la chitarra*, Torino, 1926.

Buchner, Dr. Alexander, *Musical Instruments Through the Ages*, London, c. 1955.

Buek, Fritz, *Die Gitarre und ihre Meister*, Berlin, 1926.

Burney, Charles, *An Eighteenth Century Musical Tour in France and Italy*, Scholes, Percy A., ed., London, 1959.

Cadenza, The (official monthly organ of the American Guild of Banjoists, Mandolinists and Guitarists), Boston, 1920–24.

Carcassi, Matteo, *Méthode complète pour la guitare*, Paris, c. 1840.

Carfagna, C. and Caprani, A., *Profilo Storico della Chitarra*, Ancona, 1966.

Carles y Amat, Joan, *Guitarra española y vándola*, Gerona, 1639.

Carreras y Candi, Francisco, ed., *Folklore y costumbres de España*, Barcelona, 1931.

Carulli, Ferdinando, *Méthode complète pour la guitare*, Paris, 1831.

Charters, Samuel, *The Bluesmen*, New York, 1967.

———, *Jazz New Orleans 1885–1963*, New York, 1958.

Chase, Gilbert, *America's Music*, New York, 1955.

———, *The Music of Spain*, New York, 1941.

Chauvet, Stephen, *Musique Nègre*, Paris, 1929.

Chavarri Anoujar, Eduardo L., *Folklore musical español*, Madrid, 1956.

Chilesotti, Oscar, "Intavolature di chitarra, appunti," *Le Chronache Musicali* I, Rome, 1900.

———, "Francesco Corbetta guitarrista," *Gazzetta Musicale de Milano* XLIV, 1888.

———, "Notes sur le guitariste Robert de Visée," *Sammelbände der Internationalen Musikgesellschaft*, IX, 1907–08.

Chouquet, Gustave, *Le Musée du Conservatoire National de Musique. Catalogue descriptif et raisonné*, Paris, 1875–1903.

Coelho, Olga, "The guitar in Brasil . . . and some reminiscences," *Guitar Review*, no. 21, 1957.

Contreras, Segundo N., *La guitarra*, Buenos Aires, 1927.

———, *La guitarra argentina*, Buenos Aires, 1950.

Corbett, Francisque, *La guitarre royale*, Paris, 1671.

Córdova y Oña, Sixto, *Cancionero popular de la Provincia de Santander*, Santander, 1947.

Corrêa de Azevedo, Luis-Heitor, "La guitare archaïque au Brésil," *Studia Memoriae Belae Bartok Sacra*, Budapest, 1956.

Cottin, Madeleine, *Méthode complète de guitare*, Paris, 1909.

Courlander, Harold, *Negro Folk Music U.S.A.*, New York, 1963.

Coussemaker, Edmond de, *Mémoire sur Hucbald . . . et sur les instruments de musique*, Paris, 1841.

———, "Essai sur le instruments de musique au moyen âge," *Annales archéologiques*, III, Paris, 1845.

Crescendo, The (for a time, the official monthly organ of the American Guild of Banjoists, Mandolinists and Guitarists), Boston, 1908–33.

Dart, Thurston, "The Cittern and its English Music," *Galpin Society Journal*, London, 1948.

———, "La pandore," *Le luth et sa musique*, Jacquot, Jean, ed., Paris, 1958.

Da Silva Leite, Antonio, *Estudo de guitarra*, Oporto, 1795.

Das Italienische Stilleben von den Anfängen bis zur Gegenwart, catalogue, Museum Bôymans-Van Beuningen, Rotterdam, March–April 1965; Zürich, Dec., 1964–Feb., 1965.

Deutsch, Otto Erich, "W. Matiegkas Gitarren-Trio und Schubert," *Zeitschrift für Musikwissenschaft*, XIV, 1932–33.

Dick, Friedrich, *Bezeichnungen für Saiten-und schlaginstrumente in der altfranzösischen Literatur*, Giessen, 1932.

Diderot, Denis, and Alembert, Jean Lerond d', eds., *Encyclopédie*, Paris, 1751–65.

Doizi de Velasco, Nicolao, *Nuevo modo de cifra para tañer la guitarra*, Naples, 1640.

Donington, Robert, *The Instruments of Music*, London, 1949.

Donostia, José Antonio de and Tomás, Juan, "Instrumentos de música popular española," *Anuario Musical*, I, Barcelona, 1946.

Ducamin, Jean, *Juan Ruiz Arcipreste de Hita. . . .*, Toulouse, 1901.

Duran Muñoz, García, *Andalucía y su cante*, Madrid, 1962.

Elorriaga, Luis, "The guitar," *Guitar Review*, no. 8, 1949.

Engel, Carl, *A Descriptive Catalogue of the Musical Instruments in the South Kensington Museum*, London, 1870.

Espinel, Vicente, *Relación de la vida y aventuras del escudero Marcos de Obregón*, Madrid, 1887.

Farmer, Henry George, *A History of Arabian Music*, London, 1967.

———, *Historical Facts for the Arabian Influence*, London, c. 1925.

———, *Islam* (Musikgeschichte in Bildern, Band III, Lieferung 2), Leipzig, c. 1966.

Feather, Leonard, "A History of Jazz Guitar," *Downbeat*, July 24, 1958.

Ferandiere, Fernando, *Arte de tocar la guitarra española por música*, Madrid, 1799.

Fitz-Gerald, Desmond, "The Norfolk House Music Room," *Victoria and Albert Museum Bulletin*, vol. II, no. 1, London, Jan., 1966.

Fleischhauer, Günter, *Etrurien und Rom* (Musikgeschichte in Bildern, Band II, Lieferung 5), Leipzig, c. 1964.

Galan Bergua, Demetrio, *El libro de la jota aragonesa*, Zaragoza, 1966.
Galpin, Francis William, *The Music of the Sumerians, Babylonians and Assyrians*, Cambridge, 1937.
——, *Old English Instruments of Music*, London, 1910.
——, *A Textbook of European Musical Instruments*, New York, 1937.
Galpin Society Journal, The ("An occasional publication" for "all those interested in research into the history of European musical instruments"), London, 1946– .
García Hidalgo, José, *Arte de la pintura*, Madrid, 1965.
García Marcellan, José, *Catálogo del Archivo de Música*, Madrid, c. 1945.
Garnault, Paul, *Le temperament, son histoire, son application aux violes de gambe et guitares*, Paris, 1924.
Gavaldá, Miguel Querol, *La música en las obras de Cervantes*, Barcelona, 1948.
Gavall, John, "The Guitar—an Evaluation," *Musical Times*, vol. 95, Nov, 1954.
Gavoty, Bernard, *Andrès Segovia*, Geneva, 1955.
Geiringer, Karl, "Der Instrumentenname 'Quinterne' und die mittelalterlichen Bezeichnungen der Gitarre, Mandola und Coslascione," *Archiv für Musikwissenschaft*, VI, 1924.
——, *Musical Instruments*, New York, 1945.
Giordano, Mario, *Contributo allo studio della chitarra*, Milan, 1936.
Gitarre, Die (A "monthly journal for the cultivation of lute and guitar playing"), Berlin, 1919–33.
Giulianiad, The, or Guitarist's Magazine (first guitar magazine in English; at least eight volumes appear to have been issued, with a selection of new guitar music, but some of the introductory articles seem to have been repeated in successive volumes), London, 1833–34.
González Climent, Anselmo, *Antología de poesía flamenco*, Madrid, 1961.
——, *Bibliografía flamenca*, Madrid, 1965.
——, *Flamencología*, Madrid, 1964.
Granata, Gio. Battista, *Soavi concenti di sonate musicali per la chitarra spagnuola*, Bologna, 1659.
Grunfeld, Frederic, "The Guitar," *Horizon*, IX, Summer, 1967.
Grunfeld, Jacoba, *Manuel de Falla*, Zürich, 1968.
Guitar Review, The (published by the Society of the Classic Guitar), New York, 1946–
Guthrie, Woody, *American Folksong*, New York, 1947.

Hague, Eleanor, *Latin American Music, Past and Present*, 1934.
Hamilton, Anthony, *Memoirs of Count Grammont*, London, 1905.
Hammerstein, Reinhold, *Die Musik der Engel*, Munich, 1962.
Harrison, Frank and Rimmer, Joan, *European Musical Instruments*, London, 1964.

Hayden, W. L., *Hayden's New and Improved Method for the Guitar*, Boston, 1870.

Heartz, Daniel, "Parisian Music Publishing under Henry II: A Propos of Four Recently Discovered Guitar Books," *The Musical Quarterly*, vol. XLVI, no. 4, 1960.

Hecht, Paul, *The Wind Cried*, New York, 1968.

Herz, Henri, *My Travels in America*, Madison, Wis., 1963.

Hickmann, Hans, *Ägypten* (Musikgeschichte in Bildern, Band II, Lieferung 1), Leipzig, c. 1961.

————, *45 Siècles de musique dans l'Egypte*, Paris, 1956.

Higgins, R. A., and Winnington-Ingram, R. P., "Lute-players in Greek Art," *Journal of Hellenic Studies*, vol. LXXXV, 1965.

Hildebrandt, Edmund, *Antoine Watteau*, Berlin, 1923.

Hoffmann, E. T. A., *Tales of Hoffmann*, Lazare, Christopher, ed., New York, 1946.

Hoffman, Richard, *Some Musical Recollections of Fifty Years*, New York, 1910.

Holland, Justin, *Holland's Comprehensive Method for the Guitar*, Boston, 1888.

Howe, Elias, *Howe's New American Guitar School*, Boston, 1859.

Howson, Gerald, *The Flamencos of Cádiz Bay*, London, 1965.

Jacquot, Jean, ed., *Le luth et sa musique*, Paris, 1958.

————, ed., *La musique instrumentale de la renaissance*, Paris, 1955.

Jahnel, Franz, *Die Gitarre und ihr Bau*, Frankfurt a. Main, 1963.

Jones, LeRoi, *Blues People*, New York, 1963.

Keepnews, Orrin and Grauer, Jr., Bill, *A Pictorial History of Jazz*, New York, 1955.

Keith, Richard, "La guitare royale," *"Recherches" sur la musique française classique*, vol. VI, Paris, 1966.

Kinsky, Georg, *Geschichte der Musik in Bildern*, Leipzig, 1929.

————, *Musikhistorisches Museum von Wilhelm Heyer in Cöln. Katalog*, Cologne, 1910 and 1912.

————, "Zu Schuberts Gitarren-Quartett," *Zeitschrift für Musikwissenschaft*, XI, 1928–29.

Kirby, P. R., *The Musical Instruments of the Native Races of South Africa*, London, 1934.

Kircher, Athanasius, *Musurgia Universalis*, Rome, 1650.

Kirkpatrick, Ralph, *Domenico Scarlatti*, Princeton, 1953.

Koczirz, Adolf, "Die Gitarren Kompositionen in Miguel de Fuenllanas Orphenica Lyra," *Archiv für Musikwissenschaft*, IV, 1922.

————, "Zur Geschichte der Gitarre in Wien," *Musikbuch aus Oesterreich*, Vienna, 1907.

————, "Die Fantasien des Melchior de Barberis fur die Siebensaitige Gitarre," *Zeitschrift für Musikwissenschaft*, IV, 1921–22.

Koczirz, Adolf, and Zuth, Josef, *Beiträge zur Geschichte der Gitarre und des Gitarrenspiels,* Vienna, 1919.

Körte, Oswald, *Laute und Lautenmusik bis zur Mitte des 16. Jahrhunderts,* Leipzig, 1901.

Kunst, Jaap, *Ethnomusicology,* The Hague 1959.

L'Accademico Caliginoso detto il Fvrioso (pseud.), *I qvatro Libri della Chitarra spagnola,* Verona(?), c. 1650.

La Chitarra (rivista mensile letteraria e musicale), Bologna, 1934–

Larkin, Margaret, ed., *Singing Cowboy,* New York, 1931.

Lavignac, A. and Laurencie, L. de la, *Encyclopédie et dictionnaire du conservatoire,* Paris, 1913.

Lawless, Ray M., *Folksingers and Folksongs in America,* New York, 1960.

L'Eco della musica (official bi-monthly organ of the Associazione nazionale liuteria artistica Italiana), Ancona, 1963–

Ledbetter, Huddie, *The Leadbelly Songbook,* Asch, Moses and Lomax, Alan, eds., New York, 1962.

Legouvé, Ernest, *Soixante ans de souvenirs,* Paris, 1886.

Lesure, François, "La guitare en France au XVIe siècle," *Musica Disciplina,* vol. IV, Rome, 1950.

———, *Musik and Gesellschaft im Bild,* Kassel, 1966.

Loesser, Arthur, *Men, Women and Pianos,* New York, 1954.

Lomax, Alan, *American Folk Guitar,* New York, 1957.

———, *The Folk Songs of North America,* London, 1960.

Lomax, John and Alan, *American Ballads & Folk Songs,* New York, 1934.

———, *Folk Song U.S.A.,* New York, 1960.

López Chavarri, Eduardo, *Música popular española,* Barcelona, 1927.

Lorca, Federico García, *Obras completas,* Madrid, 1965.

Lütgendorff, Willibald Leo, Freiherr von, *Die Geigen-und Lautenmacher vom Mittelalter bis zur Gegenwart,* Frankfurt a. Main, 1913.

Mahillon, Victor Charles, *Catalogue descriptif & analytique du Musée Instrumental du Conservatoire Royal de Musique de Bruxelles,* Ghent, 1893–1922.

Mairants, Ivor, *The Flamenco Guitar,* London, 1958.

Manfredi, Domingo, *Geografía del cante jondo,* Madrid, 1955.

Manzano, Rafael, *Cante jondo,* Barcelona, c. 1960.

Marchetti, Tomasso, *Il primo libro d'intavolatura della lutana spagnola,* Roma, 1660.

Marcuse, Sibyl, *Musical Instruments: A Comprehensive Dictionary,* London, 1964.

Marden, C. Carroll, ed., *Libro de Apolonio,* Princeton, 1917.

Marescot, Charles de, *La guitaromanie,* Paris, c. 1850.

———, *Instructions for the Guitar,* London, c. 1850.

Marfurt, Luitfrid, *Musik in Afrika,* Munich, 1957.

Maschkewitz, W., "Zur Geschichte der Gitarre in Russland," *Die Gitarre*, X, 1928.

Matteis, Nicola, *The False Consonances of Musick*, London, c. 1690.

Mattheson, Johann, *Das neu eröffnete Orchester*, Hamburg, 1713.

Menéndez Pidal, Ramón, *Poesía juglaresca y juglares*, Madrid, 1924.

Mersenne, Marin, *Harmonie universelle . . .* , Paris, 1636–37.

Mertens, Jacqueline, *Je joue de la guitare*, Verviers, 1964.

Milá y Fontanals, Manuel, *De los trovadores en España*, Barcelona, 1966.

Milioni, Pietro, *Corona del primo secondo e terso libro d'intavolatura di chitarra spagnola di Pietro Milioni*, Rome, 1638.

Molina Fajardo, Eduardo, *Manuel de Falla y el "Cante jondo,"* Granada, 1962.

Molina, Ricardo, *Cante flamenco*, Madrid, 1965.

Molina, Ricardo and Mairena, Antonio, *Mundo y formas del cante flamenco*, Madrid, 1963.

Moreck, Kurt, *Die Musik in der Malerei*, Munich, 1924.

Moretti, Federico, *Principios para tocar la guitarra de seis órdenes*, Madrid, 1799.

Morlaye, Guillaume, *Livre de chansons, galliardes, pavannes*, I-IV, Paris, 1551–53.

Morphy, Guillermo, *Les luthistes espagnols du XVIe. siècle*, Leipzig, 1902.

Mudarra, Alonso, *Tres libros de música en cifra para vihuela*, Seville, 1546, transcription by Pujol, Emilio, Barcelona, 1949.

Muñoz, Ricardo, *Historia de la guitarra*, Buenos Aires, 1930.

Murcia, Santiago de, *Resumen de acompañar la parte con la guitarra*, Madrid, 1714.

Museo Degli Strumenti Musicali, catalogue, Milan, 1963.

Narváez, Luis de, *El delphín de música*, Osuna, 1538, transcription by Torner, Eduardo M. in Colección de vihuelistas españoles del siglo XVI, Madrid, 1965.

Nathan, Hans, *Dan Emmett and the Rise of Early Negro Minstrelsy*, Norman, Okla., 1962.

Nicola, Isaac, "Notas históricas de la guitarra," *Conservatorio*, Madrid, April–June, 1948.

North, Roger, *Roger North on Music*, Wilson, John, ed., London, 1959.

Nowak, Leopold, *Hausmusik mit Gitarre*, Vienna, 1949.

Oliver, Paul, *Conversation with the Blues*, London, 1965.

Pahissa, Jaime, *Vida y obra de Manuel de Falla*, Buenos Aires, 1956.

Pantoja Antunez, José Luis, *Evocación de las grandes figuras del flamenco*, Jerez, 1963.

Panum, Hortense, *Stringed Instruments of the Middle Ages*, revised and edited by Pulver, Jeffrey, London, c. 1920.

Parigi, Luigi, *I Disegni musicali del gabinetto degli "Uffizi,"* Florence, 1951.

Parker, K. T. and Mathey, J., *Antoine Watteau: Catalogue complet de son oeuvre dessiné*, Paris, 1957.

Parrish, Lydia, *Slave Songs of the Georgia Sea Islands*, New York, 1942.

Pedrell, Felipe, *Cancionero musical popular español*, Barcelona, 1958.

————, *Emporio científico e histórico de organografía musical antiqua española*, Barcelona, 1901.

Pemartín, Julian, *El cante flamenco*, Madrid, 1966.

Pfandl, Ludwig, *Cultura y costumbres del pueblo español de los siglos XVI y XVII*, Barcelona, 1929.

Pico, Foriano, *Nuova scelta di sonate per la lutana spagnola*, Venice, 1608.

Pilon, Edmond and Saisset, Frédéric, *Les fêtes en Europe au XVIIIe siècle*, Paris, c. 1945.

Pohren, D. E., *The Art of Flamenco*, Jerez de la Frontera, 1962.

————, *Lives and Legends of Flamenco*, Seville, 1964.

Post, C. N., "The Origin and Growth of the Guitar, Mandolin and Banjo Industry in America," *Music Trades*, vol. 26, no. 24, New York, 1903.

Praetorius, Michael, *Syntagma musicum. II, De organographia . . . Theatrum instrumentorium*, Wolffenbüttel, 1619; reprint Kassel, 1929.

Prat, Domingo, *Diccionario biográfico, bibliográfico, histórico, crítico, de guitarras, guitarristas, guitarreros*, Buenos Aires, 1933.

Pujol, Emilio, *El dilema del sonido en la guitarra*, Buenos Aires, 1960.

————, *Escuela razonada de la guitarra*, Buenos Aires, 1956.

————, *La guitarra y su historia*, Buenos Aires, c. 1930.

————, *Tárrega*, Lisbon, 1960.

————, "Significación de Juan Carlos Amat en la historia de la guitarra," *Anuario Musical*, V, Barcelona, 1950.

————, "La guitare," *Encyclopédie de la musique et dictionnaire du conservatoire*, III, Lavignac, A. and Laurencie, L. de la, eds., Paris, 1927.

————, "The guitar in Portugal," *Guitar Review*, no. 5, 1948.

————, "Les ressources instrumentales et leur rôle dans la musique pour vihuela et pour guitare au XVIe siècle et au XVIIe," *La musique instrumentale de la renaissance*, Paris, 1955.

————, "Apporto italiano alla chitarra classica," *Quaderni dell'Accademia Chigiana*, XXIX, Siena, 1953.

Rao, Harihar, *Introduction to Sitar*, New York, 1967.

Reese, Gustave, *Music in the Middle Ages*, New York, 1942.

Reinach, Theodor, *La guitare dans l'art grec*, Paris, 1895.

Reuter, Evelyn, *Les représentations de la musique dans la sculpture Romaine en France*, Paris, 1938.

Riaño, Juan F., *Critical and Bibliographical Notes on Early Spanish Music*, London, 1887.

Ribayaz, Lucas Ruiz de, *Luz y norte musical para caminar por las cifras de la guitarra española, y arpa*, Madrid, 1677.

Ribera, Julián, *La música árabe y su influencia en la española*, Madrid, 1927.

————, *La música de las cantigas*, Madrid, 1922.

————, *Music in Ancient Arabia and Spain,* trans. Hague, E. and Leffingwell, M., Stanford, 1929.

Ricart Matas, J., *Refranero internacional de la música y de la danza,* Barcelona, 1950.

Ridge, Eric Victor, *The Birth of a Guitar,* London, 1959.

Rocamora, Manuel, *Fernando Sor,* Barcelona, 1957.

Rothschild, Germaine de, *Luigi Boccherini,* New York, 1965.

Roveri, Ercole Remo, *Maria Luisa Anido,* Milan, 1957.

Sachs, Curt, *Handbuch der Musikinstrumentenkunde,* Leipzig, 1920.

————, *The History of Musical Instruments,* New York, 1940.

————, *Real-Lexikon der Musikinstrumente,* Berlin, 1913.

————, *The Rise of Music in the Ancient World East and West,* New York, 1943.

————, "Musik der Antike," *Handbuch der Musikwissenschaft,* Bücken, E., ed., Berlin, 1923.

Saenz de la Maza, R., *La guitarra y su historia,* Madrid, 1955.

Salazar, Adolfo, *La música en Cervantes y otros ensayos,* Madrid, 1961.

————, *La música en la sociedad Europea,* Mexico City, 1942–46.

————, *Música, instrumentos y danzas en las obras de Cervantes,* Mexico City, 1948.

————, "El laud, la vihuela y la guitarra," *Nuestra Música,* 1946.

Saldoni, Baltasar, *Diccionario biográfico-bibliográfico de efemérides de músicos españoles,* Madrid, 1868.

Sampayo Ribeiro, Mário de, *Achegas para a história da música em Portugal,* Lisbon, 1932–41.

Sandburg, Carl, *The American Songbag,* New York, 1927.

Sanz, Gaspar, *Instrucción de música sobre la guitarra española,* Saragossa, 1674; facsimile by the Institución Fernando el Católico, 1952.

Sauerland, Max, *Die Musik in Fünf Jahrhunderten der Europäischen Malerei,* Königstein and Leipzig, 1922.

Scheit, Karl, "Von der Gitarre," *Musikerziehung,* Sept., 1951.

Scheurleer, Daniel F., *Iconographie des instruments de musique,* card catalogue, The Hague, 1914.

Schlesinger, Kathleen, *Early Records of the Precursors of the Violin Family,* London, 1910.

————, Articles on "Cithara," "Cittern," "Guitar" and "Guitar Fiddle" in *Encyclopædia Britannica,* 11th edition, New York, 1910.

Schlosser, Julius Ritter von, *Die Sammlung alter Musikinstrumente. Kunsthistoriches Museum in Wien,* Vienna, 1920.

Schneider, Max F., *Musik der Neuzeit in der bildenden Kunst Basels,* Basel, 1944.

Scholes, Percy A., *The Mirror of Music 1844–1944,* London, 1947.

Schweizer, Gottfried, "Die Guitarre Maria Stuarts," *Zeitschrift für Musik,* July, 1953.

Segovia, Andrés, "The Guitar and Myself," trans. Golden, Eithne, *Guitar Review*, vol. 1, no. 4, 1947.

Seligman, Janet, *Figures of Fun*, New York, 1957.

Sharpe, Albert Percy, *Make Your Own Spanish Guitar*, London, 1957.

——, *The Story of the Spanish Guitar*, London, 1954.

Silverman, Jerry, *The Folksinger's Guitar Guide*, New York, 1962.

Sing Out! ("The Folk Song Magazine," bi-monthly), New York, 1951–

Sommer, Hermann, *Die Laute*, Berlin, 1920.

——, *Laute und Gitarre*, Stuttgart, 1922.

Sor, Fernando, *Méthode pour la guitare*, Paris, 1830.

Starkie, Walter, *Spain. A Musician's Journey through Time and Space*, Geneva, 1958.

Stevens, John, *Music and Poetry in the Early Tudor Court*, London, 1961.

Straeten, Edmund van der, *The History of the Violin; Its Ancestors and Collateral Instruments*, London, 1933.

Subirá, José, *Historia de la música española e hispanoamericana*, Barcelona, 1953.

——, *Historia de la música teatral en España*, Madrid, 1945.

——, *El teatro del real palacio*, Madrid, 1950.

Terzi, Benvenuto, *Dizionario dei chitarristi e liutai italiani*, Bologna, 1937.

Tessarech, Jacques, *Resumé d'une causerie sur l'evolucion de la guitare*, Ajaccio, 1922.

Thomas, Juan M., "The Guitar and Its Renaissance," *Chesterian*, Oct., 1955.

Thompson, Thomas Perronet, *Instructions to My Daughter for Playing on the Enharmonic Guitar*, London, 1829.

Torres Villarroel, Diego de, *The Remarkable Life of Don Diego*, trans. Atkinson, William C., London, 1958.

Toscanelli, Angelina, *Il liuto: notizie esplicative e storiche*, Milan, 1921.

Trend, J. B., *The Music of Spanish History, to 1600*, Oxford, 1926.

Triana, Fernando el de, *Arte y artistas flamencos*, Madrid, 1952.

Trichet, Pierre, "Le traité des instruments de musique," *Annales Musicologiques* III and IV, Lesure, François, ed., Paris, 1955–56.

Usher, Terrence, "The Spanish Guitar in the 19th and 20th Centuries," *Galpin Society Journal*, IX, June, 1956.

Valderrábano, Enríquez de, *Libro de música de vihuela, intitulado Silva de Sirenas*, Valladolid 1547, transcription by Pujol, Emilio, Barcelona, 1965.

Valmar, Marqués de, *Estudio histórico, crítico y filológico sobre las cantigas del rey Don Alfonso el Sabio*, Madrid, 1897.

Vannes, René, *Dictionnaire universel des luthiers*, Brussels, 1951 and 1959.

Vega, Carlos, *Música sudamericana*, Buenos Aires, 1946.

——, "The Classical Guitar in Early Buenos Aires," *Guitar Review*, no. 10, 1949.

Vidal Revuelta, Benito, *La guitarra*, Madrid, 1962.

Vidal, Robert J., "Quelques grands guitaristes," *Musica*, no. 31, Paris, Oct., 1956.

Virdung, Sebastian, *Musica getutscht und auszgezogen durch Sebastianum Virdung Priesters von Amberg* . . . , Basel, 1511; facsimile ed., Schrade, Leo, ed., Kassel, 1931.

Visser, Dick, "De ontwikkeling van het gitaarspel in Nederland," *Mens en melodie*, June, 1959.

Wegner, Max, *Griechenland* (Musikgeschichte in Bildern, Band II, Lieferung 4), Leipzig, c. 1963.

Weinstock, Herbert, *Mexican Music*, New York, 1940.

Wild, N., *La vie musicale sous la regence*, Paris, 1961.

Winner, Septimus, *Winner's Eureka Method for the Guitar*, Boston, 1891.

Winternitz, Emanuel, *Musical Instruments and their Symbolism in Western Art*, London, 1967.

————, *Musical Instruments of the Western World*, London, 1966.

Work, John W., ed., *American Negro Songs and Spirituals*, New York, 1940.

————, *Folk Song of the American Negro*, New York, 1915.

Zapata, Luys, *Miscelánea*, in *Memorial histórico español*, XI, Cayangos, de P. de, ed., Madrid, 1859.

Zuth, Josef, *Handbuch der Laute und Gitarre*, Vienna, 1926.

————, *Simon Molitor und die Wiener Gitarristik*, Vienna, 1919.

Index

Numbers in italics refer to illustrations

[335]

[340]